PLUG -n- PLAY

JAVA SCRIPT

Kevin Ready, Paul Vachier & Benoit Marsot

New Riders Publishing,
Indianapolis, Indiana

Plug-n-Play JavaScript

By Kevin Ready, Paul Vachier, and Benoit Marsot

Published by:
New Riders Publishing
201 West 103rd Street
Indianapolis, IN 46290 USA

Printed in the United States of America 1 2 3 4 5 6 7 8 9 0

Library of Congress Cataloging-in-Publication Data

```
Ready, Kevin, 1962-
Plug-n-Play JavaScript / Kevin Ready, Paul Vachier, Benoit
Marsot.
p.xx  cm.xx

Includes index.
ISBN 1-56205-674-3
1. JavaScript (Computer program language)  2. World Wide
Web (Information retrieval system)
I. Vachier, Paul, 1964-
II. Marsot, Benoit, 1969-
III. Title
QA76.73.J39R43    1996
005.2—dc20
            96-33169

            CIP
```

Warning and Disclaimer

This book is designed to provide information about the JavaScript programming environment. Every effort has been made to make this book as complete and as accurate as possible, but no warranty or fitness is implied.

The information is provided on an "as is" basis. The authors and New Riders Publishing shall have neither liability nor responsibility to any person or entity with respect to any loss or damages arising from the information contained in this book or from the use of the disks or programs that may accompany it.

Publisher	*Don Fowley*
Publishing Manager	*Julie Fairweather*
Marketing Manager	*Mary Foote*
Managing Editor	*Carla Hall*

Product Development Specialist
Sean Angus

Senior Editor
Sarah Kearns

Development Editor
Christopher Cleveland

Associate Marketing Manager
Tamara Apple

Acquisitions Coordinator
Tracy Turgeson

Administrative Coordinator
Karen Opal

Cover Designer
Aren Howell

Book Designer
Sandra Schroeder

Production Manager
Kelly Dobbs

Production Team Supervisor
Laurie Casey

Graphics Image Specialists
Stephen Adams
Debra Bolhuis
Daniel Harris
Casey Price
Laura Robbins

Production Analysts
Jason Hand
Bobbi Satterfield

Production Team
Kim Cofer
Tricia Flodder
David Garratt
Scott Tullis
Megan Wade

Indexer
Christopher Cleveland

About the Authors

Kevin Ready is an author and freelance multimedia consultant. He has taught HTML and multimedia classes, in both Macintosh and PC environments, for the past five years. In addition to teaching, Kevin has designed high-bandwidth Web sites for companies such as @Home, c l net, and others, integrating rich media formats into the Web experience. His present attention is dedicated to the Blue Platypus, a sensoral experience on the Web residing at www.blueplatypus.com. This site integrates several breaking technologies, such as Shockwave and Palace into a single, multilayered Web adventure. BTW (Before the Web) Kevin freelanced for many Fortune 500 companies, including Price Waterhouse, Levi's, and others, developing custom solutions using many standard office software products.

Paul Vachier is a freelance graphic artist, HTML author, Web developer and founder of Transmit Media in San Fransisco. Paul has designed and programmed content for numerous online magazines including Word, PC World Annex, and Salon Internet. Currently he's working with @Home network and developing a Real Audio based Web site for IDG entitled Silicon Valley Radio. He has also taught classes in basic and advanced HTML at San Francisco State University's Multimedia Studies program and holds a BA degree in history and anthropology from Montclair State University in New Jersey.

Benoit Marsot, a native of Montreal, Quebec studied Physics and Computer Engineering at Laval Univerty & Montreal Polytechnic. He has worked as a C/C++ programmer in various research and development labs in cross platform environments and created Pubnet with Edouard Bernal, a Internet consulting company focused on highly interactive and high impact technology Web sites using Java, JavaScript, Perl, and various database formats. You can contact him at benoit@www.pubnet.qc.ca or see his page: **http:// www.pubnet.qc.ca/ben/start.htm**

Trademark Acknowledgments

All terms mentioned in this book that are known to be trademarks or service marks have been appropriately capitalized. New Riders Publishing cannot attest to the accuracy of this information. Use of a term in this book should not be regarded as affecting the validity of any trademark or service mark. JavaScript is a registered trademark of Netscape Communications, Inc.

Acknowledgments

In no particular order, the authors would like to thank and say hello to Sean Angus, Wendy Milanese, Chris Cleveland, Paul Barlass, David Ready, Bruce Falck, Adam Gould and the folks at Construct, Simon Smith, David Hyman, Eric Franz, Tri Le, Janine Warner, Helene Schneider, Paul's mother, Andrew Beebe, Caleb Clark, Elise Bauer, the Noend group, Jaime Levy, Rebecca Cherkoss, Lynda Weinman, Bill Weinman, Craig Thigpen, Tom, Riley, Dalton, and Karyn Greene (and the oven bun), Crystal Waters for a cool reference in an excellent book, Super Uli, Steven Warren, Mariate Lopez, Craig Barnes, Grumpy, Ty Ahmad-Taylor, Lettie from artwebb.com, Blacky, Phoenix Pop Productions, Dominique pour les incroyables massages, Kalle Wik, Genevieve Dame, Teddy Bernal, Carol Pisarczyk and the IFUSION crew, Cotton Coulson and the c I net crew, John Goecke, Malin Ask, Criss Van de Woestyne, Craig Collins, the WWWAC, Lewis Communications, Bruno Ybarra, Simona Stanzani Pini, Kristina Lloyds, Melissa and Mary from Global Dynamics, Melissa Adofaci, Tana Butler, Gipsy, Rebecca and DeAnne from Avid, Zoe Comings, David Dwyer, ACM SIGGRAPH for overseeing major ragers in the Big Easy, Digital Domain for throwing the most excellent party at the House of Blues, and Rage Against the Machine for musical inspiration. Thanks to anyone that was overlooked here who helped us over the past few months turn this book into a reality. You guys have all been great! And thank God it's over!

Contents at a Glance

Table of Contents

I

Introduction

This book is intended for Web designers and developers who want to quickly integrate JavaScript functionality into their Web sites. It is designed mainly for non-programmers, but also serves as a very complete and up-to-date JavaScript reference source for beginners and experts alike. Experienced programmers should find great use for the book as well, and much time has been spent by the authors to ensure that the data contained here is as complete and current as possible.

The examples in this book and on the CD-ROM are designed to be copied and pasted directly into your HTML documents and can be easily customized for your own needs as well as expanded upon to add further functionality. These scripts are useful regardless of your level of experience with JavaScript, although a basic familiarity with HTML is assumed. It is not necessary to read the entire book to use the examples inside, but it is recommended if you intend to design your own JavaScripts and/or have little experience with JavaScript. The first chapter and the appendices provide additional resources for those wishing to pursue JavaScript in more depth.

As the Web matures and additional functionality is made available to developers, Web authors are facing increasing demands from their clients and visitors to their sites. In the three years since Mosaic was introduced, the browser experience has progressed from the grey, left-aligned world of HTML 2, to the rich media, tables, and frames of browsers such as Navigator and Explorer. The browser's architecture has been extended to enable plug-ins,

Java, and JavaScript to surpass functionality well beyond the limitations of HTML.

JavaScript is one of the critical additions that enable Web developers to break away from the static world of HTML and move to a much more exciting and useful toolbox without learning complex programming. Although JavaScript is in essence a programming language, it is more accurately desribed as a scripting language—far easier to use than counterparts like Java or C.

In the six chapters of this book, we seek to bridge the gap for designers who are needing to implement JavaScript, but don't have the time or desire to learn a programming language. Those with more JavaScript experience will find many new and useful implementations of JavaScript not discussed anywhere else, plus a very complete and useful reference guide in Appendix A.

Chapter 1 introduces the JavaScript programming language. Chapters 2 through 5 use Event Handlers as an organizational device. These basic components of JavaScript trigger scripts in response to user actions. If you are new to JavaScript, this organization provides a simple and logical introduction to the workings of the language. For experienced programmers, this also provides a logical way of categorizing the various functionalities available for usage. Each chapter includes many examples in increasing order of complexity.

Chapter 6 will be of greatest interest to advanced users and more adventurous beginners as it provides some truly elaborate JavaScript examples including a very extensive reference form guide to JavaScript, itself created with JavaScript. These advanced scripts push the limits and illustrate JavaScript's capabilities as a very capable language for incorporating true interactivity without programming skills or the need to run server-based solutions.

One way to use this book is to browse the chapters and find a particular script that you would like to incorporate into your page. Copy the script from the included CD-ROM directly into your HTML file and make the necessary changes to personalize your script. To facilitate this, customizable portions of the scripts such as image and file names, variable names, etc. have been indicated in *this typeface*. Above all, this book is intended to help you quickly implement JavaScript into your Web pages. So what are you waiting for? Turn the page!

New Riders Publishing

The staff of New Riders Publishing is committed to bringing you the very best in computer reference material. Each New Riders book is the result of months of work by authors and staff who research and refine the information contained within its covers.

As part of this commitment to you, the NRP reader, New Riders invites your input. Please let us know if you enjoy this book, if you have trouble with the information and examples presented, or if you have a suggestion for the next edition.

Please note, though: New Riders staff cannot serve as a technical resource for **JavaScript** or for questions about software- or hardware-related problems. Please refer to the documentation that accompanies **JavaScript** or to the applications' Help systems.

If you have a question or comment about any New Riders book, there are several ways to contact New Riders Publishing. We will respond to as many readers as we can. Your name, address, or phone number will never become part of a mailing list or be used for any purpose other than to help us continue to bring you the best books possible. You can write us at the following address:

New Riders Publishing
Attn: Publisher
201 W. 103rd Street
Indianapolis, IN 46290

If you prefer, you can fax New Riders Publishing at (317) 581-4670.

You can also send electronic mail to New Riders at the following Internet address:

`ccleveland@newriders.mcp.com`

NRP is an imprint of Macmillan Computer Publishing. To obtain a catalog or information, or to purchase any Macmillan Computer Publishing book, call (800) 428-5331.

Thank you for selecting *Plug-n-Play JavaScript*.

PART I

JavaScript Fundamentals

1

JavaScript Fundamentals

This book was created by non-programmers as a tool for non-programmers, although can it can be used by anyone from novice to expert level, provided they already have a working knowledge of HTML. It is the belief of the authors that the present books available on JavaScript focus too much on programming methods and technicalities and not enough on functionality. For this reason, this book focuses its attention on useful and practical implementations of JavaScript which is currently supported by Netscape 2.0 and later and to a lesser degree Microsoft Internet Explorer 3.0 and later. All of the examples in the book are intended to be copied and pasted straight into your HTML pages. Once the JavaScripts are in your pages, they can be easily edited to suit your needs. *Words and that are replaceable without affecting the basic code are indicated by this text style.* You will generally not need to understand the programming behind the JavaScripts to be able to use them in your page, although Appendix A provides a very good introduction to JavaScript programming concepts as well as a very complete JavaScript reference source in Appendix B.

The book is structured around JavaScript's event handlers. Event handlers are keywords that instruct JavaScript to begin running a script in response to specific "events." These events consist of processes such as a button being clicked, a page being loaded, a form textbox being clicked into, a click on a hyperlink, and so on. The names of the event handlers are logically derived from the events that trigger them (such as *onClick*, *onLoad*, and *onSubmit*). The final chapter addresses advanced JavaScripts and accesses all of the previously introduced event handlers. In it, you will find examples of JavaScript and Live3D, Java, Plug-ins, cookies, and more. It is recommended that you read Appendix A if you want to gain a better understanding of the code behind the scripts.

This chapter introduces the programming elements of JavaScript. You do not have to read through this chapter to use the examples in the rest of the book, although it is a good idea to become familiar with the language and its syntax. All of the available programming elements are presented in Appendix A. To help you learn as you go, each of the examples in the following chapters will specify the page(s) in Appendix A that describe the relevant programming elements. Before jumping into the unique elements and syntax of JavaScript, a brief introduction to programming language functionality is useful.

Programming Languages

A programming language is like any other language, it follows rules of grammar and syntax and can say the same thing in many different ways. Instead of nouns, verbs, adverbs, and adjectives, an object-based programming language like JavaScript typically has objects, statements, methods, and properties. One strong distinction between programming languages and human speech is the former's intolerance of slang. Unlike spoken language, where meaning can be conveyed without the need to be syntactically correct, programming languages require strict adherence to their syntax and word usage.

A scripting language is a type of programming language. Typically, scripting languages are software extensions or operating system extensions as opposed to programming languages, which create compiled self-contained applications. AppleScript, Word Basic, VBScript, and JavaScript are examples of scripting languages. Java, C, C++, and Pascal are examples of programming languages. Scripting languages are less powerful but consequently easier to learn than true programming languages. A higher level programming language like Java, for instance, requires a very steep learning curve and a great degree of involvement to master. JavaScript is actually descended from Java, but it was developed by Netscape, originally under the name LiveScript, as a means to bring the simplicity of scripting languages to a wider audience. JavaScript, although initially developed as a server-side scripting language, expanded the functionalities and capabilities of the Netscape browser. The main difference between Java and JavaScript that will concern the readers of this book is that Java code is compiled into "applets" that are distinct from the HTML page and whose code cannot be viewed directly, whereas JavaScript code is included directly in the HTML document and can be easily modified. For the purposes mentioned here, programming languages include the subset of scripting languages, unless otherwise specified.

An object-oriented programming language enables programmers to break their code into component pieces that can be treated as logical entities by other code—kind of like Legos. An example will help to clarify this concept. An object in JavaScript could be a form element, such as a text box. By accessing the text box object's properties, you can determine what has been entered into the box, resize it, or pass the box information to another object for further processing.

Object-oriented programming languages typically have an associated object hierarchy. The object hierarchy enables you to specify exact objects and their properties that might otherwise be ambiguous. It also provides a more elegant and powerful way to work with objects and associated code than is possible without a structural relationship. This relationship is a natural extension of object-oriented programming. Consider the following:

textbox.length

This expression reflects the length of a textbox.

document.form.textbox.length

This expression reflects the length of a textbox contained within a form contained within a document.

The document, form, and textbox are each objects that have a relationship to each other that is hierarchically based. This is explained in greater detail in Appendix A, which outlines the JavaScript Object Hierarchy. Before getting to that point, you should become familiar with the programming elements of JavaScript.

JavaScript Elements

The following sections introduce the principal programming elements that will be used throughout this book. Appendix A will explain any programming terms included here that are not described below. The following elements are used by JavaScript and are representative of other programming language elements.

Arguments

Arguments are used with *methods* and *functions*. *Arguments* are either *values*, *variables*, or *objects* that the method or function requires in order to be processed. If you have designed a function called *squareroot*, for instance, that calculates the square root of a number, the function with its argument would appear:

```
function squareroot(16)
```

In this example, the number 16 is the *argument*, and the calculation returns the number 4 as the answer.

Event Handlers

Event handlers are used to initiate, or call, a JavaScript. It is actually the function that is called by the *event handler* which contains *statements* that are then executed. An example is the *onClick* event handler that is used with the <A> anchor tag to initiate an action described by a function.

```
<A HREF="link.html" onClick="functionZ()">Click Here</A>
```

The *functionZ* function is initiated by the *onClick event handler* when the "Click Here" text is clicked with the mouse. Event handlers are the elements around which the book is based. Event handlers fall into several categories, depending on the object(s) they affect. These categories have been organized in this book as button and link events, window events, form events, and image events. With Navigator 3.0, these have been augmented to include Live3D, LiveAudio, and LiveVideo events, which are discussed in Chapters 3 and 6.

Expressions

An *expression* is a set of *literals*, *variables*, *operators*, and/or *expressions* that describe a single number, string, or logical *value*. In the following example, the entire line is the expression.

```
NewNumber = FirstNumber - 10
```

In this example, *NewNumber* and *FirstNumber* are both variables. The number *10* is a *literal*. The equal sign (=) and the minus sign (-) are *operators*. Finally, *FirstNumber - 10*, itself, is an expression.

Functions

Functions are special *statements* that contain other *statements* for execution when called by an event handler. Functions are complete "fragments" of code that perform a specific operation by themselves and can be considered, along with other statements, as the rough equivalent of verbs in spoken languages. In computer languages, these might be called subroutines or procedures. The function statements are contained between curly braces (*{}*).The placement of the curly braces (*{}*) is generally done above and beneath the code fragments for better legibility, although in the example below, they could have been placed on the same line as the *alert()* method. Their inclusion in the function definition is mandatory and the function will not work if it does not have both opening and closing braces, although their exact placement is not critical so long as the code fragment has an opening and closing brace to indicate where it begins and ends. Many scripts contain multiple functions and the curly braces serve as way to isolate the fragments into self-contained pieces of code for easy identification. The following is a very small function.

```
function testmessage()
{
alert ("This is a very small function.")
}
```

The *testmessage* function uses the *alert() method* to display a warning box with the text *"This is a very small function."* This function could also have been written with the curly braces in a different location without affecting the way it operates:

```
function testmessage() {
alert ("This is a very small function.")
}
```

Literals

Literals are representations of *values*. Literals can be integers, floating point numbers, Boolean values, or strings. Unlike *variables*, *literals* are inferred and not declared. Declaring a variable means actually stating *a=45*, where *a* is the variable. The number *45* is implied as a numeric value and does not need an expression to declare its value. Any real number can be considered a literal—either an integer (1) or floating point (1.3333)—if it is not a whole number. A Boolean value is either true or false (actually, one or zero), and a string value is defined as some string of text. All of the preceding examples can be literals because they possess a value in and of themselves.

Methods

Methods are special types of functions, associated with *objects*, that require *arguments*. Due to their association with *objects* (noun), and their function (verb) characteristics, methods are often thought of as the programming counterpart of adverbs. Like *properties*, which correspond to adjectives in human languages and are descriptive in nature, methods are directly associated with *objects*, yet they require processing of the object, not defining its characteristics. Methods are predefined and are listed in Appendix A. You can easily recognize a method because it is made up of a word followed by parentheses such as in the example: *open()*. Although functions also use the parentheses, they are preceded by the word function and followed by a set of opening and closing curly braces: {}. One of the simplest methods is the *alert()* method. Its syntax is as follows:

```
alert("The alert method displays a warning dialog box.")
```

Objects

Objects are the principal elements that are affected or interpreted using JavaScript. The spoken language counterpart of an *object* is a noun. An example of an object is the location (the URL) of the current page, or a checkbox element in a form. There are built-in objects, and you can also make your own objects as well. In the example below, the *document* object is being used to write a line in the HTML page. It is the *write()* method of the document object that is invoked to perform the task.

```
document.write("This text will show up in the browser window.")
```

Operators

There are two types of *operators* in JavaScript. Assignment operators, as the name implies, assign *values* to the operand on the left side of the operator. The other types of operators consist of arithmetic, string, and logical operators. Broadly stated, operators affect or interpret values of one or more operands. Examples of operators include the equal sign (=), the plus sign (+) and minus sign (−).

Warning

An operand is simply a value being used in an equation. In the equation A+B=C, there are three operands (A, B, and C) and two operators (+ and =).

Properties

Properties can be considered as adjectives that describe objects. In many cases, these may function as objects themselves. For instance, the document object is a property of the window object. Similarly, the forms *property* of the document object is also treated as an object with properties like checkboxes, which are, likewise, objects with properties.

Statements

Statements are responsible for directing the flow of the code. The classic example, with a spoken counterpart, is the if...then statement. If condition X is true, then the statement(s) following the if...then statement will be executed. In JavaScript, if...then is actually if...else, as seen in the following example.

```
<SCRIPT>
X= 9
Y = 10
function bottomofpage()
{
if( X > Y)
        {
        alert("X is greater than Y.")
        }
else
        {
        alert("Y is greater than or equal to X.")
        }
}
</SCRIPT>
```

The function *bottomofpage()* uses two global *variables*. The variables X and Y are tested by the *if(X>Y)* statement. If this statement is true, the *alert()* method will invoke a warning dialog box with the text "X is greater than Y." However, in this case it is not true, and the warning box displays the text "Y is greater than or equal to X." The *else* statement contains the *alert()* method and the text content for this dialog box. Finally, two closing braces are needed; one for the *else* statement, and the other for the function *bottomofpage()* itself.

Values

JavaScript recognizes four types of *values* (also known as data types): numbers, Boolean (logical), strings, and null (nothing, no value). JavaScript also recognizes a date value data type that is accessed through the built-in date object of JavaScript. Each type of value will be treated differently by JavaScript. It is important that only legitimate value types are used in expressions, statements, and other elements. If you try to add a number to a word, for instance, JavaScript will not be able to perform the calculation.

Variables

Variables are representations of values that are explicitly set using an expression. The variable is placed to the left of the operator, and its assigned value is placed to the right of the operator. Variables can be either global or local. Global means that all functions within <SCRIPT> </SCRIPT> tags can use the variables. Local means that the variable was declared within a function and is only available to that specific function. Making a variable global requires declaring the variable before the first function within <SCRIPT> </SCRIPT> tags. In the following example, a global and a local variable are declared.

```
<SCRIPT>
var globalvar1=5
function fivetimestwo()
{
var localvar1 = 2  * globalvar1
alert ("Five times two is " + localvar1)
}
</SCRIPT>
```

The global variable is called *globalvar1*, and is declared before the function *fivetimestwo()* is defined. The local *variable*, *localvar1*, is able to use the value of *globalvar1* and multiply it by two. The *alert()* method is then used to display a warning box with the text "Five times two is 10." If a second function followed *fivetimestwo()*, it would be able to use the *globalvar1 variable*, but the *localvar1 variable* would not be recognized. The var keyword should only be used for declaring a variable so that once you declare: var globalvar1 = 5, if you want to change the value later in the script you would simply say: globalvar1 = 8.

There, now that wasn't so bad. The programming elements are the nuts and bolts of JavaScript. Using a linguistic metaphor, you have been introduced to the grammatical components of JavaScript. The final thing to cover in this chapter is the syntax that JavaScript needs to adhere to in an HTML page in order to function properly.

JavaScript Syntax and HTML

For the most part, JavaScript is contained within the HTML document (an exception to this rule is server-side scripting using LiveWire or the as yet unsupported capability to reference JavaScripts in the href tag as a document on the server, but this doesn't affect the scripts you'll be dealing with in this book). You will generally write your JavaScript within the <SCRIPT> and </SCRIPT> tags in the Web page. It is recommended that the script be included in the <HEAD> section of the document. This way the script will be loaded before it is called by the event handler in the <BODY> section, which is important because if the event handler loaded first it wouldn't have any code to invoke. Refer to the following example:

```
<HTML>
<HEAD>
<TITLE>Small Script</TITLE>
<SCRIPT>
function alertOne(){
    alert("This is a small script.")
        }
</SCRIPT>
</HEAD>
<BODY>
<FORM>
<INPUT TYPE=BUTTON VALUE="Click Here" onClick="alertOne()">
</FORM>
</BODY>
</HTML>
```

This example shows that the <SCRIPT>...</SCRIPT> paired tags are contained within the <HEAD>...</HEAD> section. The JavaScript consists of a function that contains one method and its argument. In the <BODY>...</BODY> section, the input button is described by *<INPUT TYPE=BUTTON VALUE="Click Here" onClick="alertOne()">*. When you click on the button, the *onClick* event handler initiates the *alertOne()* function. The *alertOne()* function has one argument that is supplied by the *alert()* method. This argument is "This is a small script."

alert() is a predefined method that produces a warning window box. Because it is predefined, the following code could have been substituted for the function:

```
<INPUT TYPE=BUTTON VALUE="Click Here" onClick=alert("This is a small
script.")>
```

Typically, a function will be used to respond to event handlers, but for predefined methods, you can ignore convention and simply insert the method. As a rule of thumb, place the JavaScript within the <HEAD>...</HEAD> section, and the event handlers that call them within the <BODY>...</BODY> section.

The Rest of the Book

The examples in the following chapters are based on event handlers. These, as well as all other JavaScript programming elements, are described in Appendix A. It is strongly recommended that you become familiar with the material in Appendix A, although, for the most part, the book is designed to enable you to implement JavaScript with very little programming knowledge.

The JavaScripts are introduced in progressively more difficult fashion. The usage of the event handler as the element around which the book is based is arbitrary. Most of the scripts that are called with one event handler can be called by any of the others. If you see a script that performs from an *onClick* handler, you can copy and paste the function into a page to support *onLoad*, *onBlur*, or most other handlers, depending on which event you want to trigger the action.

Chapter 2 has the simplest examples, and reviewing it will familiarize you with the way that JavaScripts are implemented. Any programming elements on the page will be referenced to the page number where they are defined in Appendix A. Most of the scripts in Chapters 5 and 6 require Navigator 3.0, which is still in a late Beta state as of this book's writing. These utilize functionality that was not built into earlier versions. When a script cannot be executed in all versions and platforms of Navigator and Internet Explorer, it will be noted in its description.

PART II

Link and Button Events

2

Chapter

Link and Button Events: onClick, onMouseOut, onMouseOver

This chapter is an introduction to event handlers. Event handlers can be considered the most basic components of JavaScript as they are the means by which scripts are initiated in response to user events. Without event handlers a script would exist on a page but it would never execute as it would have no way of knowing when to begin executing. Because event handlers constitute the basic building blocks of JavaScript, the chapters in this book have been organized according to the various event handlers available and the types of page components that they interact with.

One of the most basic event handlers is *onClick*, which initiates a script, as its name implies, when a user clicks on a link in the browser window. All of the other event handlers work in this same manner by evaluating a user action, then calling a script that executes some code. The event handlers introduced in this chapter are associated with text and image hyperlinks and the button form object. The *onClick* and *onMouseOver* event handlers are part of the original Navigator 2.0 specifications introduced by Netscape while the *onMouseOut* handler is new to Navigator 3.0 and does not function with previous versions. *OnMouseOut* and *onMouseOver*, like *onClick*, refer to the location of the mouse pointer in relation to a hyperlink. If you're a JavaScript newcomer, starting off with these three event handlers will provide you with a good basis for understanding the inner workings of JavaScript and for utilizing the rest of the examples in this book. In subsequent chapters, you will learn more powerful ways to use event handlers and build upon the basic knowledge acquired here.

Although this book organizes event handlers based on the types of functions they generally carry out, in truth any event handler can be used to perform virtually any function. The manner in which functions are associated with particular event handlers is rather arbitrary, although it is implemented in this book in a manner that complements the function's anticipated usage. This is done in order to clarify and help organize them as well as to provide a source for readers to access scripts in a plug-and-play fashion without having to really learn any programming. Here's a brief look at some of the basic types of functions that you could implement with the *onClick*, *onMouseOver* and *onMouseOut* event handlers.

☐ Bring up an alert message when a user clicks on a picture or hyperlink.

☐ Send an e-mail message by clicking on a button rather than hypertext.

☐ Provide a button to navigate backward and forward through your URL history.

☐ Display some text in the status bar of the window as the mouse rolls across a hypertext link.

☐ Call up a new window when a user clicks on a button.

The examples and chapters in this book are presented in increasing complexity. As the examples progress you will see more than one event handler occurring within a page, and even within a single HTML tag. For now, this chapter will demonstrate how to create a simple alert box, a simple forward and backward navigation button, a confirmation box, a new window, and status bar messages. This chapter will also demonstrate how the *open()* and *close()* methods are used with the window object. By familiarizing yourself with the basic event handlers introduced in this chapter, you will be able to use any of the other event handlers included in the examples in this book and be well on the way toward understanding the basic concepts behind scripting in JavaScript.

As with all scripts in this book, the following examples can be included directly into your HTML and expected to work if implemented as described here. Each script can easily be modified to suit your own needs without affecting the underlying programming structure and the user-changeable variables have been indicated in `this typeface` to help facilitate this. The scripts can be pulled directly off the CD, which contains all of the chapter examples.

onClick Alert Message

01.htm

The onClick alert message script creates an alert message in response to a mouse click.

The *onClick* event handler is one of the most basic and commonly used JavaScript components available to incorporate into your scripts. The following script utilizes the *onClick* event handler to generate an alert message in the browser. Alert messages can be used creatively for numerous purposes, such as the example here that uses an alert box to provide brief information about a link without having to load the hyper-linked page. Alert messages serve the purpose of providing a means for displaying text using information in a dialog box in response to a user action. They are generated via the *alert()* method, which is a built-in function of JavaScript and is available to any event handler (see methods in Appendix A).

The alert is generated by calling the *alert()* method, which invokes the browser's alert dialog box. This method is defined in the *pushbutton()* function that is called by the *onClick* event handler.

HTML code for the onClick alert message JavaScript:

```
<HTML>
<HEAD>
<TITLE>OnClick alert message</TITLE>
<SCRIPT LANGUAGE="JavaScript">
function pushbutton() {
alert("This section of our web site is still under construction but have a
look around anyway");
}
</SCRIPT>
</HEAD>
<BODY>
<CENTER>
<H1>
<A HREF="http://www.transmitmedia.com" onclick="pushbutton()">Visit our
Home Pages!</A>
</H1>
</CENTER>
</BODY>
</HTML>
```

Terminology

event handler: *onClick*-page 187-188

method: *alert( )*-page 241, 254

Figure 2.1

Invoking an alert box

Navigation Buttons

02.htm

The Navigation Buttons script creates forward and backward navigation elements to move between the URLs in the browser's history list.

The Navigation Buttons script implements the *onClick* event handler to initiate the *go( )* method of the *history* object to enable backward and forward navigation through the URL history. There are actually two ways of doing this same task and this script includes both methods.

The *history.go( )* object method takes an integer, in this case *+1* or *–1*, and loads the link the corresponding number of places forward or backward in the navigation history. This method is included in the function *nav(x)*, where *x* becomes the value in the *nav( )* function of the button that is clicked. To design your own buttons, you could do the same thing with the <A> tag as illustrated in the last part of the script beginning with the line: <A HREF=javascript:history.go(-2). This line introduces the usage of a JavaScript object as the target of the HREF attribute in an <A> tag. While most JavaScripts utilize code between the <SCRIPT></SCRIPT> tags, in the second part of the example, the HREF of the custom button is some JavaScript code, indicated by the use of *javascript:history.go(-2)*. This is just another way to do the same thing as the first part of the script which utilizes a more common and familiar method.

HTML code for the Navigation Buttons JavaScript:

```
<HTML>
<HEAD>
<TITLE>History Buttons</TITLE>
<SCRIPT LANGUAGE="JavaScript">
function nav(x) {
history.go(x);
}
</script>
</HEAD>
<BODY>
<CENTER>
<h1>History Buttons</h1>
<h2>Here are the two buttons made with navigator form buttons: </h2><P>
<FORM>
<INPUT TYPE="button" VALUE="GO BACK" onClick="nav(-1)">
```

```
<INPUT TYPE="button" VALUE="GO FORWARD" onClick="nav(1)">
</FORM>
<P>
<h2>And here is a custom button with a javascript link.</h2><P>
<A HREF=javascript:history.go(-2)><IMG SRC="back2.gif" BORDER=0></A>
</CENTER>
</BODY>
</HTML>
```

Terminology

event handler: *onClick*-page 187-188

method: *go()*-page 243

object: *history*-page 213

Figure 2.2

Navigator Buttons

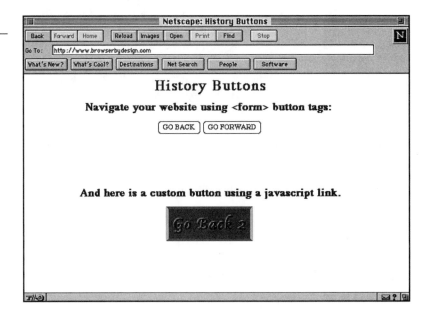

Dialog Box with Confirm

03.htm

The Dialog Box with Confirm asks the viewer for confirmation before opening a link and leaving the current page.

This uses the *onClick* event handler to call the *confirm( )* method. The *confirm( )* method brings up a dialog box with a choice of either "yes" or "no" enabling the users to confirm whether or not they wish to leave the page. This script could thus function as a exit point announcing that the user is about to leave the current site and travel to a new URL, providing a way to clearly delineate the "boundaries" of the current Web site. The text displayed in the confirm message can be easily be customized.

 Browser Warning

> The ability of onClick to return both true and false conditions is new to Navigator 3.0 and not supported by 2.0.

This script uses a new attribute of the *onClick* event handler, enabling the event handler to return a "false" condition via the *confirm( )* method when the return statement is included in the script. Normally the onClick event generates a true condition, but in this case since the choices in the confirm box are "yes" or "no," a value of either true or false can be returned based on the input of the user. This process has the effect of canceling the loading of the new page with the click event when a false condition is generated by clicking on "no."

HTML code for the Dialog Box with Confirm JavaScript:

```
<HTML>
<HEAD>
<TITLE>Confirm Dialog Box</TITLE>
</HEAD>
<BODY BGCOLOR=FFFFFF>
<CENTER>
<H1>Confirm Dialog Box</H1><P>
<A HREF = "http://www.browserbydesign.com/" onClick="return confirm('Are
you sure you're ready to leave the safe confines of our website')"When you
click, a confirm dialog box displays. </a>
</CENTER>
</BODY>
</HTML>
```

Terminology

event handler: *onClick*-page 187-188

method: *confirm( )*-page 242, 255

statement: *return*-page 270

Figure 2.3

Setting up a Confirm dialog box

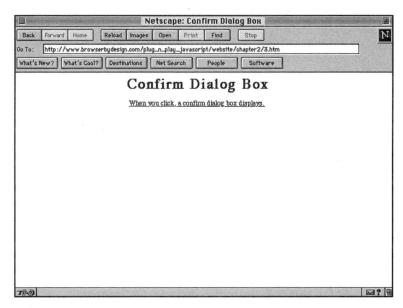

Figure 2.4

Invoking a Confirm dialog box

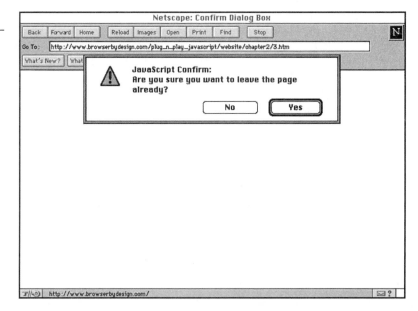

E-mail Button

04.htm

The E-mail Button script sends an e-mail message using a button form entry instead of a text hyperlink.

This script uses the *onClick* event handler in conjunction with a clickable button to invoke the *mailto:* HTML command, invoking a standard browser mail message window in the window that called it. This script enables you to incorporate a submit style button rather than just a text link in order to send an e-mail message. This serves primarily an aesthetic function, as buttons can be more interesting and dynamic than standard hyperlinked text. You can easily substitute an URL instead of a mail address.

The script utilizes the *self.location* window object property, which accesses a specified link (in this case a mail link) in the current window.

HTML code for the E-mail Button JavaScript:

```
<HTML>
<HEAD>
<title>E-mail button</title>
<HEAD>
<FORM>
<INPUT TYPE="button" VALUE="send e-mail"
onClick="self.location='mailto:person@place.com'">
</FORM>
</BODY>
</HTML>
```

Terminology

event handler: *onClick*-page 187-188

object: *window*-page 232-233

Figure 2.5

*Providing a button to
send e-mail*

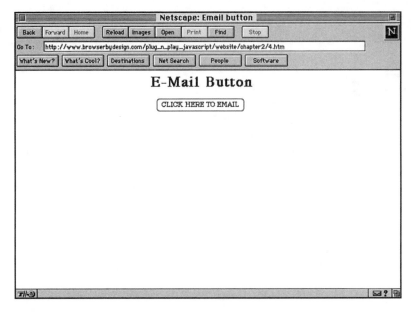

Figure 2.6

*Invoking an e-mail
message box*

New Window

05.htm

The New Window script creates a new window by clicking on a button.

In the following example, the *onClick* event handler is used to open a new window, while retaining the original browser window. The new window is fully functional, navigable, and provides an excellent way to jump to a new URL without losing the original page linked from. This technique is a useful way to retain the original URL, allowing visitors to return easily to your page, while giving them access to another page or Web site. When the user closes this new browser window, the original page or Web site will remain in view. This example uses the *open()* method of the window object.

HTML code for the New Window JavaScript:

```
<HTML>
<HEAD>
<title>Open New Window</title>
</HEAD>
<body bgcolor=FFFFFF>
<CENTER>
<h1>Open New Window</h1>
<P>
<FORM>
<INPUT TYPE="button" VALUE="CLICK HERE TO OPEN A NEW WINDOW"
onClick=window.open("http://www.3pdesign.com")>
</FORM>
</CENTER>
</BODY>
</HTML>
```

Terminology

event handler: *onClick*-page 187-188

method: *open()*-page 240, 242, 255-256

Figure 2.7

*Providing a button to
open additional
windows*

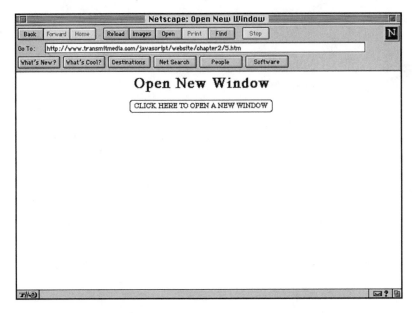

Figure 2.8

*Opening another
window*

New Window with Controllable Options

06.htm

The New Window with Controllable Options script opens a new window with the toolbar, location bar, directory buttons, and other features enabled or disabled.

Besides calling up a new window, JavaScript enables you to define certain properties of the new window such as its size and whether the window has a toolbar, menubar, directory buttons, scrollbars, and so on. The following script shows an example of a new window created with a predetermined size and no menu bars. This particular example illustrates how to incorporate a button into your Web site, say an art gallery, and bring up a new window containing artwork to display in a custom-sized window. Each button can link to a different image and size the window to be big enough to just include the artwork. This capability provides added aesthetic appeal for your Web pages.

This example uses the *open()* method of the window object with user-definable window parameters. The syntax for indicating the parameters with the *open()* method is as follows:

```
window.open("URL", "window
name","parameter1","parameter2","parameter3","etc. ")
```

Note that writing *window.open()* in it's entirety is optional, you can simply write *open()*, because the *open()* method belongs to the *window* object by default. Also note that the window parameters need to be separated by a comma *without* a space between them, unlike the URL and window name arguments. In addition, these parameters only affect the new window being opened and not the parent window. The following is a list of valid property arguments to use when modifying the window parameters:

Property Arguments for Modifying Window Parameters	
Property Arguments	Effect on Window Parameters
toolbar=yes/no	toggles toolbar buttons on or off
location=yes/no	toggles location bar on or off
directories=yes/no	toggles directory buttons on or off
status=yes/no	toggles status bar on or off

continues

Property Arguments for Modifying Window Parameters, **continued**	
Property Arguments	Effect on Window Parameters
menubar=yes/no	toggles menubar on or off (Windows only)
scrollbars=yes/no	toggles scrollbar on or off
resizeable=yes/no	determines whether the window can be resized
width=pixels	width in pixels
height=pixels	height in pixels

The following example demonstrates how the syntax is used with a function to open a new window with specific attributes. This can be an extremely useful tool when defining an exact-sized window for galleries, control pads, and other purposes.

HTML code for the New Window with Controllable Options script:

```
<HTML>
<HEAD>
<TITLE>Open new custom window</TITLE>
<SCRIPT LANGUAGE="JavaScript">
function NewWindow() {
window2=window.open("http://www.somewhere.com", "New Window",
"toolbar=no,directories=no,menubar=no,width=200,height=200");
}
</SCRIPT>
</HEAD>
<BODY>
<FORM>
<input type="button" value="New Window" onclick=NewWindow()>
</FORM>
</BODY>
</HTML>
```

Terminology

event handler: *onClick*-page 187-188

method: *alert()*-page 241, 254

method: *open()*-page 240, 242, 255-256

Figure 2.9

Providing a button to open a customized window

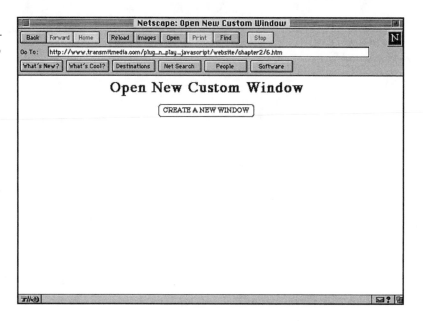

Figure 2.10

Opening a customized window

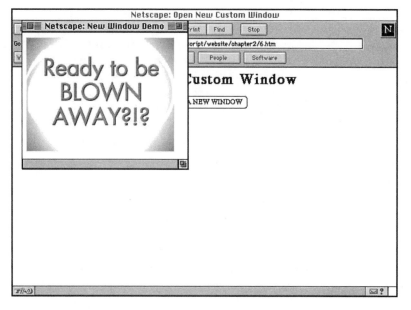

New Window with Controllable Options and Close Box

The New Window with Controllable Option and Close Box script enables the opening and closing of windows via the open() and close() methods.

Another method associated with the window object is the *close()* method, which performs exactly like the *open()* method except that it closes windows. The following example uses the *close()* method in the new window that was created in the preceding script example. This example includes an additional window to illustrate how this particular script can be utilized for a page that needs to call up several different images in a predefined window size. The benefit of a script like this is that it enables interaction with separate windows without affecting the parent window. This could be very useful in an art gallery, commercial, or adult site, or simply to provide a large number of image links without having to exit the page that references them.

Notice that this is the first time that the *write()* method is being used. As you move to more complex JavaScripts, you will see this method used more frequently. One benefit of using the *write()* method to open new windows is that there is less server interaction involved (except for loading of images and other non-text files) as the page is generated on-the-fly rather then retrieved via a hyperlink reference. This eliminates the small delay when a server has to load the new HTML page—since it is now generated on the client side. If the document contains no hyper-referenced images or other files, the loading is instantaneous.

 Warning

A precautionary note about this script: Without the *hrefloc=this.location* line, along with the *<BASE HREF="* + *hrefloc* reference, locally referenced files (that is, files that exist on your local hard drive and not a server) will not load. This is only a problem when testing files locally. To test a file locally that has supporting files residing primarily on a single server, you need to include a reference to the folder in which the the files are contained.

In the following example, two functions are defined: *newWindow()* and *newWindow2()*, each of which pertain to a different window and button. To add more windows, simply copy and paste a new function with a unique name then call it from your new button.

HTML code for the New Window with Controllable Options and Close Box script:

```
<HTML>
<HEAD>
<TITLE>Open/close new custom window</TITLE>
<SCRIPT LANGUAGE="JavaScript">

hrefloc=this.location
// this assigns the current URL to the global variable hrefloc, called
later in the script as a workaround for a problem involving accessing files
from a local disk.

function NewWindow1()   //this defines the first window, accessed by
button#1
{
window1=window.open("", "NewWindow1",
"toolbar=no,directories=no,menubar=no,scrollbars=no,width=200,height=225");
window1.document.write("<HTML><HEAD><BASE HREF=" + hrefloc + ">");
                       //if calling images on the web and not local drive
                       //remove the tag: <BASE HREF=" + hrefloc + ">
window1.document.write("<TITLE>Clock</TITLE>");
window1.document.write("</HEAD><BODY  BGCOLOR=FFFFFF>");
window1.document.write("<CENTER><img src='images/clock.jpg'>");
window1.document.write("<FORM><INPUT TYPE='button' VALUE=Close
onClick='window.close()'></FORM></CENTER>");
window1.document.write("</BODY></HTML>");
}
function NewWindow2()//this defines the second window, accessed by
button#2{
window2=window.open("",
"NewWindow2","toolbar=no,directories=no,menubar=no,scrollbars=no,width=200,height=225");
window2.document.write("<HTML><HEAD><BASE HREF=" + hrefloc + ">");
window2.document.write("<TITLE>Java</TITLE>");
window2.document.write("</HEAD><BODY  BGCOLOR=FFFFFF>");
window2.document.write("<CENTER><img src='images/cup.jpg'>");
window2.document.write("<FORM><INPUT TYPE='button' VALUE='Close' " +
"onClick='window.close()'></FORM></CENTER>");
window2.document.write("</BODY></HTML>");
}
</script>
</HEAD>
<BODY BGCOLOR=FFFFFF>
<FORM>
```

```
<input type="button" value="SELECTION 1" onclick=NewWindow1()>
<P>
<input type="button" value="SELECTION 2" onclick=NewWindow2()>
</FORM>
</BODY>
</HTML>
```

Terminology

object: *document*-page 206

object: *location*-page 218-219

event handler: *onClick*-page 187-188

method: *open()*-page 240, 242, 255-256

method: *close()*-page 240, 242, 255

method: *write()*-page 240-241

Figure 2.11

Navigating multiple windows with buttons

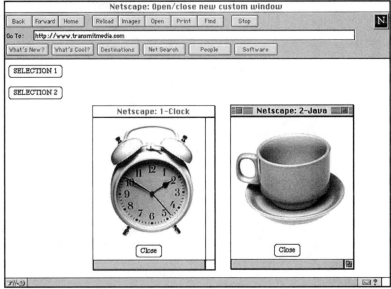

Status Bar Message

08.htm

The Status Bar Message script displays a message in the status bar window.

The *onMouseOver* event handler registers a call when the user moves the mouse pointer directly over a link object. This script utilizes *onMouseOver* to recognize the presence of the mouse over an area of text and produces a predefined message that appears in the status bar of the browser window. In the following example, two links are used to illustrate how different links can bring up different messages in the status bar. This serves the function of giving your readers information about the link they are about to click on without having to actually open the link. You could just as easily add or subtract links to your page using as many *onMouseOver* messages as deemed necessary.

This example also introduces the *window.status* property, where status refers to a property of the *window* object. The *status* property displays the assigned text in the status bar (in the lower left corner) of the document window. The script must include the statement: return *true* from the *onMouseOver* event handler in order to correctly set the status.

HTML code for the Status Bar Message JavaScript:

```
<HTML>
<HEAD>
<TITLE>Status message with text link</TITLE>
</HEAD>
<BODY BGCOLOR=FFFFFF>
<CENTER>
<A HREF="link1.html" onMouseOver="window.status='Link #1 message
here';return true"><H1>Link #1</H1></A>
<P>
<A HREF="link2.html" onMouseOver="window.status='Link #2 message
here';return true"><H1>Link #2</H1></A>
<P>
<A HREF="link1.html" onMouseOver="window.status='This is a clock';return
true"><img src="images/clock.jpg"></A>
<A HREF="link2.html" onMouseOver="window.status='This is a cup of
java';return true"><img src="images/cup.jpg"></A>
</CENTER>
</BODY>
</HTML>
```

Terminology

event handler: *onMouseOver*-page 189

object: *window*-page 232-233

property: *window.status*-page 233

Figure 2.12

Status bar message with mouse over text

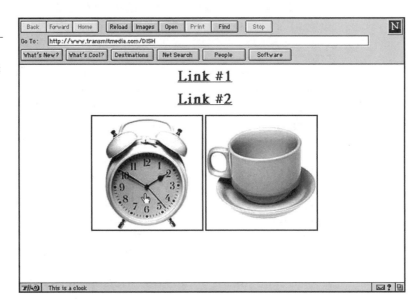

Figure 2.13

Status bar message with mouse over image

Alert Message onMouseOver

The Alert Message onMouseOver script alerts visitors when they drag the mouse over an anchored area.

The *onMouseOver* event handler can be used to call any of the methods provided by JavaScript. The following example uses the *alert()* method to bring up an alert message during the *onMouseOver* state. This is another way to provide information about a link without actually opening that link. A useful implementation of this could include links to sites still under construction or links that just serve as temporary placeholders while a page is being constructed.

HTML code for the Alert Message onMouseOver JavaScript:

```
<HTML>
<HEAD>
<title>MouseOver Alert</title>
</HEAD>
<SCRIPT LANGUAGE="JavaScript">
function AlertText() {
alert("This site is still in progress, try again in a few days");
}
</SCRIPT>
</HEAD>
<BODY>
<CENTER>
<a href="link.html" onMouseOver="AlertText()"><H1>Our new improved web
site!</H1></a>
</CENTER>
</BODY>
</HTML>
```

Terminology

event handler: *onMouseOver*-page 189

method: *alert()*-page 241, 254

Figure 2.14

*Providing alert
messages for
hyperlinks*

Alert Message onMouseOut

10.htm

The Alert Message onMouseOut script brings up an alert message during the onMouseOut state.

The *onMouseOut* event handler looks for the instance when the mouse leaves the predefined hyperlink—in effect the opposite of *onMouseOver*—and then brings up an alert box using the *alert()* method. In order for the *onMouseOut* event to occur, the mouse must first enter the area defined in the hyperlink. This type of script could serve useful in online game situations or on sites with one opening image requiring the user to click the image in order to proceed.

HTML code for the Alert Message onMouseOut JavaScript:

```
<HTML>
<HEAD>
<TITLE>MouseOut Alert</TITLE>
<BODY>
<CENTER>
<A HREF="http://www.transmitmedia.com" onMouseOut='alert("You must click on
an image in order to proceed!")'><IMG SRC="art/cup.jpg"></A>
</CENTER>
</BODY>
</HTML>
```

Terminology

event handler: *onMouseOut*-page 189

method: *alert()*-page 241, 254

Figure 2.15

*Image prior to
mouseOut*

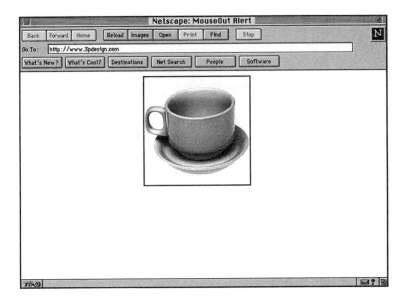

Figure 2.16

*Alert message
displays when mouse
leaves hyperlink*

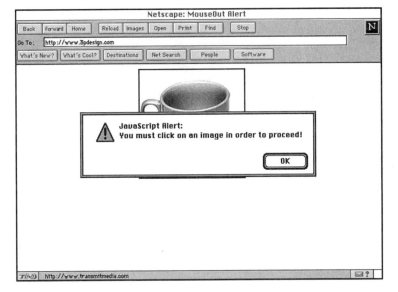

onMouseOver and onMouseOut

11.htm

The onMouseOver and onMouseOut script activates different scripts based on the mouse location over an object.

The following example presents a link object that uses two different event handlers. As the mouse moves over the image, the status window displays a text message. When the mouse moves off the image, a different text message appears. When creating a series of images, each having *onMouseOver* and *onMouseOut* event handlers, you can create an interesting page for developing hand-eye coordination for those just getting used to using the mouse. Other uses could include children's sites or training applications.

HTML code for the onMouseOver and onMouseOut JavaScript:

```
<HTML>
<HEAD>
<TITLE>onMouseOver and onMouseOut</TITLE>
<SCRIPT>
function message1{
window.status='Pucker up, big boy!';return true
}
function message2{
window.status='Oh, come on! We were just getting started!';return true
}
</SCRIPT>
<BODY BGCOLOR=FFFFFF>
<CENTER>
<H1>onMouseOver and onMouseOut</H1><P>
<H2>Use this to perform different functions based on mouse position.</H2>
<P>
<A HREF=anchor.self onMouseOver="message1" onMouseOut="message2">
<IMG SRC="lips.jpg"></A>
</CENTER>
</BODY>
</HTML>
```

Terminology

event handler: *onMouseOut*-page 189

event handler: *onMouseOver*-page 189

method: *alert()*-page 241, 254

Figure 2.17

An idle image

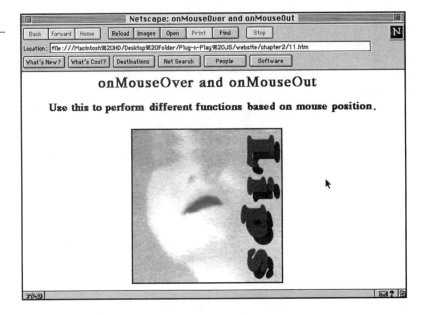

Figure 2.18

MouseOver generates status bar message

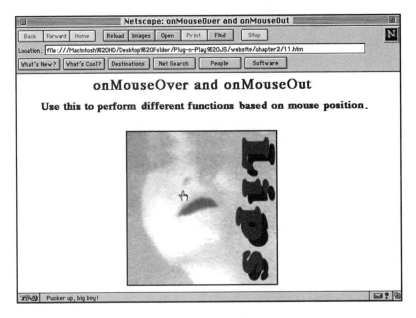

Figure 2.19

MouseOut generates
alert message

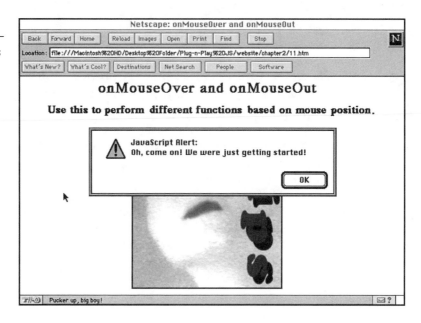

onClick with Input Tags

The onClick with Input Tags script provides immediate response to user interaction with a page. The following example demonstrates a simple multiple choice test.

This example presents the radio type of input button used to perform a function through the *onClick* event handler. The event handler activates three different alert messages based on user selection. If the visitor to your page selects Peoria as the capital of Illinois, they are alerted that it is an incorrect answer. The benefit of this script is that all of its functionality is provided entirely on the client side. Prior to JavaScript, this type of interaction was only available using server side interaction and Perl or CGI scripting. You could easily expand on this example and create a much more in-depth type of test. In Chapter 4, covering form event handlers, a complete test with multiple choice, essay questions, true-false, and other question types is presented.

HTML code for the onClick with Input Tags JavaScript:

```
<HTML>
<HEAD>
<TITLE>Using onClick with Input Tags</TITLE>
</HEAD>
<BODY BGCOLOR=FFFFFF>
<H1>Using onClick with Input Tags</H1><P>
<H2>Immediate response to visitor clicks on your page reduces server
workload.</H2>
<P>
<FORM>
<STRONG><FONT SIZE=5>What is the capital of Illinois?</FONT><STRONG>
<FONT SIZE=4><P>
<INPUT TYPE=RADIO onClick="alert('Chicago is the largest city, but not the
capital.')">Chicago<BR>
<INPUT TYPE=RADIO onClick="alert('You are right! Springfield is the
capital.')">Springfield<BR>
<INPUT TYPE=RADIO onClick="alert('Peoria is the supposed home of the
Nielsen families for demographic purposes.')">Peoria<BR>
</FONT>
</FORM>
</BODY>
</HTML>
```

Terminology

event handler: *onClick*-page 187-188

method: *alert()*-page 241, 254

Figure 2.22

Providing input radio buttons for user interaction

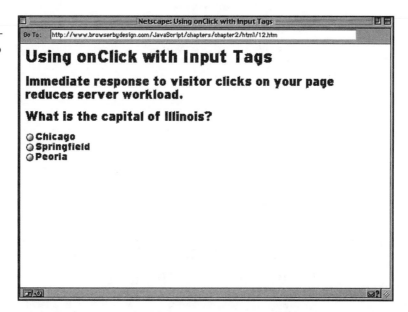

Figure 2.23

Choosing the wrong answer generates an alert message

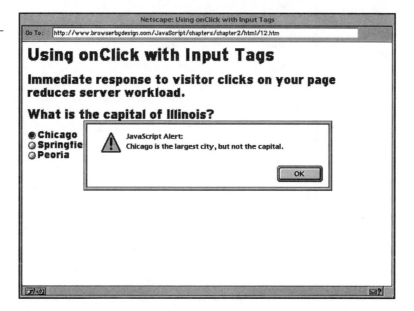

Figure 2.24

Choosing the right answer generates an alert message

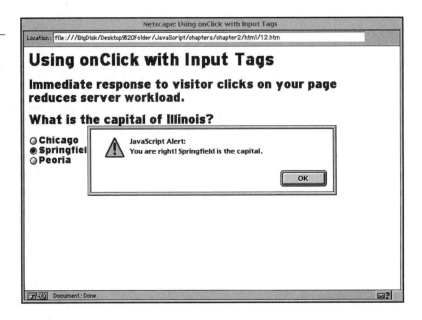

Figure 2.25

Wrong answer again generates alert message

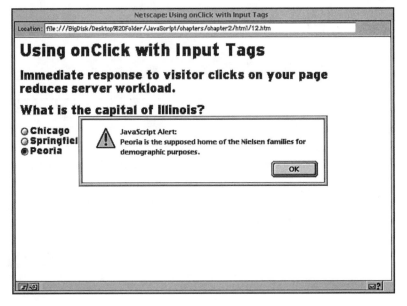

If you've followed along with the examples in this chapter, you should have a good understanding of how to implement basic JavaScript event handlers to trigger various actions within your scripts. In addition, you should be able to cut, paste, and modify the included examples to suit your needs, since these basic link and button events can be reused in countless ways. The *onClick*, *onMouseOver*, and *onMouseOut* event handlers are just few of the ways in which you will learn how to harness the power of JavaScript in this book. The next chapter will present window events—demonstrating even more of the useful functions available to event handlers in JavaScipt.

PART III

Window Events

3

C h a p t e r

Window Events: onLoad, onUnload (onBlur, onFocus)

This chapter will introduce a few window events. Window events can be defined as events triggered by some activity of the browser window such as a document loading or unloading, or *onBlur* and *onFocus* which occur when a window becomes activated or inactivated. These events apply not only to windows, but also to frames. Frames are almost identical to windows in their syntax usage and the choice of using a single window or multiple frames is primarily a question of aesthetics, although frames can provide some practical functionalities as well. In HTML, the event handlers for window events are contained within the <BODY> and <FRAMESET> tags. They appear in the HTML document as follows:

```
<BODY onLoad="functionx()"> for window without frames
```

or

```
<FRAMESET ROWS="*,*" onUnload="alert('Thanks for visiting our page.')"> for
window with frames
```

In the top example, the *onLoad* event handler calls the function *functionx()* when the document loads. In the frameset document, used to create a page with frames, a visitor will see an alert box (activated by the *onUnload* event handler) when leaving the page. These two event handlers thus function when entering or leaving a page and allow execution of a script during either of these two events.

With the introduction of Navigator 3.0, two other methods that the window object and frame object are able to use—the *blur( )* method and the *focus( )* method—have been made available. In conjunction with these methods there are two additional event handlers, *onBlur* and *onFocus*, that are now available to window objects when using Navigator 3.0, although these have previously been available to form elements and are discussed in this context in Chapter 4. Currently there aren't any truly practical implementations for *onBlur* and *onFocus* as window events so no examples have been included. However using *blur( )* and *focus( )* as window methods can be useful as illustrated in the last example, the Open Control Pad Window with Frames script, where the *focus( )* method is used to return focus to a window after a certain period of time elapses.

Browser Test

13.htm

The Browser Test script indicates to the visitor which browser they are using.

The *onLoad* event handler enables JavaScript to trigger actions as a page is loaded into the browser. The following example references the *navigator* object. Three navigator object properties (*appName*, *appVersion*, and *appCodeName*) are accessed and displayed in the alert box. The *appName* property refers to the name of the browser, *appVersion* the version number, and *appCodeName* the code name used by the company making the browser, in the case of Netscape this is Mozilla. In Chapter 6, "Advanced JavaScripts," these properties will be used to determine which page the browser loads, as accessing these properties allow Web site designers to direct viewers to different pages depending on the type of browser people are entering the site with. The following script simply shows how to display an alert box, telling the visitor which browser and version they are using, an easy way of providing customized feedback to your viewers depending on what browser they have.

As shown in figure 3.2, Microsoft's Internet Explorer 3.0 also recognizes JavaScript. For reasons of maintaining compatibility with Netscape's browser, Internet Explorer also identifies itself as Mozilla to the server. For certain browser statistics, this will confuse the server, and it will indicate that more Navigator (Mozilla) visitors have arrived than is actually the case. This needs to be taken into account when reading browser statistics that usually rely on application code names. Using the application name and version will consequently give much more reliable information than the code name.

This example utilizes the *alert()* method to call the *browsertest()* function. This function passes the three object properties *appName*, *appVersion*, and *appCode* to three different variables which are then displayed in the alert message. The script is initiated using the *onLoad* event handler which executes when the page loads into the window.

HTML code for the Browser Test JavaScript

```
<HTML>
<HEAD>
<TITLE>Testing All Browsers</TITLE>
<! This actually only tests browsers that understand JavaScript. You would
probably use this to direct non-enabled browsers somewhere else.>
<SCRIPT>
function browsertest() {
thisapp=navigator.appName
thisversion=navigator.appVersion
thisappcodename=navigator.appCodeName
alert("You are using " + thisapp + " version " + thisversion + ", which is
code named " + thisappcodename + ".")
}
</SCRIPT>
</HEAD>
<BODY onLoad="browsertest()" bgcolor=FFFFFF>
<CENTER>
<H1>Testing All Browsers</H1>
<H2>You can modify this script and use it to direct your JavaScript visi-
tors in one direction, and other visitors elsewhere.</H2>
</CENTER>
</BODY>
</HTML>
```

Terminology

event handler: *onLoad*-page 189

method: *alert()*-page 241, 254

object: *navigator*-page 221-222

property: *appCodeName*-page 221

property: *appName*-page 221

property: *appVersion*-page 221, 274-275

Figure 3.1

*Netscape Navigator
2.0 recognition alert*

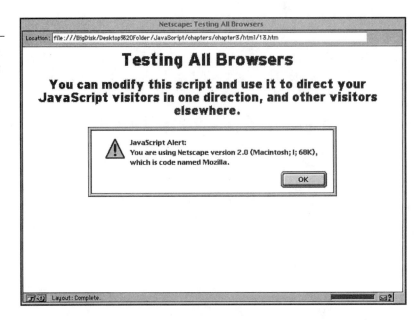

Figure 3.2

*Netscape Navigator
3.0 recognition alert*

Figure 3.3

*Internet Explorer
3.0 recognition alert*

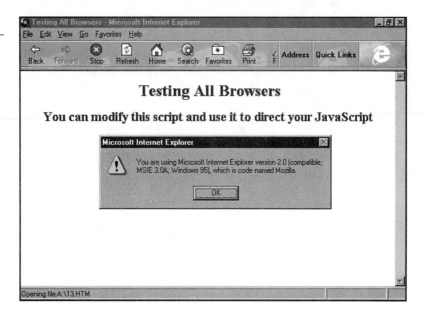

Date and Time Display

14.htm

The Date and Time Display script presents a textbox that displays the current time and date.

The *onLoad* event handler in conjunction with the *date()* method enables this script to display the local date and time in a form window. The local time and date refer to the viewer's machine, not the server which could be located in another time zone. This script thus serves as another way to customize content for the viewer.

This script presents a form entry box that displays the time and date by calling a function from the *onLoad* event handler. The date object is created using the *new date()* method and it's value is stored in the *today* variable. The *toString()* method takes the variable and produces the string output displayed in the form. The 1,000 argument represents 1,000 milliseconds, or 1 second—the time it takes the date's value to update in the window via the *timeout()* method creating the illusion of a progressive digital clock.

HTML code for the Date and Time Display JavaScript:

```
<HTML>
<HEAD>
<TITLE>Date and Time Display</TITLE>
<SCRIPT LANGUAGE="JavaScript">
function TimeOutfunc() {
timeout=window.setTimeout("TimeOutfunc()", 1000);
var today = new Date();
document.forms[0].elements[0].value = today.toString();
}
</SCRIPT>
</HEAD>
<BODY BGCOLOR=FFFFFF ONLOAD="timeout = setTimeout('TimeOutfunc()',1000);">
<CENTER>
<H1>Date and Time Display
<FORM>
<INPUT TYPE="text" NAME="disp" VALUE="" SIZE="25">
</FORM>
<P>
Today's date is visible in the textbox.</H1>
</CENTER>
</BODY>
</HTML>
```

Terminology

event handler: *onLoad*-page 189

object: *date*-page 206

Figure 3.4

*Providing a date and
time display*

Page Load with Alert Message

15.htm

The Page Load with Alert Message script generates an alert message before a page loads.

The *onLoad* event handler enables JavaScript to trigger actions as a page is loaded into the browser. This script brings up an alert message as the page is loaded and then displays the predefined message. This enables you to include pertinent information about a site as it loads, for instance that it requires a particular plug-in, or you could even include a greeting or display the time and date in conjunction with the previous script example as another example of providing custom content to the user. Clicking on OK will finish loading the page.

This example uses the *onLoad* event handler in the <BODY> tag to trigger the *alert()* method.

HTML code for the Page Load with Alert Message JavaScript:

```
<HTML>
<HEAD>
<TITLE>Entry Alert</title>
<SCRIPT LANGUAGE="JavaScript">
function entryAlert(){
alert("This site requires the shockwave plugin!")
return " "
}
</SCRIPT>
</HEAD>
<BODY BGCOLOR=FFFFFF onLoad = entryAlert()>
body text here
</BODY>
</HTML>
```

Terminology

event handler: *onLoad*-page 189

method: *alert()*-page 241, 254

object: *document*-page 206

statement: *return*-page 270

Figure 3.5

*Providing an alert
message during page
loading*

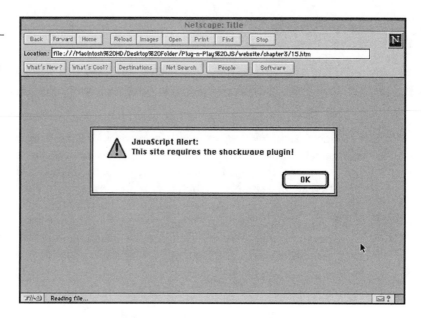

Confirm Before Load

The Confirm Before Load script enables the visitor to confirm whether they want to visit a particular page as it loads.

This script uses the *onLoad* event handler to trigger a *confirm()* box with a message asking the user whether they would like to continue to view the site, or return to the original page they linked from. The confirmation box appears as the page is loaded. A script like this provides important information about a site before the viewer enters it, enabling them to confirm whether they wish to continue or not. A perfect implementation of this script would be a site with mature or potentially offensive material, where the confirm box would function as a disclaimer. Another implemention could be a warning about a site that requires a high-bandwith connection or some other type of warning or disclaimer that would affect whether or not a viewer would wish to continue viewing the site.

The *entryConfirm()* function is defined with the inclusion of an *if* statement, which evaluates user interaction and proceeds accordingly. Clicking "yes" returns a *true* value, which then loads the page. Clicking "no" returns a *false* value, which then executes history.go(-1) an implementation of the *go()* method of the *history* object to return to the previous URL in the browser's history list.

 Warning

> The *history* object refers to the browser's history of URLs accessed.

HTML code for the Confirm Before Load JavaScript:

```
<HTML>
<HEAD>
<TITLE>Confirm on entry</TITLE>
<SCRIPT LANGUAGE="JavaScript">
function entryConfirm() {
if (!confirm
("You must be 18 or over to view this web site, are you at least 18 years
old?"))
history.go(-1);return " "
}
</script>
</HEAD>
```

```
<BODY onload = entryConfirm()>
body text here
</BODY>
</HTML>
```

Terminology

event handler: *onLoad*-page 189

method: *confirm()*-page 242, 255

method: *writeln()*-page 240

method: *go()*-page 243

object: *document*-page 206

object: *history*-page 213

statement: *if*-page 269

Figure 3.6

Providing a confirmation box prior to page loading

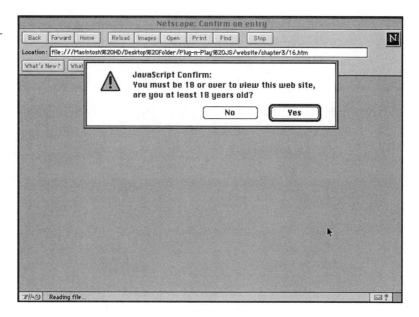

Scrolling Status Bar Message

17.htm

The Scrolling Status Bar Message script displays a scrolling message along the bottom of the browser window.

Many scripts exist for creating scrolling messages along the status bar of the currently active window. Although scrolling messages in the status bar can be annoying because they flash when the mouse is moved, they still provide a very practical implementation of JavaScript in that they present information in an attention-getting manner. Any kind of textual information can be made to scroll and the speed of the scroll can be modified easily within the script.

Like the *onMouseover* example in Chapter 2, this script utilizes the *status* property of the *window* object to display the status bar message. By manipulating the message length and adding a delay using the *setTimeout( )* method, a new message is displayed every 100 milliseconds (1 second), creating the effect of a scroll from right to left.

HTML code for the Scrolling Status Bar Message JavaScript:

```
<HTML>
<HEAD>
<TITLE>Scrolling status bar</TITLE>
<SCRIPT LANGUAGE="JavaScript">
//  Stephan Mohr <stephan.mohr@uni-tuebingen.de>
var timed = 0;
var scrollGo = false;
var delay=80; //make this variable lower to speed scrolling, higher to
slow it down
var space=100;

function scroll_start(){
var i=0;
msg="Write in a message here to scroll across the screen";
for (i=0;i<space;i++) msg=" "+msg;
scrollGo=true;
timerid=window.setTimeout("scrollmsg(0)",delay);
}

function scrollmsg(pos) {
var out = "";
scrollGo=false;
```

```
if (pos < msg.length) self.status = msg.substring(pos, msg.length);
else pos=-1;
++pos;
scrollGo=true;
timerid=window.setTimeout("scrollmsg("+pos+")",delay);
}
</SCRIPT>
</HEAD>
<BODY BGCOLOR=FFFFF onLoad="scroll_start()">
<CENTER>
<H1>body text here</H1>
</CENTER>
</BODY>
</HTML>
```

Terminology

event handler: *onLoad*-page 189

method: *setTimout()*-page 243, 256

method: *subString()*-page 252

property: *length*-page 204, 213-215

property: *status*-page 212, 233

Figure 3.7

*Scrolling text in
status bars*

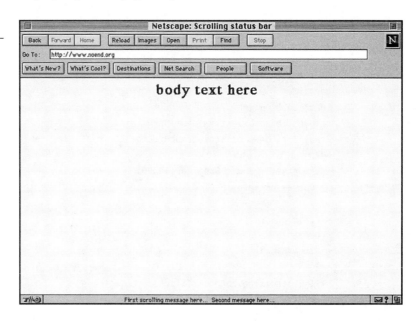

Scrolling Banner

18.htm

The Scrolling Banner script places a scrolling marquee style banner in your page.

JavaScript also enables you to build scrolling banners or "marquees" into the body of your page. Microsoft's Internet Explorer provides a simpler way of doing this via the <marquee> tag, but to accomplish this in Netscape you need to implement JavaScript. A scrolling banner differs from a scrolling status message in that it displays in the body of the page as opposed to the status window. Scrolling banners also offer an attention grabbing method of displaying information as people tend always to read messages that scroll across pages. Advertising sites, sports sites, and stock tickers are perfect candidates for this type of banner.

This script uses a similar method to the Scrolling Status Bar Message script by taking a user-defined string value and scrolling it in a text type form box. Again, the *setTimeout()* method is used as a way of controlling the scroll speed.

HTML code for the Scrolling Banner JavaScript:

```
<HTML>
<HEAD>
<TITLE>Scrolling Banner</TITLE>
<SCRIPT LANGUAGE="JavaScript">
var ScrollString="This text can be changed for you to enter your own. It
will scroll across the page from right to left."
var timer = 0
function Scrollon() {
document.box.boxtext.value = ScrollString
ScrollString=ScrollString.substring(1,ScrollString.length) +
➥ScrollString.charAt(0)
timer = setTimeout("Scrollon()",50)
// decrease timeout value (50) to speed up, increase to slow down
}
</SCRIPT>
</BODY>
</HTML><HTML>
<HEAD>
<TITLE>Scrolling Banner</TITLE>
<SCRIPT LANGUAGE="JavaScript">
```

```
var ScrollString="This text can be changed for you to enter your own. It
will scroll across the page from right to left."
var timer = 0
function Scrollon() {
document.box.boxtext.value =ScrollString
ScrollString=ScrollString.substring(1,ScrollString.length) +
ScrollString.charAt(0)
timer = setTimeout("Scrollon()",100)
}
</SCRIPT>
<BODY BGCOLOR=FFFFFF onLoad = Scrollon()>
<FORM NAME = "box" onSubmit = "0">
<CENTER>
<INPUT TYPE="text" NAME="boxtext" SIZE="45" VALUE="">
</CENTER>
</BODY>
</HTML>
```

Terminology

event handler: *onLoad*-page 189

method: *setTimout()*-page 243, 256

method: *subString()*-page 252

method: *charAt()*-page 249

Figure 3.8

Creating a scrolling banner

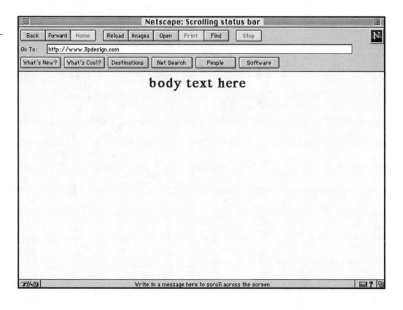

Open Control Panel Window

19.htm
panel.htm

The Open Control Panel Window script enables site navigation using a small second window to alter the contents of the first window.

Utilizing the the same technique as the new window example seen in Chapter 2 (the New Window with Controllable Options script), a new window can be loaded that acts as a control panel for navigating in the original window. The new window remains in place as a navigational element, much like a frame would work in a single window, allowing targeting of the opening window in order to access different URLs. This kind of implementation works very well as a navigitional "control pad" for a site and makes it easy to display a site's table of contents in a custom-sized window for easy navigation through the site. The types of links included in the control pad could easily be local files, images, thumbnails, sounds, Shockwave movies, and so on.

This example is composed of two HTML documents, one for the initial window (19.htm) and one for the "control pad" (panel.htm). When the first window opens, the *open()* method is utilized to create a new window with predefined sizing parameters via the *NewWindow()* function, called using the *onLoad* event handler in the <BODY> tag of the opening window. The *open()* method also instructs the browser to open the URL *panel.htm* by including this as the first argument in quotes in the *open()* method.

From here the new window opens with the predefined size parameters and content as indicated in the HTML. Form buttons have been included here but these could easily be replaced with hypertext or images. The links register a call to the *search()* function using the *onClick* event handler. Notice that the argument is different in the *search()* function for each link, this gives the function a variable (URL) which is then used by the statement: opener.location.href = URL. This *opener* object targets the opening window but it is Navigator 3.0 specific and won't work in previous versions. If compatibility with 2.0 is required you would have to build the first window with frames and then use the target="name of frame" command to target the new URL to the frame as illustrated in the next example, Open Control Panel Window using frames.

HTML code for the Open Control Panel Window:

First Window: 19.htm

```
<HTML>
<HEAD>
<TITLE>Open Control Panel Window</TITLE>
<Script Language="JavaScript">
function NewWindow()  {
window.open("panel.htm", "NewWindow",
"toolbar=no,directories=no,menubar=no,scrollbars=no,width=100,height=225");
window.open("panel.htm", "NewWindow",
"toolbar=no,directories=no,menubar=no,scrollbars=no,width=100,height=225");
}
</script>
</head>
<BODY BGCOLOR=FFFFFF onLoad=NewWindow()>
<CENTER>
<h1>Small Window Navigation</h1>
<h2>Use the small window to navigate through the big window</h2>
</CENTER>
</HTML>
```

Second Window: panel.htm

```
<HTML>
<HEAD>
<TITLE>Control Panel</TITLE>
<SCRIPT>
function search(URL){
opener.location.href = URL
}
</SCRIPT>
</HEAD>
<BODY  BGCOLOR=FFFFFF TEXT=000000>
 <h1>
<FORM>
<INPUT type=button value="Yahoo"  onClick="search('http://www.yahoo.com')">
<P>
```

```
<INPUT type=button value="Altavista"    onClick="search('http://
➥www.altavista.digital.com')">
<P>
<INPUT type=button value="Lycos"    onClick= "search('http://
➥www.lycos.com')">
<P>
<INPUT type=button value="Big Book"    onClick=" search('http://
➥www.bigbook.com')">
</BODY>
</HTML>
```

Terminology

event handler: *onLoad*-page 189

method: *open()*-page 240, 242, 255-256

Figure 3.9

*Using a control
panel for browser
window navigation*

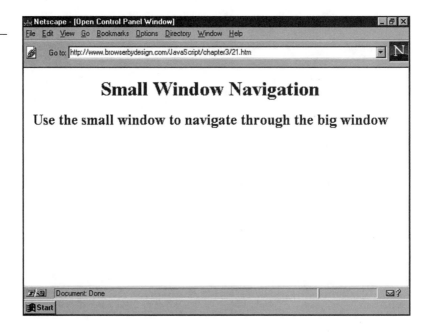

Figure 3.10

*Navigating browser
windows with a
control panel*

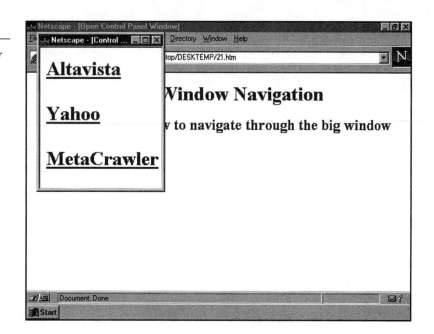

Open Control Panel Window with Frames

20.htm

20frame1.htm

20frame2.htm

20panel.htm

The Open Control Panel Window script enables site navigation using a small second window to alter the contents of a frame in the first window.

This script is similar to the the Open Control panel Window script that preceded this script. In this example, the small control pad targets a frame called "main" in the original opening window rather than a full window. It is useful for sites employing frames in their layout and numerous sites using control pads as a navigational tool, which are beginning to show up on the Web with more frequency. Control pads provide an excellent way to implement a unified navigational control within a site or to provide links to outside sources within the current frame. The following example uses links to various different search engines that target the main frame.

 Browser Warning

> This script is fully compatible with Navigator 2.0 and later.

There are four HTML files in this example. The first file, 20.htm, is the main file and defines 2 frame sources whose content is contained in the files 20frame1.htm and 20frame2.htm. The 20frame1.htm file contains the JavaScript that opens the control panel using the *onLoad* event handler and uses the *window.open()* method to open the file 20panel.htm in a new custom sized window. The 20panel.htm file is for the control pad containing the URLs to open in the first window's frame. The <HREF> tags in this file use the target="frame1" statement to target the frame called "frame" that is contained in the first window. Notice also that the following statement has been included in the HREF tags of the 20panel.htm file: setTimeout("self.focus()",2000). This statement instructs the browser to return the focus to the control pad window after 2 seconds (2000 milliseconds) so that it remains the active window.

HTML code for the Open Control Panel Window with Frames:

Main Document: 20.htm

```
<HTML>
<HEAD>
<TITLE>Frame document</TITLE>
</HEAD>
```

```
<frameset cols="*,100">
<frame src="20frame1.htm"  name="frame1">
<frame src="20frame2.htm"  name="frame2">
</frameset>
</HTML>
```

Frame 1: 20frame1.htm

```
<HTML>
<HEAD>
<TITLE>Open Control Panel Window</TITLE>
<Script Language="JavaScript">
function NewWindow()  {
window.open("20panel.htm", "NewWindow",
"toolbar=no,directories=no,menubar=no,scrollbars=no,width=100,height=225");
window.open("20panel.htm", "NewWindow",
"toolbar=no,directories=no,menubar=no,scrollbars=no,width=100,height=225");
}
</script>
</head>
<BODY BGCOLOR=FFFFFF onLoad=NewWindow()>
<CENTER>
<h1>Small Window Navigation with Frames</h1>
<h2>Use the small window to navigate through the framed window</h2>
</CENTER>
</HTML>
```

Frame 2: 20frame2.htm

```
<HTML>
<HEAD>
<TITLE>Frame 2</TITLE>
</HEAD>
<BODY BGCOLOR=FFFFFF>
Your content here
</BODY>
</HTML>
```

Control pad: 20panel.htm

```
<HTML>
<HEAD>
<TITLE>Control Panel</TITLE>
</HEAD>
```

```
<BODY  BGCOLOR=FFFFFF TEXT=000000>
<FORM>
<A HREF="http://www.yahoo.com" target="frame1" onClick =
'setTimeout("self.focus()",2000)' >Yahoo</A>
<P>
<A HREF="http://www.altavista.digital.com" target="frame1" onClick =
'setTimeout("self.focus()",2000)' >Altavista</A>
<P>
<A HREF="http://www.lycos.com" target="frame1" onClick =
'setTimeout("self.focus()",2000)' >Lycos</A>
<P>
<A HREF="http://www.bigbook.com" target="frame1" onClick =
'setTimeout("self.focus()",2000)' >Big Book</A>
</FORM>
</BODY>
</HTML>
```

Figure 3.11

A control panel to target frames in a different window

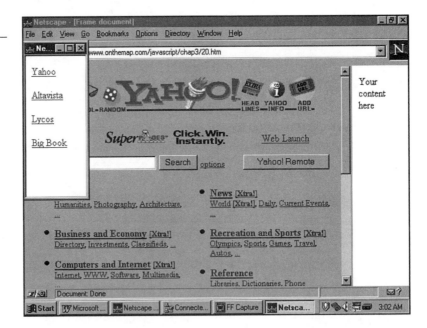

Summary

This chapter introduced the *onLoad* and *onUnload* event handlers and how they interact with window events. Using the basic scripts included in this chapter, you can modify them in countless ways to implement dynamic content and functionality into your Web pages. Experiment with the *window.open()* method to create new windows with different ways of interacting with the original window and use it in conjunction with the rest of the scripts in the book. With a little ingenuity you can make some really innovative things happen in your Web pages.

The next chapter introduces form events—HTML form elements and how to interact with them using JavaScript. Form elements really provide a tremendous way of customizing an interactive page and JavaScript can unleash their power without the need for server-side scripting.

PART IV

Form Events

4

Form Events: onBlur, onChange, onFocus, onSelect, onSubmit Event Handlers

Forms enable users to enter or access information through a Web page. Before JavaScript, interacting with form elements was only available through back-end programming that processed information through a program running on a host server. JavaScript enables users to interact with forms on the client side. Although more limited in function than server-side form processing, client-side form processing makes the response to your visitor's clicks almost instantaneous.

Unlike CGI scripts, which reside on the server and have access to programs located there, JavaScript presently is not integrated with other software applications. This is also changing, and you can expect increased functionality from JavaScript as it becomes a more open development environment.

Many, if not most, of the implementations of JavaScript on the Web today are based on form interaction. This can be in response to the following:

A change in the option selected in a <SELECT> group.

The entry or exit of a form field.

The submission of the entire form.

In this chapter you will be introduced to the handlers that react to several events associated with form elements. The form elements are: <INPUT>, <TEXTAREA>, <SELECT>, and <OPTION>, all of which must be contained within the <FORM> tags in order to display and function.

☐ *onBlur*:

onBlur initiates a script when a form field is exited. This handler functions with the <INPUT>, <TEXTAREA>, and <SELECT> form fields. Use this to execute a script when a form field loses the focus, represented by the cursor or mouse.

☐ *onChange*:

onChange works with the <INPUT>, <TEXTAREA>, and <SE-LECT> form fields and initiates a script when the contents of one of these fields is changed. Use this to execute a script once the form field contents have been changed.

☐ *onFocus*:

onFocus works with the <INPUT>, <TEXTAREA>, and <SELECT> form fields and is the opposite of *onBlur*, activating a script when a form field is entered. Use this to execute a script when the form field is entered, or receives the focus as represented by the cursor or mouse.

☐ *onSelect*:

onSelect works only with the <TEXTAREA> and <INPUT> tags and activates the script when text is selected. Use this to execute a script when text within a textarea or text-type input tag has been selected. This is often confused with onFocus, described above.

☐ *onSubmit*:

onSubmit is used in conjunction with the <FORM> tag and initiates upon submission of a form. Use this to execute a script when a form is submitted.

Alert onFocus

23.htm

The Alert onFocus JavaScript creates an alert when entering text in an input form.

This script uses the *onFocus* event handler to detect when a user clicks or tabs into a form field. In this example, clicking into the social security number field alerts the viewer that entering text in this field is optional. Any function can be inserted in the place of the *alert()* method.

The *onFocus* event handler is included in the <INPUT> tag of the social security field, triggering the *alert()* method during an *onFocus* event. The <TABLE> tags have been included in order to align the text and text entry boxes.

HTML code for the Alert onFocus JavaScript:

```
<HTML>
<HEAD>
<TITLE>Alert onFocus</TITLE>
</HEAD>
<BODY BGCOLOR=FFFFFF>
<CENTER>
<H1>Alert onFocus</H1>
<P>
<H2>Please enter your personal data here:</H2>
<P>
<FORM>
<TABLE>
<TR>
        <TD>Name:</TD>
        <TD><INPUT type="text" name="name" size=35></TD>
</TR>
<TR>

        <TD>Address:</TD>
        <TD><INPUT type="text" name="address" size=35></TD>
</TR>
<TR>

        <TD>City:</TD>
        <TD><INPUT type="text" name="city" size=35></TD>
</TR>
<TR>
```

```
        <TD>State:</TD>
        <TD><INPUT type="text" name="state" size=17 >  Zip: <INPUT
        type="text" name="zip" size=12></TD>
</TR>
<TR>
        <TD>SS#:</TD>
        <TD><INPUT type="text" name="SS#" size=35 onFocus="alert('Entering
        your Social Security number is optional')"></TD>
</TR>
</TABLE>
</FORM>
</CENTER>
</BODY>
</HTML>
```

Terminology

event handler: *onFocus*-page 188

method: *alert()*-page 241, 254

Figure 4.1

Browser with text input form field

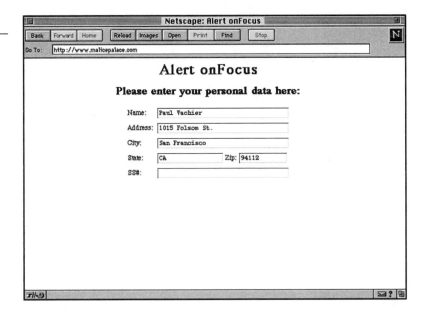

Figure 4.2

Generating alert messages with onFocus via text input

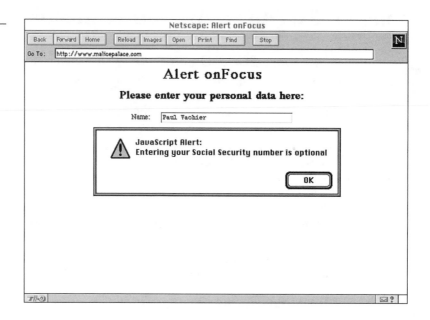

Change **BGCOLOR** Attribute onBlur

24.htm

The Change BGCOLOR attribute onBlur JavaScript changes the background color of your page using onBlur.

This script enables you to change the background color of the document dynamically by clicking into and then leaving any of the text fields. In this example, special color names are used. It is also possible to use the hexadecimal equivalent to the color's RGB value.

bgColor is a property of the *document* object. By assigning a *bgColor* value different from what is specified in the <BODY> tag, the value can be changed with an event handler, in this case *onBlur*. During *onBlur*, when the focus changes to another text field, the specified value is passed to the *bgColor* property, subsequently changing the current background color of the document. This example can use any property that JavaScript affects.

HTML code for the Change BGCOLOR attribute onBlur JavaScript:

```
<HTML>
<HEAD>
<TITLE>Change BGCOLOR onFocus</TITLE>
<BODY BGCOLOR=FFFFFF text=000000>
<CENTER>
<H2>Change the background color with onBlur</H2>
<P>
<FORM>
<INPUT Type="text" Name="bgred" value="red" onFocus=
"document.bgColor='red'">
<P>
<INPUT Type="text" Name="bggreen" value="green" onFocus=
"document.bgColor='green'">
<P>
<INPUT Type="text" Name="bgblue" value="blue" onFocus=
"document.bgColor='blue'">
<P>
<INPUT Type="text" Name="bgyellow" value="yellow" onFocus=
"document.bgColor='yellow'">
</FORM>
</CENTER>
</BODY>
</HTML>
```

Terminology

event handler: *onBlur*-page 187

object: *document*-page 206

property: *bgColor*-page 207

Figure 4.3

Changing document background color by clicking on a text box

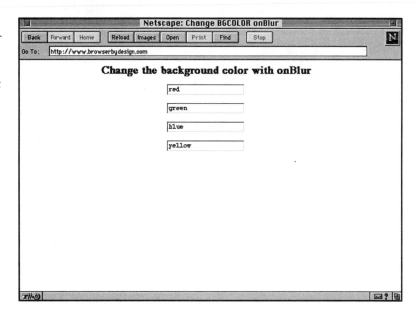

Testing Form Entry Values

25.htm

The Testing Form Entry Values JavaScript tests the validity of text input into a form.

The following script verifies and ensures that text input conforms to specific requirements before it is accepted as a form submission. This works well for fixed length numbers such as phone numbers, zip codes, social security numbers, and so on. This example tests to ensure that a phone number is entered using the standard 10 digit format.

The *onChange* event handler is used in the phone number field. When the text in this box is changed, the event handler invokes the *checkNum* function that is defined in the beginning of the script.

The *checkNum* function assesses the text that is entered—*this.value* and passes it to the variable "phone," which converts to a string object. At this point, an *if* statement verifies that the input is not blank (if it is, an alert pops up). When a string value is sent, *if* looks for three conditions in the string:

1. The first dash *does not* occur three digits into the string.

2. The second dash *does not* occur four digits later.

3. The length of the string *does not* equal 12 digits.

The three conditions are separated by the | | symbol, which is a logical operator meaning OR. The *indexOf()* method searches a string for a specified character at the specified position. In the first two conditions mentioned previously, *indexOf()* checks for the "-" dashes. If the length of the string does not equal 12 digits, *indexOf()* uses the *length* property to compare the string with the required length (12 characters).

HTML code for the Testing Form Entry Values JavaScript:

```
<HTML>
<HEAD>
<TITLE>Form entry testing</TITLE>
<BODY BGCOLOR=FFFFFF>
<SCRIPT>

function checkNum(phone){
        if(phone=="")
```

```
                {
                alert("You must input your three digit area code and 7 digit phone
                number in the following format: 415-555-5555")
                }
                else    {
                        if (phone.indexOf("-") != 3 || phone.indexOf("-", 4) != 7
     ||                      phone.length != 12 )
                                {
                                alert("You must input your three digit area code
                                and 7 digit phone number in the following format:
                                415-555-5555")
                                }
                        }
        }
</SCRIPT>
<CENTER>
<FORM>
<TABLE>
<TR>
        <TD>Name:</TD>
        <TD><INPUT type="text" name="name" size=35></TD>
</TR>
<TR>

        <TD>Address:</TD>
        <TD><INPUT type="text" name="address" size=35></TD>
</TR>
<TR>

        <TD>City:</TD>
        <TD><INPUT type="text" name="city" size=35></TD>
</TR>
<TR>

        <TD>State:</TD>
        <TD><INPUT type="text" name="state" size=17 >  Zip: <INPUT
        type="text" name="zip" size=12></TD>
</TR>
<TR>

        <TD>Phone #:</TD>
        <TD><INPUT type="text" name="phone" size=35
        onChange="checkNum(this.value)"></TD>
</TR>
</TABLE>
</FORM>
</CENTER>
</BODY>
</HTML>
```

Terminology

event handler: *onChange*-page 187

method: *indexOf( )*-page 250

statement: *this*-page 270

Figure 4.4

*Testing phone
number fields to
ensure format
compliance*

Figure 4.5

*Generating alert box
for field format non-
compliance*

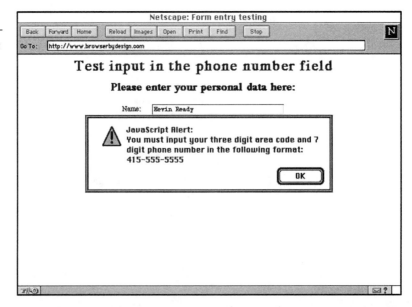

Choose a Trait Using onSelect

26.htm

The Choose a Trait Using onSelect JavaScript initiates a script or alert message when text is selected in a text box.

This script presents the user with four descriptive text boxes which they can select to describe themselves. Selecting the text in either box will generate an alert.

When using the *onSelect* event handler, it is important to realize that it is limited to responding to the text that is actually selected and only works within the <TEXTAREA> and text type <INPUT> tags. Due to its awkward implementation and misleading name, it is not advised to use the *onSelect* event handler. It generally reacts to the same events as the *onFocus* event handler.

HTML code for the Choose a Trait Using onSelect JavaScript:

```
<HTML>
<HEAD>
<TITLE>Choosing a trait with onSelect</TITLE>
<BODY BGCOLOR=FFFFFF>
<CENTER>
<H1> Using onSelect </H1>
<P>
<H2>Select some attributes which describe you:</H2>
<P>
<FORM>
<INPUT TYPE=TEXT onSelect="alert('Oh, come on! Dont be modest.')"
name="sample text" size=20 value="average">
<BR>
<INPUT TYPE=TEXT onSelect="alert('Well, at least you are honest.')"
name="sample text2" size=20 value="pompous">
<BR>
<INPUT TYPE=TEXT onSelect="alert('What is your phone number?')"
name="sample text3" size=20 value="attractive">
<BR>
<INPUT TYPE=TEXT onSelect="alert('Please wait a few minutes...')"
name="sample text3" size=20 value="patient">
</FORM>
</CENTER>
</BODY>
</HTML>
```

Terminology

event handler: *onSelect*-page 190

method: *alert()*-page 241, 254

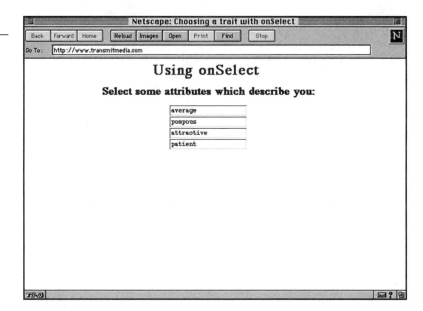

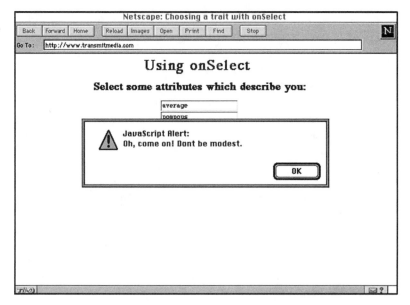

Test for Complete Response Before Submitting

27.htm

The Test for Complete Response Before Submitting script ensures that a form has been completely filled out before it is submitted.

This script is modeled just like the *Testing Form Entry Values* script and tests the input to ensure that there aren't any blank fields. When a field is left blank it creates an alert informing the viewer that they must finish completing the form. The input from this form can then be sent to a CGI application residing on the server in order to process.

This example makes use of the *onSubmit* event handler that is placed in the <FORM> tag and called when the submit button is clicked. Submitting the form invokes the *testform()* function which looks for blank values in the form fields. The value typed into each field is represented by the object attribute `document.forms[x].elements[x].value`. Because there is only one form in this script, the forms array uses the value 0, which stands for the first form. The elements are numbered similarly and represent each of the fields in the form.

In order to recognize a blank field, the comparison operator == evaluates equality to an empty string—"" and the | | (OR) operator allows for multiple conditions. Thus, when a value contains no data (==""), the alert method is initiated with the appropriate alert message, in this example, "You must fill in all the information in this form."

HTML code for the Test for Complete Response Before Submitting JavaScript:

```
<HTML>
<HEAD>
<TITLE>Test for completeness</TITLE>
<BODY BGCOLOR=FFFFFF>
<SCRIPT>
function testform(){
if(document.forms[0].elements[0].value==""
|| document.forms[0].elements[1].value==""
|| document.forms[0].elements[2].value==""
|| document.forms[0].elements[3].value==""
|| document.forms[0].elements[4].value==""
|| document.forms[0].elements[5].value=="")  {
        alert("You must fill in all the information in this form")
        }
```

```
}
</SCRIPT>
<CENTER>
<FORM method=post onSubmit="return testform()">
<TABLE>
<TR>
        <TD>Name:</TD>
        <TD><INPUT type="text" name="name" size=35></TD>
</TR>
<TR>

        <TD>Address:</TD>
        <TD><INPUT type="text" name="address" size=35></TD>
</TR>
<TR>

        <TD>City:</TD>
        <TD><INPUT type="text" name="city" size=35></TD>
</TR>
<TR>

        <TD>State:</TD>
        <TD><INPUT type="text" name="state" size=17 >
          Zip: <INPUT type="text" name="zip" size=12></TD>
</TR>
<TR>

        <TD>Phone #:</TD>
        <TD><INPUT type="text" name="phone" size=35></TD>
</TR>
</TABLE>
<INPUT type="submit" name="submit button" value="submit" >
</FORM>
</CENTER>
</BODY>
</HTML>
```

Terminology

event handler: *onSubmit*-page 190-191

attribute: *value*-page 204-206

array property: *elements[]*-page 209

array property: *forms[]*-page 208

object: *document*-page 206

Figure 4.8

Verifying form field input

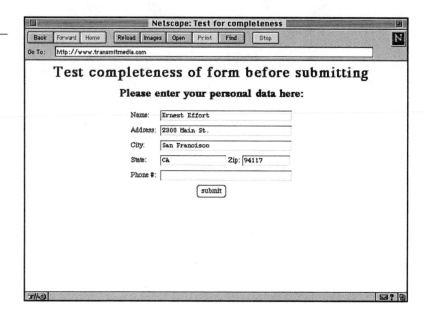

Figure 4.9

Generating alert boxes for neglected fields during form submission

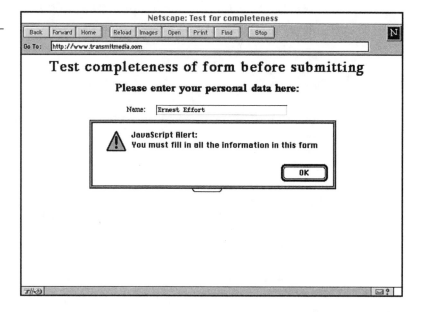

Pulldown Navigation Menu

28.htm

The Pulldown Navigation Menu JavaScript enables the user to navigate a Web site from a pulldown menu.

This script provides a way to list URLs in a pulldown menu. This is an excellent way to navigate a Web site or provide a way of visiting other URLs in a convenient and easily accessible manner. Put your own URLs into the value= tag in order to customize the script. Chapter 5, "Image Events: onAbort, onError, onLoad" also contains a variation of this script that can be used to change images on a page without reloading.

This script utilizes the *onChange* event handler located in the <SELECT> tag of the document form. *onChange* invokes the *formHandler()* function which extracts and passes the value from the selected option item (Altavista, in this example) to the URL variable. This value is then read by the *href* attribute of the *window.location* object which accesses the new URL.

HTML code for the Pulldown Navigation Menu JavaScript:

```
<HTML>
<body bgcolor = ffffff>
<script language = "JavaScript">
function formHandler(){
var URL =
document.pulldown.selectname.options[document.pulldown.selectname.selectedIndex].value
window.location.href = URL
}
</script>
Choose a search engine:
<FORM name = "pulldown">
<SELECT NAME="selectname" SIZE=1 onChange ="formHandler()">
<OPTION VALUE="http://www.yahoo.com">Yahoo
<OPTION VALUE="http://www.metacrawler.com">Metacrawler
<OPTION VALUE="http://www.altavista.digital.com">Altavista
<OPTION VALUE="http://www.webcrawler.com">Webcrawler
<OPTION VALUE="http://www.lycos.com">Lycos
</SELECT>
</body>
</HTML>
```

Terminology

event handler: *onChange*-page 187

object: *window*-page 232-233

object: *location*-page 218-219

property: *selectedIndex*-page 223, 228

attribute: *HREF*-page 187-188

Figure 4.10

*Selecting an URL
from the pulldown
menu*

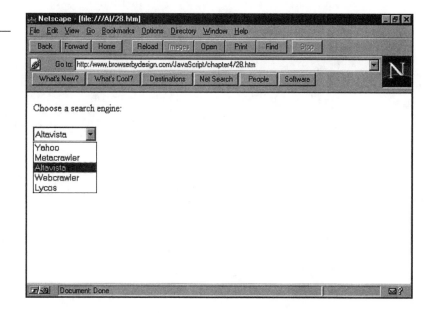

Large Form Example

The Large Form Example JavaScript accepts multiple input from form fields for data acquisition.

This script is an extended example of several of the scripts and event handlers discussed previously in the chapter. It demonstrates JavaScript's capability to extract user input values and manipulate them as data items. This script also utilizes the *prompt( )* method to prompt the user for additional information before submitting the final form.

The script begins by declaring several variables using empty quotes "" in order to assign them as string values. The functions in the script are called by the onBlur and onFocus event handlers. The name and social security fields use onBlur and onFocus to validate the entries.

HTML code for the Large Form Example JavaScript:

```
<HTML>
<HEAD>
<TITLE>Multiple Event Handlers in a Single Form</TITLE>
<SCRIPT>

var alertTest=0
var photo=""
var   prem=""
var   dir=""
var   debab=""
var   quark=""

function checkStatus1() {
if(this.document.forms[0].Single.checked) {
        this.document.forms[0].Married.checked=0;
        return true;
        }
}


function checkStatus2() {
if(this.document.forms[0].Married.checked) {
        this.document.forms[0].Single.checked=0;
        return true;
        }
}
```

```
function alertOnce() {
if(alertTest==0) {
        alert('Entering this information is optional.')
        alertTest=1
        }
}

function ConfirmMe() {
if (this.document.forms[0].elements[0].value=="") {
        alert("You must enter your name.")
        this.document.forms[0].elements[0].focus()
        }
}

function testProgVer() {
for (x=0; x<5; x++)
{
if(this.document.forms[0].softProg.options[x].selected==1) {
        var myVersion=prompt("What version of " +
➥this.document.forms[0].softProg.options[x].value + " do you use?", "");
                if(x==0) {
                photo=myVersion
                };
                if(x==1) {
                prem=myVersion
                };
                if(x==2) {
                dir=myVersion
                };
                if(x==3) {
                debab=myVersion
                };
                if(x==4) {
                quark=myVersion
                };
        }
}
alert("You specified:   Photoshop " + photo + ",  Premiere " + prem + ",
Director  " + dir + ",  Debabelizer " + debab + ", Quark  " + quark);
}
</SCRIPT>
</HEAD>
<BODY BGCOLOR=FFFFFF>
```

```
<H1>Employee Information</H1>
<CENTER>
<FORM NAME=empForm METHOD=POST>
<TABLE BGCOLOR=FFCCCC>
<TR>
<TD width=50% VALIGN=TOP>
<TABLE BORDER=5 CELLPADDING=5 CELLSPACING=2 BGCOLOR=FFFFCC WIDTH=100%>
<TR>
<TD HEIGHT=130>
Please Enter Your Name
<BR>
<INPUT NAME="empname" TYPE="text" SIZE=30 onBlur="ConfirmMe()">
<P>
What is your title?<BR>
<INPUT NAME="emptitle" TYPE="text" SIZE=30>
<P>
My Social Security Number is
<BR>
<INPUT TYPE="text" onFocus=alertOnce()>
</TD>
</TR>
</TABLE><TABLE BORDER=5 CELLPADDING=5 CELLSPACING=2 BGCOLOR=CCCCFF
WIDTH=100%>
<TR>
<TD HEIGHT=145>
Select software programs that you know well. More than one program can be
selected by using the shift key and/or command or control keys.
<P>
<SELECT NAME="softProg" MULTIPLE SIZE=5>
<OPTION VALUE="Photoshop" NAME="PShop">Photoshop
<OPTION VALUE="Premiere" NAME="Prem">Premiere
<OPTION VALUE="Director" NAME="Dir">Director
<OPTION VALUE="DeBabelizer" NAME="Debab">DeBabelizer
<OPTION VALUE="QuarkImmedia" NAME="Quark">QuarkImmedia
</SELECT>
</TD>
</TD>
</TR>
</TABLE>
</TD>
<TD width=50% valign=top>
```

```
<TABLE BORDER=5 CELLPADDING=5 CELLSPACING=5 BGCOLOR=CCFFFF WIDTH=100%>
<TR>
<TD HEIGHT=135>
Please check all that are appropriate:
<P>
<INPUT TYPE="checkbox" name="Single" onClick="checkStatus1()">Single
<INPUT TYPE="checkbox" name="Married" onClick="checkStatus2()">Married
<INPUT TYPE="checkbox" name="Living Together">Living Together
<P>
I work in the following capacity:
<BR>
<INPUT NAME="position" TYPE="radio" VALUE="Mgr">Manager
<INPUT NAME="position" TYPE="radio" VALUE="Tech">Technical
<INPUT NAME="position" TYPE="radio" VALUE="Admin">Administrative
<INPUT NAME="position" TYPE="radio" VALUE="Lab">Laborer
</TD>
</TR>
</TABLE><TABLE BORDER=5 CELLPADDING=5 CELLSPACING=5 BGCOLOR=CCFFCC
WIDTH=100%>
<TR>
<TD HEIGHT=128>
Which operating systems do you use?<P>
<INPUT TYPE=checkbox VALUE=mac NAME=mac>Macintosh
<INPUT TYPE=checkbox VALUE=win NAME=win>Windows
<INPUT TYPE=checkbox VALUE=uni NAME=uni>Unix
<P>
<P>
<INPUT TYPE="submit" VALUE="Send Employee Information"
onClick="testProgVer()">
</TD>
</TR>
</TABLE>
</TD>
</TR>
</TABLE>
</FORM>
</CENTER>
</BODY>
</HTML>
```

Temperature Conversion

30.htm

The Temperature Conversion JavaScript converts Fahrenheit to Celsius and Celsius to Fahrenheit.

This is a temperature conversion script using *onChange* and *onClick* and demonstrates mathematical functions as well as the checked attribute of the form object.

The script can be activated one of two ways:

via the *onClick* event handler with the radio buttons, or

via the *onChange* event handler with the input form field.

Either one of these events calls the displayTemp() function that checks to see which radio button is checked using the *checked* property. The input value by the user is passed to the *tempVal* variable. Depending on which button was checked, the appropriate math calculation is performed and passed to the variable *finalC* or *finalF*. This number is then rounded off using the *math.round()* method and passed to the *finalTemp* variable, which is then displayed in the result window.

HTML code for the Temperature Conversion JavaScript:

```
<HTML>
<HEAD>
<TITLE>Temp Converter</TITLE>
<script language = "JavaScript">
function displayTemp(){

if (document.forms[0].elements[1].checked){
        var tempVal = document.forms[0].yourInput.value
        var finalC = (tempVal-32)*5/9
        var finalTemp = Math.round(finalC) + " degrees Celsius"
        }

if (document.forms[0].elements[2].checked){
        var tempVal = document.forms[0].yourInput.value
        var finalF = (tempVal*9/5)+32
        var finalTemp =Math.round(finalF) + " degrees Fahrenheit"
        }
document.forms[1].result.value = finalTemp;
}
```

```
</SCRIPT>
</HEAD>
<BODY BGCOLOR=FFFFFF>
<CENTER>
<FORM>
<INPUT TYPE="text" NAME="yourInput" SIZE=8 VALUE=""
onChange="displayTemp();">
<INPUT type="radio" NAME="F" SIZE=1 onClick="displayTemp();">Fahrenheit
<INPUT type="radio" NAME="F" SIZE=1 onClick="displayTemp();">Celsius
</FORM>
<P>
<FORM name=buttons>
<BR>
<BR>
Is equal to:<P>
<INPUT TYPE="text" NAME="result" SIZE=30 VALUE="">
</FORM>
</CENTER>
</BODY>
</HTML>
```

Terminology

event handler: *onChange*-page 187

event handler: *onClick*-page 187-188

property: *checked*-page 205, 226

method: *round()*-page 246

Figure 4.11

*Converting
temperatures to/from
Fahrenheit/Celsius*

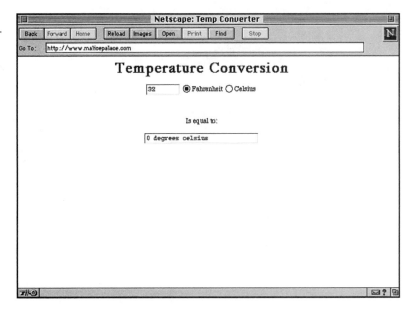

Metric Length Conversions

31.htm

The Metric Length Conversions script converts lengths from metric to English or from English to metric values.

This relatively complex script provides conversions for length measurements. It is included here to provide a more powerful example of the programming capabilities of JavaScript utilizing form elements. It is best used when pasted directly into an html document without code modifications.

This script makes use of the *onChange* and *onClick* event handlers in addition to arrays to provide conversion formulas.

 Note

> Arrays in JavaScript are a way of indexing information as an ordered collection of data. Arrays in the current release of JavaScript are not fully developed and this script contains a slight workaround (the Array object is actually created).

In this case the conversion formulas are "stored" and later accessed when needed by the script.

HTML code for the Metric Length Conversions JavaScript:

```
<HTML>
<HEAD>
<TITLE>Length Equivalents</TITLE>
<!-- Copyright 1996, Infohiway Server Network, http://www.infohiway.com.
Restricted use is hereby granted (both personal and commercial use OK so
long as this code is not *directly* sold), providing this notice is buried
somewhere deep in your HTML document.-->
<SCRIPT LANGUAGE="JavaScript">

function initArray() {
  this.length = initArray.arguments.length;
  for (var i = 0; i < this.length; i++) {
    this[i] = initArray.arguments[i];
    }
  }
var isn01 = new initArray("4b","5b","8b","8b");
isn01[0] =
➥"~01~10.3937~20.03281~30.01094~40.01~50.0004971~60.00001~70.000006214~8";
```

```
isn01[1] =
➥"~02.540~11~20.08333~30.02778~40.0254~50.001263~60.0000254~70.00001578~8";
isn01[2] =
➥"~030.48~112~21~30.3333~40.3048~50.01515~60.0003048~70.0001894~8";
isn01[3] = "~091.44~136~23~31~40.9144~50.04545~60.0009144~70.0005682~8";
isn01[4] = "~0100~139.37~23.281~31.0936~41~50.04971~60.001~70.0006214~8";
isn01[5] = "~02012~1792~266~322~420.12~51~60.0212~70.0125~8";
isn01[6] = "~0100000~139370~23281~31093.6~41000~549.71~61~70.6214~8";
isn01[7] = "~0160934~163360~25280~31760~41609~580~61.609~71~8";

function lenCon() {
  // First, get the variables checked by the user
  for (var i = 0; i < 8; i++) {
    if (document.isnform01.leni[i].checked) {
      leni = i;
      leninm = document.isnform01.leni[i].value;
      }
    }
  for (var i = 0; i < 8; i++) {
    if (document.isnform01.leno[i].checked) {
      leno = i;
      lenonm = document.isnform01.leno[i].value;
      }
    }
  // Now grab the number input by user and parse to be sure numeric
  useri = document.isnform01.leninp.value;
  if (useri == 0) {
    useri = 1;
    document.isnform01.leninp.value = useri;
    }
  mulstr = isn01[leni];
  picker = "~" + leno;
  ps = mulstr.indexOf(picker);
  leno++;
  picker = "~" + leno;
  ps1 = mulstr.indexOf(picker);
  mulstr = mulstr.substring((ps + 2),ps1);
  ps = (useri * mulstr);
  picker = "";
  picker += ps
  ps1 = picker.indexOf(".");
  if (ps1 > -1) {
    // Correct for binary/floating point conversion error
    ps = ps + .000001;
```

```
      picker = "";
      picker += ps;
      ps2 = picker.indexOf("e");
      if (ps2 < 0) {
        picker = picker.substring(0,(ps1 + 6));
        }
      if (ps2 == 0 || ps2 > 0) {
        ps3 = picker.indexOf("00000");
        if (ps3 > 0) {
          picker = picker.substring(0,ps3 + 1) +
picker.substring(ps2,picker.length);
          }
        }
      }
  picker = useri + " " + leninm + " = " + picker + " " + lenonm
  document.isnform01.lenout.value = picker;
  }

// End Hiding -->
</SCRIPT>
</HEAD>
<BODY BGCOLOR="white">
<CENTER>
<TABLE BORDER=1 WIDTH=486>
<TR><TD COLSPAN=9 ALIGN=CENTER><FORM NAME="isnform01"><FONT
COLOR="blue"><B>Length Equivalents</B></FONT></TD></TR>
<TR><TD COLSPAN=9 VALIGN=TOP><FONT SIZE=1><B>First, type the number you
wish converted here: </B>
<INPUT TYPE="text" NAME="leninp" SIZE=30 VALUE=""
onChange="lenCon();"><BR><B>Then, click radio buttons for desired conver-
sion:</B></FONT></TD></TR>
<TR><TD ALIGN=CENTER><FONT COLOR="red" SIZE=1><B>From:</B></FONT></TD>
<TD ALIGN=CENTER VALIGN=TOP><FONT SIZE=1>Centimeters<BR><INPUT TYPE="radio"
NAME="leni" VALUE="Centimeters" CHECKED onClick = ""></TD>
<TD ALIGN=CENTER VALIGN=TOP><FONT SIZE=1>Inches<BR><INPUT TYPE="radio"
NAME="leni" VALUE="Inches" onClick = ""></TD>
<TD ALIGN=CENTER VALIGN=TOP><FONT SIZE=1>Feet<BR><INPUT TYPE="radio"
NAME="leni" VALUE="Feet" onClick = ""></TD>
<TD ALIGN=CENTER VALIGN=TOP><FONT SIZE=1>Yards<BR><INPUT TYPE="radio"
NAME="leni" VALUE="Yards" onClick = ""></TD>
<TD ALIGN=CENTER VALIGN=TOP><FONT SIZE=1>Meters<BR><INPUT TYPE="radio"
NAME="leni" VALUE="Meters" onClick = ""></TD>
```

```
<TD ALIGN=CENTER VALIGN=TOP><FONT SIZE=1>Chains<BR><INPUT TYPE="radio"
NAME="leni" VALUE="Chains" onClick = ""></TD>
<TD ALIGN=CENTER VALIGN=TOP><FONT SIZE=1>Kilometers<BR><INPUT TYPE="radio"
NAME="leni" VALUE="Kilometers" onClick = ""></TD>
<TD ALIGN=CENTER VALIGN=TOP><FONT SIZE=1>Miles<BR><INPUT TYPE="radio"
NAME="leni" VALUE="Miles" onClick = ""></TD></TR>
<TR><TD ALIGN=CENTER><FONT COLOR="red" SIZE=1><B>To:</B></TD>
<TD ALIGN=CENTER VALIGN=TOP><FONT SIZE=1>Centimeters<BR><INPUT TYPE="radio"
NAME="leno" VALUE="Centimeters" onClick = ""></TD>
<TD ALIGN=CENTER VALIGN=TOP><FONT SIZE=1>Inches<BR><INPUT TYPE="radio"
NAME="leno" VALUE="Inches" CHECKED onClick = ""></TD>
<TD ALIGN=CENTER VALIGN=TOP><FONT SIZE=1>Feet<BR><INPUT TYPE="radio"
NAME="leno" VALUE="Feet" onClick = ""></TD>
<TD ALIGN=CENTER VALIGN=TOP><FONT SIZE=1>Yards<BR><INPUT TYPE="radio"
NAME="leno" VALUE="Yards" onClick = ""></TD>
<TD ALIGN=CENTER VALIGN=TOP><FONT SIZE=1>Meters<BR><INPUT TYPE="radio"
NAME="leno" VALUE="Meters" onClick = ""></TD>
<TD ALIGN=CENTER VALIGN=TOP><FONT SIZE=1>Chains<BR><INPUT TYPE="radio"
NAME="leno" VALUE="Chains" onClick = ""></TD>
<TD ALIGN=CENTER VALIGN=TOP><FONT SIZE=1>Kilometers<BR><INPUT TYPE="radio"
NAME="leno" VALUE="Kilometers" onClick = ""></TD>
<TD ALIGN=CENTER VALIGN=TOP><FONT SIZE=1>Miles<BR><INPUT TYPE="radio"
NAME="leno" VALUE="Miles" onClick = ""></TD></TR>
<TR><TD COLSPAN=9 ALIGN=CENTER VALIGN=TOP><FONT SIZE=1><INPUT TYPE="button"
VALUE=" Click for Conversion " onClick="lenCon();"> <INPUT TYPE="reset"
VALUE=" Reset Values "><BR><INPUT TYPE="text" NAME="lenout" SIZE=60
VALUE="" onClick="lenCon();">
</FONT></TD></TR>
</TABLE></FORM>
<P>
</BODY>
</HTML>
```

Terminology

objects: *array*-page 204

event handlers: *onClick*-page 187-188

event handlers: *onChange*-page 187

property: *checked*-page 205, 226

property: *length*-page 204, 213-215

Figure 4.12

*Converting length to/
from English/Metric*

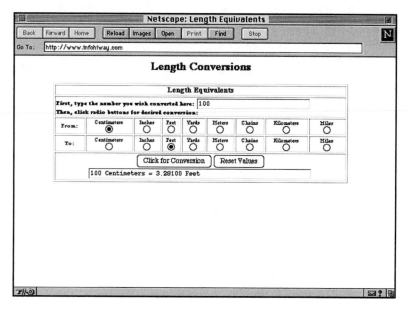

Math Functions

32.htm

The Math Functions JavaScript calculates various trigonometric functions.

This script demonstrates some of the many mathematical functions available in JavaScript. In addition to the ones illustrated here, inverse trigonometric calculations are possible, as well as the value of pi( ), Euler 's constant, the natural logarithms of 2 and 10, and the square root of 0.5 and 2.

This script is initiated by the *onBlur* event handler in the <INPUT> tag of the field used to enter the angle being converted. The function targeted—*checkNum( )* first determines if no value has been entered using an *if* statement and the *value==""* statement. If this condition is true, an alert message is generated and the entry field is reselected using the *focus( )* method. This method focuses the cursor back to the specified field. If the condition is not true (a value *has* been entered into the field), the *else* part of the script takes the value entered, applies the trigonometric function to it and then passes this to the variable using the *new( )* method in conjunction with the *string( )* method. This creates a new instance of the variable. This new variable becomes the value passed to the appropriate field; however, because the number is a floating point value with many digits to the right of the decimal, the *substring( )* method is used to a shorten this number to seven digits.

The function of the *substring( )* method is to extract a range of characters from the first position indicated, up to, but not including the last character. Because character positions in JavaScript are zero-based, the 0 in *substring(0,8)* represents the first character and the 8 represents the seventh character, thus extracting the first seven characters of the string. The resulting string is then displayed in the appropriate field.

HTML code for the Math Functions JavaScript:

```
<HTML>
<HEAD>
<TITLE>Common Trigonometric Functions</TITLE>
<SCRIPT>

var varc=""
var vars=""
var vart=""
```

```
function checkNum() {
        if(this.document.forms[0].elements[0].value=="") {
        alert("You must enter a numeric value");
        this.document.forms[0].elements[0].focus();
        }

        else {
        varc=new String(Math.cos(this.document.forms[0].elements[0].value))
        vars= new
        ➥String(Math.sin(this.document.forms[0].elements[0].value))
        vart= new
        ➥String(Math.tan(this.document.forms[0].elements[0].value))

        this.document.forms[0].c1.value=(varc.substring(0,8));
        this.document.forms[0].s1.value=(vars.substring(0,8));
        this.document.forms[0].t1.value=(vart.substring(0,8));
        }
}
</SCRIPT>
</HEAD>
<BODY BGCOLOR=FFFFFF>
<CENTER>
<H1>Trigonometric Functions</H1>
</CENTER>
<FORM>
<CENTER>
<TABLE WIDTH=350>
<TR>
        <TD WIDTH=40% ROWSPAN = 6 VALIGN=top>
        Enter the degree of the angle in radians:
        <P>
        <INPUT TYPE="text" Name="text1" SIZE=10 VALUE="" onBlur=checkNum()>
        <BR>
        </TD>
        <TD align=right>cosine:</TD>
        <TD><INPUT TYPE="text" SIZE=8 NAME=c1></TD>
</TR>
<TR>
        <TD align=right>sine:</TD>
        <TD><INPUT TYPE="text" SIZE=8 NAME=s1></TD>
</TR>
```

```
<TR>
        <TD align=right>tangent:</TD>
        <TD><INPUT TYPE="text" SIZE=8 NAME=t1></TD>
</TR>
</TABLE>
<P>
</CENTER>
</FORM>
</BODY>
</HTML>
```

Terminology

event handler: *onBlur*-page 187

method: *focus()*-page 242, 247-248, 254-255

method: *string()*-page 108

method: *substring()*-page 252

statement: *new*-page 269-270

statement: *else*-page 269

statement: *if*-page 269

Figure 4.13

Trigonometric functions

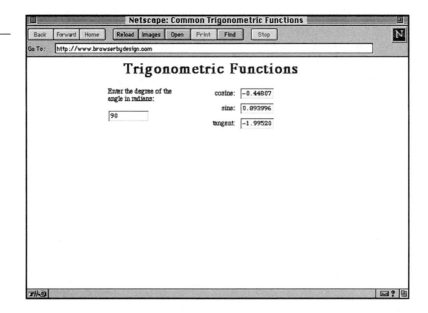

Number Functions

The Number Functions JavaScript converts a number to binary, octal, or hexadecimal values.

This script demonstrates another mathematical function of JavaScript using the *parseInt()* method. In this example, the *parseInt()* method takes an integer and returns its binary (base 2), octal (base 8) or hexadecimal (base 64) values.

This script is initiated by the *onBlur* event handler in the <INPUT> tag of the field where the number to be converted is located. The targeted *checkNum()* function determines if no value has been entered using an *if* statement and the *value=="'"* statement. If this condition is true, an alert message is generated and the entry field is reselected using the *focus()* method which focuses the cursor back to the specified field. If the condition is not true (a value *has* been entered into the field), the *else* part of the script takes the value entered and passes it to the *MyVar* variable. *MyVar* is then parsed using the *parseInt()* method for bases 2, 8, and 16. These values are then passed to the appropriate variables (*base2Num, base8Num* or *base16Num*) which are then displayed in the appropriate field.

HTML code for the Number Functions JavaScript:

```
<HTML>
<HEAD>
<TITLE>Converting Numbers Into Binary, Octal, and Hexadecimal Values
</TITLE>
<SCRIPT>

function checkNum() {
if (this.document.forms[0].inputNum.value=="") {
        alert("You must enter a numeric value");
        this.document.forms[0].inputNum.focus();
        }
else    {
        var MyVar = new String(this.document.forms[0].inputNum.value);
        base2Num=parseInt(MyVar, 2);
        base8Num=parseInt(MyVar, 8);
        base16Num=parseInt(MyVar, 16);
```

```
                    this.document.forms[0].b2.value=(base2Num);
                    this.document.forms[0].b8.value=(base8Num);
                    this.document.forms[0].b16.value=(base16Num);
                    }
            }
</SCRIPT>
</HEAD>
<BODY BGCOLOR=FFFFFF>
<CENTER>
<H2>Converting Numbers Into Binary, Octal, and Hexadecimal Values</H2>
<FORM>
<CENTER>
<TABLE WIDTH=90%>
<TR>
        <TD colspan=3>
        Enter a number to see how it appears in binary, octal, and hexa
        decimal numbering systems. Any number unrecognized is ignored
        along with the numbers following it.
        <INPUT NAME=inputNum TYPE="text" SIZE=5 VALUE=""
        onBlur=checkNum()><P>
        </TD>
</TR>
<TR>   <TD ROWSPAN=3 WIDTH=40% VALIGN=top> This example demonstrates how
       to convert base 10 numbers into other number types.<BR></TD>
        <TD align=right WIDTH=30%>Base 2: </TD>
        <TD WIDTH=30%><INPUT TYPE="text" SIZE=8 NAME=b2></TD>
</TR>
<TR>
        <TD align=right>Base 8: </TD>
        <TD><INPUT TYPE="text" SIZE=8 NAME=b8></TD>
</TR>
<TR>
        <TD align=right>Base 16: </TD>
        <TD><INPUT TYPE="text" SIZE=8 NAME=b16> </TD>
</TR>
</TABLE>
</CENTER>
</FORM>
</BODY>
</HTML>
```

Terminology

event handler: *onBlur*-page 187

method: *focus()*-page 242, 247-248, 254-255

method: *parseInt()*-page 257

statement: *else*-page 269

statement: *if*-page 269

Figure 4.14

Converting number values with the parseInt() method

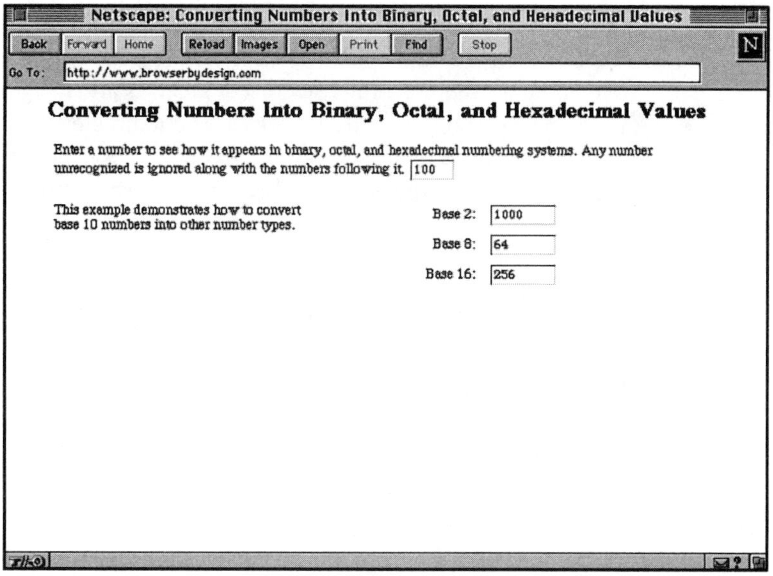

True and False Quiz

34.htm

This script creates a true and false quiz.

This script utilizes the *onSubmit* event handler to accept true and false answers from a list of quiz questions and provides feedback based on the responses. This script could be easily modified to provide an online quiz in an educational situation.

The script uses radio buttons to accept the user input for each of the questions posed. Clicking the submit button generates the *onSubmit* event handler which calls the function *tester()*. This function begins by declaring five variables representing the correct answers and assigning them with a value of zero. The script then looks at the radio element containing the correct answer using the *checked* attribute of the *elements[]* object to determine if it has been clicked. If it has (==true) the corresponding variable is given a value of 1. This process continues for each element and at the end the total values of the variables are added and passed to the variable total. This total is then assessed using comparison operators ==5, or < 5 and, depending on the result, produces the appropriate alert message.

HTML code for the True and False Quiz JavaScript:

```
<HTML>
<HEAD>
<TITLE>Date Functions</TITLE>
<SCRIPT LANGUAGE=JavaScript>

function tester() {
var a = 0
var b = 0
var c = 0
var d = 0
var e = 0

        if(document.forms[0].elements[0].checked==true) {
        a = 1
        }
        if(document.forms[0].elements[3].checked==true) {
        b = 1
        }
        if(document.forms[0].elements[5].checked==true) {
        c = 1
        }
```

```
            if(document.forms[0].elements[6].checked==true) {
            d = 1
            }
            if(document.forms[0].elements[9].checked==true) {
            e = 1
            }
total = a + b + c + d + e

            if(total == 5) {
            alert("5 out ot 5 correct, Great Job!")
            }

            if(total < 5) {
            alert("You got " + total + " out of 5 correct, try again!")
            }
}
</SCRIPT>
</HEAD>
<BODY BGCOLOR=FFFFFF>
<CENTER>
<H1>True/False Question form</H1>
</CENTER>
<FORM method=post onSubmit=tester()>
1. George Washington was the first president of the United States.
<INPUT type=radio name=aa>True
<INPUT type=radio name=aa>False
<BR>
<BR>
<BR>
2. Tucson is the capital of Arizona.
<INPUT type=radio name=bb>True
<INPUT type=radio name=bb>False
<BR>
<BR>
<BR>
3. Guam is an island in the Carribean.
<INPUT type=radio name=cc>True
<INPUT type=radio name=cc>False
<BR>
<BR>
<BR>
4. JavaScript is easier to learn than Java.
<INPUT type=radio name=dd>True
<INPUT type=radio name=dd>False
```

```
<BR>
<BR>
<BR>
5. Mhz refers to how much memory a computer has.
<INPUT type=radio name=ee>True
<INPUT type=radio name=ee>False
<BR>
<BR>
<BR>
<CENTER>
<Input type=submit value="get score">
<Input type="reset" value="clear">
</CENTER>
</FORM>
</BODY>
</HTML>
```

Terminology

event handler: *onSubmit*-page 190-191

attribute: *checked*-page 205, 226

array object: *elements[]*-page 209

comparison operator: ==-page 264

comparison operator: <-page 264

Figure 4.15

Evaluating responses to a true/false quiz with onSubmit

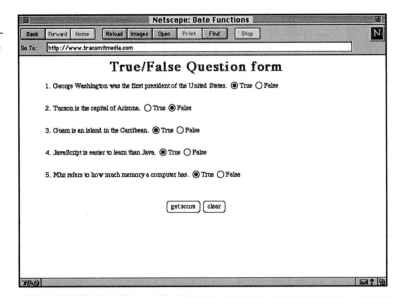

Figure 4.16

Generating an alert message to indicate not all questions have been answered correctly

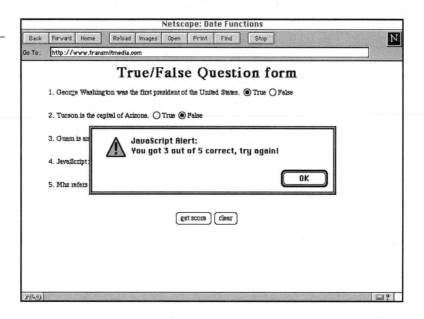

Figure 4.17

Generating an alert message to indicate all questions have been answered correctly

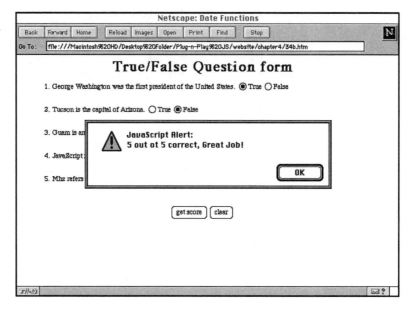

Summary

In this chapter, you have seen how scripts are initiated using form events. Much of the power built into JavaScript is derived from its treatment of form elements and the information they contain. Checking form entry is one of the simplest, yet most effective, uses of JavaScript. Implementing JavaScript in form checking scenarios greatly reduces the workload on the server hosting the HTML documents. By performing the form checking in the browser, major time drags associated with the transfer of information from the server are avoided.

If you are using the form events to administer a test, or to test your visitor for entry information, remember that a visitor can use a browser that does not support JavaScript (or disables JavaScript from Navigator) to view the information that you wish to keep confidential. In other words, if a password is needed to enter a site, and client-side JavaScript programming is all that is used for security, another browser can be used to visit the site and view the document source. The correct password can be found in the JavaScript, and unintended visitors will get through the thin line of security.

In the next chapter, image events are introduced. These features are built into Navigator 3, but are unavailable in earlier versions of Navigator. When designing pages using these features, be aware that a portion of your Navigator audience may not be able to view the page as you intended.

PART V

Image Events

5

Image Events: onAbort, onError, onLoad

This chapter will present some new event handlers and event handler functions introduced with Netscape Navigator 3.0. The new handlers are *onAbort* and *onError*, which interact with the image object, represented by the <IMG> tag in HTML. Although the *onLoad* event handler was introduced in Chapter 3, "Window Events," this chapter will examine its usage as an image event—initiating a script when an image loads. The new handler *onAbort* works similarly in that it initiates a script when an image load is aborted—triggered by selecting another URL, clicking the stop button, pressing the back button, hitting the escape key, or some other means of canceling the image load. The other new handler, *onError*, is triggered when an image referenced in the script or HTML cannot be found by the browser. In other words, what occurs when you see a broken .gif or .jpg icon on your page. Utilizing these three image events enables some useful functionality not previously available with JavaScript.

When working with images and JavaScript, an important detail to remember is that you should always include the height and width modifiers of the image in your HTML tags. Neglecting to do so can result in erratic script behavior or break functionality. In any case, it's always a good idea to include the height and width modifiers because they provide for quicker and more efficient page display in your browser.

Change Image Using src (source) Property

35.htm

The Change Image Using src (source) Property script changes the <img src> of an image on your page without reloading the page.

This example actually uses the *onClick* event handler to demonstrate the functionality of the *src* property of the image object. The HTML equivalent of the src property is the SRC attribute of the <IMG> tag. By clicking on a button shown in the following figure you can change the image displaying on your page without loading a new page. This is a great way of dynamically including multiple image links into a page without having to open any new windows or load new pages. It is excellent for art galleries and portfolios, photo exhibits, image databases, and so on.

 Note

> Changing an image source by utilizing the src property always results in an image displaying in the same height and width dimensions as the first image regardless of the size of the second image. For this reason it is best to use images of exactly equal height and width values with this type of script.

The *imageURL* variable is used in the example to represent the URL for the requested image. Notice that its value is declared before the function uses it, meaning that it is global and set once (for example, the *imageURL* variable's value is not reset every time the function is called). The *changeImage()* function uses a simple *if...else* statement to test the condition of the *imageURL* variable which corresponds to the image displayed in the HTML code for this script. When the visitor clicks on the button defined in the <INPUT> tag, the *onClick* event handler calls the *changeImage()* function. It tests the value of *imageURL* using the == comparison operator, which produces a Boolean value of true or false as required in the *if...else* conditional statement. Because it is equal to "*clock.jpg*," (or false) it ignores the statements passed by the *if...* part of the statement and proceeds to execute the statements following the *else...* part of the statement. The *else...* part instructs the browser to load the new image "*cup.jpg.*" The new image is loaded by changing the *src* property of the *images* array object.

HTML code for the Change Image Using src (source) Property script:

```
<HTML>
<HEAD>
```

```
<TITLE>Change image using source attribute</TITLE>
</HEAD>
<BODY BGCOLOR="#FFFFFF">
<SCRIPT>
imageURL="clock.jpg"
function changeImage(){
        if(imageURL=="cup.jpg") {
        imageURL = "clock.jpg";
        }
        else{
        imageURL = "cup.jpg"
        }
document.images[0].src =imageURL
}
</SCRIPT>
<P>
<CENTER>
<H2>Changing an Image Using the onClick Event Handler</H2>
<FORM>
<INPUT TYPE=Button VALUE="Change the image source" onClick="changeImage()">
</FORM>
<P>
<IMG SRC="clock.jpg" width=180 height=180 NAME="myImage">
</CENTER>
</BODY>
</HTML>
```

Terminology

event handler: *onClick*-page 187-188

object: *document*-page 206

array property: *images*-page 208

comparison operator: ==-page 264

property: *src*-page 215

statement: *if…else*-page 269

Figure 5.1

Browser window prior to clicking button

Figure 5.2

Browser window with new image after clicking button

Alert visitor onAbort

36.htm

The Alert visitor onAbort script brings up an alert box when a user aborts an image load.

The *onAbort* event handler triggers a message when a user aborts an image load which can be useful if the image is a critical part of the Web page, such as an image map. It primarily serves as a way to alert the viewer to some important aspect of the aborted image. Aborting the loading of an image is always a user initiated action and can be triggered by selecting another URL, clicking the stop button, pressing the back button, hitting the escape key, or some other means of canceling the image load. In this example a simple alert box will be called up when the load is aborted.

The script utilizes *onAbort* by placing it in the <IMG> tag, where it calls the function *imageAlert()*. This function is defined at the beginning of the script and contains the call to the *alert()* method.

HTML code for the Alert visitor onAbort JavaScript:

```
<HTML>
<HEAD>
<TITLE>Alert visitor onAbort</TITLE>
<SCRIPT LANGUAGE="JavaScript">
function imageAlert(){
alert("You have not loaded the main image map of this page, this image is
approximately 26K and must be completely loaded in order to navigate the
rest of this website.");
return " "
}
</SCRIPT>
</HEAD>
<BODY BGCOLOR="FFFFFF">
<CENTER>
<H2>Alert Visitor when aborting and image load</H2>
<IMG SRC="image.jpg" width=252 height=289 onAbort=imageAlert()>
</CENTER>
<BODY>
</HTML>
```

Terminology

event handler: *onAbort*-page 186

method: *alert()*-page 241, 254

Figure 5.3

Alert message generated by aborting an image load

Catalog Example with onError

The Catalog Example with onError script selects multiple image sources from a pull-down menu and generates an alert when a non-existent image is accessed.

For this example, the *onChange* handler introduced in Chapter 4 is used with a pull-down menu, in conjunction with the *onError* tag for the event handler. This could be implemented for an online catalog, where users would be able to choose a picture of an inventory item. If the inventory item was not in stock—the image file was not present—they would receive the predefined error message.

In this example, both the options array and the images array are employed. First, the *pullchoice* variable is defined using the options array value property which gets its value based on the option choosen by the user. The images array is then used in the line following the variable declaration to refer to the source of the first image in the document (in this case there is only one). Thus when the variable is changed by a different selection, the source changes as well.

HTML code for the Catalog Example with onError JavaScript:

```
<HTML><HEAD><TITLE>Catalog Example</TITLE></HEAD>
<BODY BGCOLOR="#FFFFFF">
<SCRIPT LANGUAGE=JavaScript>
function changeImage() {
var pullchoice =
document.pull.selector.options[document.pull.selector.selectedIndex].value
document.images[0].src=pullchoice;
}
function imageAlert(){
alert("The item you selected is not in stock, please choose another item");
}
</SCRIPT>
<body>
<P>
<FORM name = "pull">
<SELECT NAME="selector" onChange="changeImage()" SIZE=1>
<OPTION VALUE="default.gif" NAME="default">Choose a computer model
```

```
<OPTION VALUE="100mhz.gif" NAME="option1">100MHz
<OPTION VALUE="166mhz.gif" NAME="option2">166MHz
<OPTION VALUE="180mhz.gif" NAME="option3">180MHz
<OPTION VALUE="200mhz.gif" NAME="option4">200MHz
</SELECT>
</FORM>
<P>
<IMG SRC="default.gif" align=right width=194 height=208
onError=imageAlert()>
</BODY>
</HTML>
```

Terminology

event handler: *onChange*-page 187

event handler: *onError*-page 188

method: *alert()*-page 241, 254

property: *src*-page 215

object: *document*-page 206

array property: *images*-page 208

array property: *options*-page 228

Figure 5.4

Initial pull-down menu option

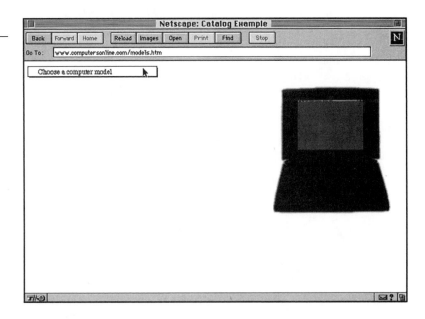

Figure 5.5

Browser window with new image after another menu option has been selected

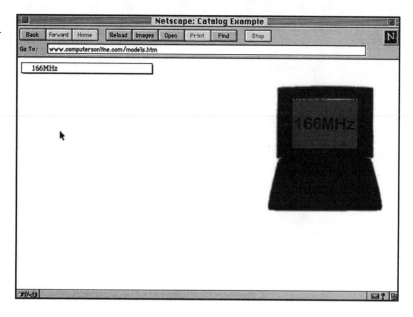

Figure 5.6

Browser window when non-existent image has been selected

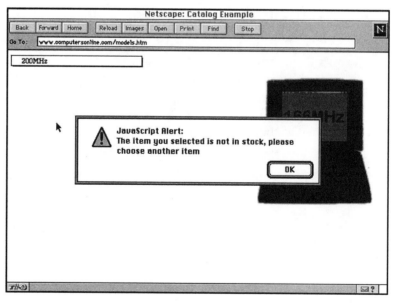

Animation Using onLoad Event Handler

38.htm

The Animation Using onLoad Event Handler script creates anima-tions using the onLoad event handler of the <IMG> tag.

This example provides a JavaScript implementation for animating an image sequentially through changing the *src* property of the *image* object. Though image animation is possible using Java, this example provides a method which is much more accessible to the non-programmer and easier to modify as well. It demonstrates the usefulness and robustness of the src property in JavaScript and can be used in various other ways to control or invoke an animation via any event handler. Thus, by changing the event handler you can initiate or stop the animation at any time via *onClick, onMouseOver,* and so on—something not possible using traditional gif89a animation.

When the initial image has loaded, the *onLoad* event handler invokes the *startAnim()* function. Two variables, *animImage* and *x*, are initialized before the function definition in order to give a value type to the variables, and to prevent them from being reset each time the function is called. The *startAnim()* function then defines the *animImage* variable to enable sequen-tial image numbering for reloading purposes by increasing the value of the variable. This is accomplished using the statement x++, which increases the value of x by 1 until until it reaches 31. The *if (x <= 31)* statement tests for the highest numbered image, and stops the reloading process once that image (in this case: *"images/image31.jpg"*) has been loaded. For your own animation, you need to change the number 31 to indicate the number of the last image in the animation you plan to use.

HTML code for the Animation Using onLoad Event Handler JavaScript:

```
<HTML>
<HEAD>
<TITLE>Animation Using onLoad Event Handler</TITLE>
</HEAD>
<BODY BGCOLOR="#FFFFFF">
<SCRIPT LANGUAGE=JavaScript>
// initial variable values are set
var animImage=""
var x=1
```

```
function startAnim() {
animImage="images/image" + x + ".jpg"
//the first argument is the file name minus the number and file extension,
the second adds a number, the third the extension name of your animation
files (.gif or .jpg)
        if (x<=31) {
        x++
        document.images[0].src=animImage ;
        }
}
</SCRIPT>
<BODY BGCOLOR=FFFFFF TEXT=000000>
<IMG align=right SRC="images/image1.jpg" width=160 height=120
onLoad="startAnim()">
<H1>Animation Using JavaScript</H1>
<HR SIZE=4>
<H2>The animation starts when the image loads. Each time the image loads,
it calls the startAnim function.</H2>
<BR CLEAR=ALL>
<CENTER><HR SIZE=4 WIDTH=90%></CENTER>
</BODY>
</HTML>
```

Terminology

event handler: *onLoad*-page 189

object: *document*-page 206

array object: *images*-page 208

property: *src*-page 215

statement: *if*-page 269

statement: *var*-page 270

Figure 5.7

*Animation using
onLoad event
handler*

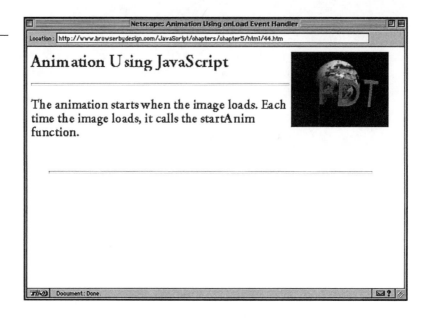

Load Default Image onError

The Load Default Image onError script loads a preselected image when the first image can't be loaded.

This script performs a function similar to the <IMG *Alt = alternate text*> tag in HTML, which displays pre-defined text when the image referenced in the <IMG> tag cannot be loaded. The difference is that this script provides a way of calling up an alternate image rather than just displaying text when an image can't load. You can easily create a custom icon or .gif, perhaps with a company logo or small animated .gif to display when an image can't load rather than just showing the ugly broken image icon and a text description.

The error produced by referencing a non-existant image in the <IMG> tag calls the *altImage()* function via the *onError* event handler. This function designates the new image source using the *images.src* property as in the previous example.

HTML code for the Load Default Image onError JavaScript:

```
<HTML>
<HEAD>
<TITLE>Catalog Example</TITLE>
</HEAD>
<BODY BGCOLOR="#FFFFFF">
<SCRIPT LANGUAGE="JavaScript">
function altImage() {
document.images[0].src="cup.jpg";
}
</SCRIPT>
<body>
<P>
<IMG SRC="clockerr.jpg" width=180 height=180 onError=altImage()>
</BODY>
</HTML>
```

Terminology

event handler: *onError*-page 188

property: *src*-page 215

object: *document*-page 206

object: *image*-page 213

Figure 5.8

Loading an alternate image

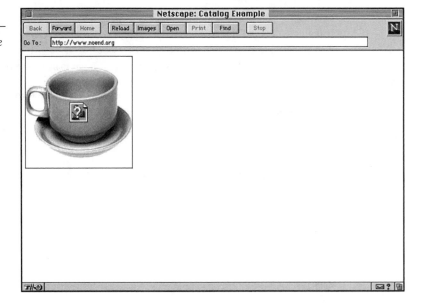

Confirm Window onAbort

The Confirm Window onAbort script asks for confirmation when someone attempts to stop loading your image.

In this example, a new window is created with a confirmation message that attempts to convince the visitor not to leave the page. This may be irritating to some visitors, so use it sparingly, but it is useful where the image is essential to the Web experience.

This example uses several methods from previous examples, and uses the opener property of the window object to communicate from the smaller window to the original one. The script is initiated by the *onAbort* event handler placed in the <IMG> tag of the main image. When invoked, this triggers the function *DontKillWindow()*, which opens another window and writes HTML directly to it using the *write()* method. The new window presents two buttons, each of which performs a different task via *onClick*. Clicking "yes" simply closes the window and returns to the aborted image window, while clicking "no" continues loading the image by using *history.go(0)*, which continues loading the current URL because it is the first item in the history list.

Browser Warning

This script works in Navigator 3.0 and later only.

HTML code for the Confirm Window onAbort JavaScript:

```
<HTML>
<HEAD>
<TITLE>Confirm Window onAbort</TITLE>
</HEAD>
<BODY BGCOLOR="#FFFFFF">
<SCRIPT LANGUAGE=JavaScript>
function DontKillWindow() {
myWindow = window.open("", "ConfirmWindow",
"toolbar=no,directories=no,menubar=no,scrollbars=no,width=250,height=200");
myWindow.document.write("<HTML><HEAD><TITLE>Confirm...</TITLE>");
myWindow.document.write("</HEAD><BODY  BGCOLOR=FFFFFF><CENTER>");
myWindow.document.write("<H1>Are you sure you want to stop loading the
document?</H1>");
```

```
myWindow.document.write("<FORM><INPUT TYPE='button' VALUE='Yes'
onClick='window.close()'>");
myWindow.document.write("<INPUT TYPE='button' VALUE='No'
onClick=opener.history.go(0)><BR>");
myWindow.document.write("<INPUT TYPE='button' VALUE='Close Window'
onClick=window.close()>");
myWindow.document.write("</FORM></CENTER>");
myWindow.document.write("</BODY></HTML>");
}
</SCRIPT>

<BODY BGCOLOR=FFFFFF TEXT=000000>
<CENTER>
<H1>Confirm Window onAbort</H1>
<H2>When you attempt to abort, a confirm dialog box appears.</H2>
<HR SIZE=4>
<IMG SRC="open.jpg" onAbort="DontKillWindow()"><BR>
<HR SIZE=4 WIDTH=90%></CENTER>
</BODY>
</HTML>
```

Terminology

event handler: *onClick*-page 187-188

event handler: *onAbort*-page 186

method: *write()*-page 240-241

method: *open()*-page 240, 242, 255-256

method: *close()*-page 239, 241, 255

object: *document*-page 206

object: *window*-page 232-233

Gallery Image Picker

41.htm

gallery.htm

The Gallery Image Picker script loads a new window with a directory of links that will change the source image of the original window.

This script produces a new window with several links of artists' names for a virtual artist's gallery. Clicking on one of the artists' names will change the image source of the original image of the opening page. The new window remains as a static navigation tool to affect the image source of the larger window.

This example is comprised of 2 HTML files: 41.htm and gallery.htm. The main script is contained in 41.htm that generates a new window by using the *window.open()* method to open the html file "gallery.htm". This occurs when 41.htm loads using the *onLoad* event handler. Although in previous examples the *open()* method has been used to open new windows independent of any existing HTML files, this example opens an HTML file-dependent window by looking at the first argument in quotes—"gallery.htm" in the *open()* command which appears like this:

```
window.open("gallery.htm", "MakeGalleryCtrlWindow",
"toolbar=no,directories=no,menubar=no,scrollbars=no,width =200,height
=225").
```

By including a file name in the quotes, the browser uses this for the source HTML of the new window. This file provides three hyperlinks that call the *changeImage()* function using the *onClick* event handler. The changeImage function creates a string such as: "images/picasso.jpg" based on the value *nameofImage* that is defined by which of the three hyperlinks are selected. This URL is then passed to the *imgChange* variable, which becomes the image source file for the opening window via the *src* property. The *opener.document.images[0].src* command indicates where to apply this source file, the opener object indicating the window which opened the current one.

HTML code for the 41.htm file of the Gallery Image Picker script:

```
<HTML>
<HEAD><TITLE>Gallery-Image Picker</TITLE>
</HEAD>
```

```
<SCRIPT>
function MakeGalleryCtrlWindow() {
GalleryControl=window.open("gallery.htm", "MakeGalleryCtrlWindow",
"toolbar=no,directories=no,menubar=no,scrollbars=no,width=200,height=225");
}
</SCRIPT>
<BODY BGCOLOR="#FFFFFF">
<P>
<CENTER>
<H2>Creating a New Window when Image is Loaded</H2>
<P>
<IMG SRC="images/main.jpg" width=200 height=200 NAME="myImage"
onLoad=MakeGalleryCtrlWindow()>
</CENTER>
</BODY>
</HTML>
```

HTML code for the gallery.htm file of the Gallery Image Picker script:

```
<HTML>
<HEAD>
<TITLE>Gallery Control</TITLE>
</HEAD>
<SCRIPT>
imgChange=""
function changeImage(nameofImage) {
imgChange="images/" + nameofImage + ".jpg";
opener.document.images[0].src=imgChange;
}
</SCRIPT>
<BODY  BGCOLOR=FFFFFF TEXT=000000>
<h2><a ." name="Picasso" onClick="changeImage('picasso')">Picasso</A></h2>
<h2><a href="#" name="Rembrandt"
onClick="changeImage('rembrandt')">Rembrandt</A></h2>
<h2><a href="#" name="Van Gogh" onClick="changeImage('vangogh')">Van Gogh</
A></h2>
</BODY>
</HTML>
```

Terminology

Figure 5.10

*Browser window
with new control
window when page
first loads*

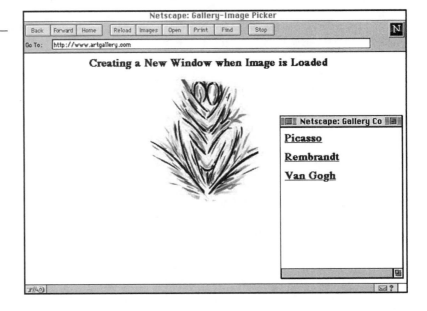

Figure 5.11

Changing the image source of the main image

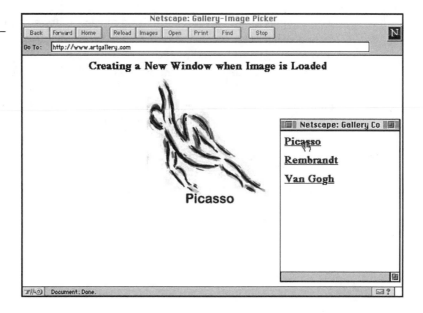

Figure 5.12

Calling another image by clicking on a different hyperlink

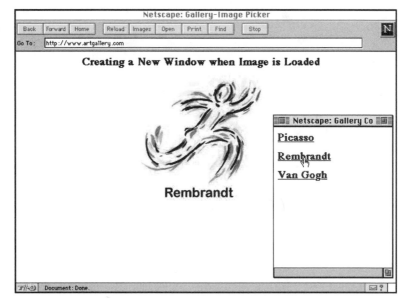

This chapter introduced implementing image events with JavaScript. The examples here provide concrete methods for building dynamic functionality into a Web site and detail new ways of working with images. Image display is one of the most important components of browsing the Web, and you should be able to customize the basic code presented here to suit your needs, or build upon it to create some really powerful functionality. All it takes is a little imagination and persistence. In the next chapter, the JavaScript envelope will really be pushed through exploring some of the latest and more advanced capabilities available to JavaScript programmers. You'll discover some of the powerful potential only beginning to emerge as JavaScript's capabilities expand to increasingly higher levels of functionality.

PART VI

Advanced JavaScripts

6

Chapter

Advanced JavaScripts

This chapter covers advanced implementations of JavaScript, most of which require Navigator version 3.0 and later. The event handlers introduced in the first five chapters of the book are integrated with additional Web entities, such as Java and plug-ins. Several examples here use more than one event handler to perform JavaScript execution. The JavaScript Reference script is particularly useful for not only seeing several event handlers working in tandem, but it also contains a complete JavaScript online reference. This is contained on the CD-ROM that accompanies the book.

Most of the examples in previous chapters have been relatively basic. The following examples will provide more developed models of what is possible and a peek into the future of JavaScript. Here you will see how the language currently works with cookies, plug-ins, MIME-types, advanced forms, and frames.

Advanced Forms

Page Loader with Multiple Frames and Forms

The Page Loader with Multiple Frames and Forms script utilizes two frames and multiple select forms, which all other HTML pages based on user selections.

43.htm

43top.htm

43pers.htm

43tech.htm

43exp.htm

43more.htm

This script illustrates an advanced usage of select forms in a two frame layout to provide an online resumé. The top frame contains a multiple select form that lists HTML links to load into the bottom frame. Each of the pages loaded in the bottom frame contains multiple select forms to access different data pertinent to the resumé.

This example consists of six HTML files, the primary one being **43.htm**, which indicates the main page layout and frame sources. The top frame displays **43top.htm**, which contains a select form with several displayed options using the **<select multiple>** tag to display them all. Each of these links to HTML documents, which are displayed in the lower frame. All of the files in this example use arrays to define the different data types available in the select forms. The following line contains the names of the HTML links to be accessed in the select form of the top frame:

```
<select multiple name="sel_subject"
onChange='show_subject(this,"43pers.htm","43tech.htm","43exp.htm","43more.htm");'>
```

Notice the names of the HTML files included as arguments in the *show_subject()* function. This is where you define to which files the links will take you. The options below them indicate the names assigned to the files in the form. These names are selected and accessed using the *selectedIndex* property and initiated using the *onChange* event handler.

Each of the included link pages in the bottom frame: **43pers.htm**, **43tech.htm**, and **43exp.htm** are variations on one template. Any HTML page can be loaded, but the included examples contain a select form used to display the resumé information. Again, an array is created to handle the data. In these examples, the selected index item displays data in a **<textarea>** form box.

To create linebreaks in the **<textarea>** form the **/n** or **/r/n** commands are assigned to the nl variable representing a new line. Because the usage of **/n** versus **/r/n** to indicate a new line in a text area is platform specific, the *windPlat( )* function has been included to determine if the user has a Windows browser by looking for the "W" character in the appVersion property.

HTML code for the Page Loader JavaScript:

Main document: 43.htm

```
<HTML>
<HEAD>
<TITLE>Pulldown list with frames</TITLE>
</HEAD>
<FRAMESET rows="110,*">
<FRAME src="43top.htm" NAME="topframe" MARGINWIDTH=0 SCROLLING=NO>
<FRAME src="43pers.htm" NAME="botframe" MARGINWIDTH=10>
</FRAMESET>
</HTML>
```

Top frame: 43top.htm

```
<HTML>
<HEAD>
<SCRIPT LANGUAGE="JavaScript">
<!--

function MakeArray(n)
  {
  this.length = n;
  for(var i = 1; i <= n; i++)
    {
    this[i] = 0;
    }
  return this;
  }

function show_subject(asubject)
  {
  subject = new MakeArray(show_subject.arguments.length);

  for(var i=1;i<show_subject.arguments.length;i++)
    {
    subject[i-1]=show_subject.arguments[i];
    }
```

```
    top.frames[1].location=subject[asubject.selectedIndex];
    }

//-->

</SCRIPT>
</HEAD>
<BODY bgcolor=ffffff>
<CENTER>
<H1>Mary Smith's Resume</H1>
<P>
<FORM>
  <table border=0>
    <TR>
      <td valign=top>
        <select multiple name="sel_subject"
onChange='show_subject(this,"43pers.htm","43tech.htm","43exp.htm","43more.htm");'>
          <option selected>Personal information
          <option>Technical summary
          <option>Professional experience
          <option>More info
        </select>
      </TD>
    </TR>
  </TABLE>
</FORM>
</CENTER>
</BODY>
</HTML>
```

Bottom frame link: 43pers.htm (43tech.htm, 43exp.htm, 43more.htm)

```
<HTML>
<HEAD>
<TITLE>Personal Info</TITLE>
<SCRIPT LANGUAGE="JavaScript">
<!--

var nl;

function windPlat(){
return navigator.appVersion.charAt(navigator.appVersion.indexOf("(")+1) ==
"W";
}
```

```
function MakeArray(n){
this.length = n;

        for(var i = 1; i <= n; i++) {
        this[i] = 0;
        }


return this;
}



function show_data(ainfo)  {
info = new MakeArray(3);
        //newline for Windows platforms
        if(windPlat()){
        nl="\r\n";
        }

     //newline for other platforms
        else {
        nl="\n";
        }

     // first textarea data item
        info[0]="MA - Computer Science, Stanford University - (1994)."
        +nl+nl+"BA - Mathematics, Washington Universtiy - (1992).";

     // second textarea data item
        info[1]="Bilingual:"
        +nl+"- French"
        +nl+"- English";

     // third textarea data item
        info[2]="- Marital Status:  Single"
        +nl+"- Nationality:  American"
        +nl+"- Age:  26"
        +nl+"- Birth:  St. Louis, MO";

document.form1.txt_info.value=info[ainfo.selectedIndex];
}
//-->
</SCRIPT>
</HEAD>
```

```
<BODY onload="show_data(document.form1.sel_personal)" BGCOLOR=ffffff>
<CENTER>
<br>
<font size=5>Mary Smith</font>
<br>456 Jones St.
<br>San Jose, CA 95335
<br>(408)735-4114
<br>
<A HREF="mailto: msmith@stanford.edu">e-mail: msmith@stanford.edu</A>
<FORM name="form1">
<TABLE bgcolor="FFFFEC" border=2>
   <TR>
     <td colspan=2>
        <CENTER><b><font size=5 color="#000000">Personal information</
font></b></CENTER>
      </TD>
   <TR>
     <TD width=40%>
       <CENTER>
        <select multiple name="sel_personal" onChange="show_data(this);">
        <option selected>Education
        <option>Written and spoken languages
        <option>Personal Information
        </select>
        </CENTER>
     </TD>
     <TD>
       <CENTER>
         <TEXTAREA name="txt_info" rows=6 cols=35 wrap=physical>
         </TEXTAREA>
       </CENTER>
     </TD>
   </TR>
</TABLE>
</FORM>
<br>
</CENTER>
</BODY>
</HTML>
```

Terminology

event handler: *onLoad*-page 189

event handler: *onChange*-page 187

property: *length*-page 204, 213-215

property: *selectedIndex*-page 223, 228

property: *appVersion*-page 221, 274-275

keyword: *this*-page 270

keyword: *return*-page 270

method: *charAt()*-page 249

Figure 6.1

Online resumé using multiple frames and form items

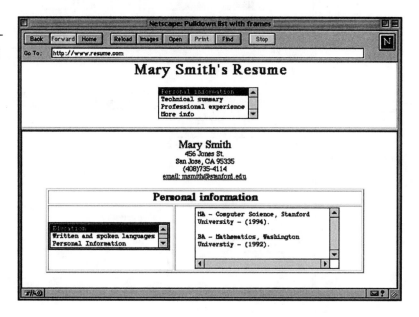

Figure 6.2

Selecting a new item to display in the right textarea box

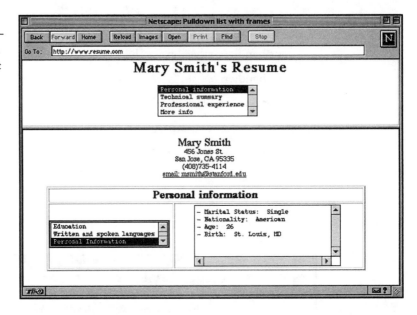

Figure 3.10

Selecting a different document to display in the lower frame

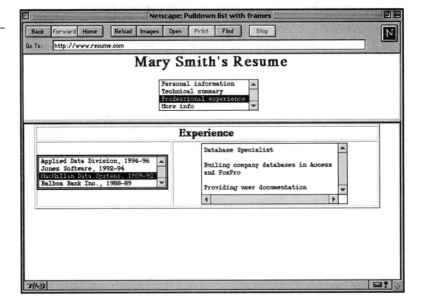

Online Order Form

The Online Order Form script provides an online order form to calculate the price of selected items and then submits the form via e-mail.

This script illustrates an advanced usage of select forms to provide an online order form. Users can select multiple items from the pulldown menus, have totals calculated, tax information included, and then submit the information to a predefined e-mail address using the submit button. Information sent via e-mail can be parsed by an application or database at the client's end to handle the incoming data.

HTML code for the Online Order Form JavaScript:

```
<HTML>
<HEAD>
<TITLE>Online Order Form</TITLE>

<SCRIPT LANGUAGE="JavaScript">
<!-- hide

function MakeArray(n)
{
this.length = n;
for(var i = 1; i <= n; i++)
   {
   this[i] = 0
   }
return this
}


function f_tax(num)
{

if(num)
  {
  if(document.input.TAX.checked)
    {
    // this line modifies the local tax amount
    document.input.f_res.value=Math.round(8.25*num)/100;
    }
```

```
  else
    {
    document.input.f_res.value=0;
    }
  }
cal_gtot();
}

function cal_gtot()
{
var tamp=0;

if(document.input.f_stot.value.length != 0)
  {
  tamp+=parseFloat(document.input.f_stot.value);
  }
if(document.input.f_res.value.length != 0)
  {
  tamp+=parseFloat(document.input.f_res.value);
  }

document.input.f_gtot.value=tamp;
}

function process(sel)
{
var t_price = new MakeArray(process.arguments.length);
var line=sel.name.charAt(sel.name.length-1);


for(var i=1;i<process.arguments.length;i++)
  {
  t_price[i-1]=parseFloat(process.arguments[i]);
  }

if(document.input["f_qty"+line].value.length != 0)
  {
  var fv=parseFloat(document.input["f_qty"+line].value);

  if(navigator.appVersion.charAt(navigator.appVersion.indexOf("(")+1) ==
"W" || navigator.appVersion.charAt(navigator.appVersion.indexOf("(")+1) ==
"M")
    {
```

```
    if(fv == 0)
      {
      line++;
      alert("the qty at line "+line+" must be a number");
      return;
      }
    }
  else
    {
    if(isNaN(fv))
      {
      line++;
      alert("the qty at line "+line+" must be a number");
      return;
      }
    }

  if(sel.name.substring(0,sel.name.length-1)=="product")
    {
    document.input["f_tot"+line].value=eval(t_price[sel.selectedIndex]*fv);
    document.input["f_price"+line].value=t_price[sel.selectedIndex];
    }
  else
    {
    document.input["f_tot"+line].value=eval(t_price[document.input["product"+line]
    ➥.selectedIndex]*fv);
    document.input["f_price"+line].value=t_price[document.input["product"+line]
    ➥.selectedIndex];
    }
  }

var i=0;
var total=0;
while(document.input["f_tot"+i])
  {
  if(document.input["f_tot"+i].value.length != 0)
    {
    total+=parseFloat(document.input["f_tot"+i].value);
    }
  i++;
  }
```

```
document.input.f_stot.value=total;
f_tax(total);
cal_gtot();
}

function f_send()
{
if(   document.input.f_name.value.length == 0
   ||document.input.f_addr.value.length == 0
   ||document.input.f_stat.value.length == 0
   ||document.input.f_country.value.length == 0
   ||document.input.f_zip.value.length == 0
   ||document.input.f_phone.value.length == 0)
   {
   alert("You must complete the form first!");
   return;
   }
if (confirm("Press ok to send the order"))
   {
   document.input.submit();
   }
}

//-->
</SCRIPT>
</head>
<body bgcolor="#ffffff">
<center>
<FONT SIZE=5><B>Online Order Form</B></FONT>
<form name=input METHOD="post" ACTION="mailto:kready@onthemap.com">
 <table>
  <TR>
   <TH ALIGN=right>Name</TH>
   <TD COLSPAN=5><INPUT NAME="f_name" value="" SIZE=59></TD>
  </TR>
  <TR>
   <TH ALIGN=right>Address</TH>
   <TD COLSPAN=5><INPUT NAME="f_addr" value="" SIZE=59></TD>
  </TR>
  <TR>
   <TH ALIGN=right>City</TH>
   <TD><INPUT NAME="f_city" value="" maxlength = 20 SIZE=20></TD>
   <TH ALIGN=right>State/Province</TH>
```

```
        <TD COLSPAN=3><INPUT NAME="f_stat" value="" maxlength = 30 SIZE=20></TD>
       </TR>
       <TR>
        <TH ALIGN=right>Country</TH>
        <TD><INPUT NAME="f_country" value=""          maxlength = 20 SIZE=20></TD>
        <TH ALIGN=right>Zip/Postal Code</TH>
        <TD COLSPAN=3><INPUT NAME="f_zip" value="" maxlength = 10 SIZE=20></TD>
       </TR>
       <TR>
        <TH ALIGN=right>Billing Phone</TH>
        <TD><INPUT NAME="f_phone" value="" maxlength = 21 SIZE=12></TD>
        <TH ALIGN=right>E-mail Address</TH>
        <TD COLSPAN=3><INPUT NAME="f_e-mail" value="" maxlength = 100 SIZE=20></
td>
      </tr>
      <tr>
       <td colspan=2 align=center>
        <INPUT TYPE="submit" name="f_submit" value="     SUBMIT     "
onClick='f_send();'>
       </td>
       <td colspan=4 align=center>
        <INPUT TYPE="RESET"  value="RESET">
       </td>
      </tr>
      <tr>
       <td ROWSPAN=8><pre>       </pre></td>
       <th align=right>Qty .</th>
       <th align=center>Product</th>
       <th align=center>Price</th>
       <th align=center>Total</th>
       <th ROWSPAN=8><pre>        </pre></td>
      </tr>
      <tr>
       <td valign=top align=right><input type=text name="f_qty0" size=3
onChange='process(this, "1.55", "2.25", "3.52", "4.79", "5.99", "6.99",
"7.56", "8.25", "9.99", "10.99");'>
</td>
       <td valign=top>
        <SELECT name="product0" onChange='process(this, "1.55", "2.25",
"3.52", "4.79", "5.99", "6.99", "7.56", "8.25", "9.99", "10.99");'>
        <option>product 1 <option>product 2 <option>product 3
        <option>product 4 <option>product 5 <option>product 6
➥<option>product 7
```

```
    <option>product 8 <option>product 9 <option>product 10
<option selected>select a product
    </select>
    </td>
    <td valign=top><input type=text name="f_price0" size=8
onFocus="this.blur();"></td>
    <td valign=top><input type=text name="f_tot0" size=8
onFocus="this.blur();"></td>
    </tr>
    <tr>
    <td valign=top align=right><input type=text name="f_qty1" size=3
onChange='process(this, "1.55", "2.25", "3.52", "4.79", "5.99", "6.99",
"7.56", "8.25", "9.99", "10.99");'>
</td>
    <td valign=top>
     <SELECT name="product1" onChange='process(this, "1.55", "2.25",
"3.52", "4.79", "5.99", "6.99", "7.56", "8.25", "9.99", "10.99");'>
      <option>product 1 <option>product 2 <option>product 3
      <option>product 4 <option>product 5 <option>product 6
➥<option>product 7
      <option>product 8 <option>product 9 <option>product 10
<option selected>select a product
     </select>
    </td>
    <td valign=top><input type=text name="f_price1" size=8
onFocus="this.blur();"></td>
    <td valign=top><input type=text name="f_tot1" size=8
onFocus="this.blur();"></td>
    </tr>
    <tr>
    <td valign=top align=right><input type=text name="f_qty2" size=3
onChange='process(this, "1.55", "2.25", "3.52", "4.79", "5.99", "6.99",
"7.56", "8.25", "9.99", "10.99");'>
    <td valign=top>
     <SELECT name="product2" onChange='process(this, "1.55", "2.25",
"3.52", "4.79", "5.99", "6.99", "7.56", "8.25", "9.99", "10.99");'>
      <option>product 1 <option>product 2 <option>product 3
      <option>product 4 <option>product 5 <option>product 6
➥<option>product 7
      <option>product 8 <option>product 9 <option>product 10
<option selected>select a product
     </select>
    </td>
```

```
    <td valign=top><input type=text name=f_price2 size=8
onFocus="this.blur();"></td>
    <td valign=top><input type=text name=f_tot2 size=8
onFocus="this.blur();"></td>
   </tr>
   <tr>
    <td></td>
    <td></td>
    <th>Subtotal</th>
    <td><input type=text name=f_stot size=8 onFocus="this.blur();"></td>
   </tr>
   <tr>
    <th colspan=2 align=right>CA Residents <input type=checkbox name=TAX
onClick="f_tax(document.input.f_stot.value);"></th>
    <th>Taxes</th>
    <td><input type=text name=f_res size=8 onFocus="this.blur();"></td>
   </tr>
   <tr>
    <td></td>
    <td></td>
   </tr>
   <tr>
    <td></td>
    <td></td>
    <th>Total</th>
    <td><input type=text name=f_gtot size=8 onFocus="this.blur();"></td>
   </tr>
  </table>
 </form>
</center>
</body>
</html>
```

Figure 6.4

Calculating item totals and submitting orders via e-mail in an online order form

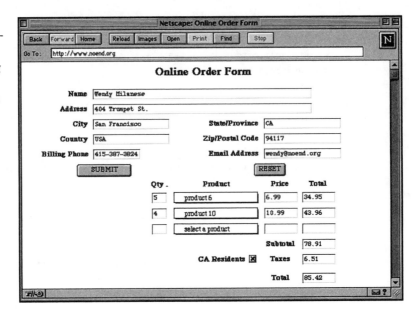

JavaScript Reference

The JavaScript Reference script provides a complete JavaScript reference source using frames and pulldown menus.

This example provides a complex usage of frames and synchronized event handlers, as well as an online reference source for JavaScript. It includes all of the programming references from Appendix A. The principal HTML files are included here. Reference the CD-ROM for the complete HTML documentation.

Mainfram.htm

```
<HTML>
<HEAD>
<TITLE>
JavaScript Programming Reference
</TITLE>

<! This is the page that defines the frames for the manual.>

</HEAD>

<FRAMESET COLS="160,*">
        <FRAMESET ROWS="*, 70">
                <FRAME NAME="model" SRC="model.htm" MARGINHEIGHT=0
                    MARGINWIDTH=0 SCROLLING=VERTICAL NORESIZE>
                <FRAME NAME="optf" SRC="option.htm" MARGINHEIGHT=0
                    MARGINWIDTH=0 SCROLLING=NO NORESIZE>
        </FRAMESET>
        <FRAMESET ROWS="40, *">
                <FRAME NAME="selections" SRC="details.htm" MARGINHEIGHT=0
                    MARGINWIDTH=0 SCROLLING=NO NORESIZE>
                <FRAME NAME="infoff" SRC="bodytext.htm" MARGINHEIGHT=0
                    MARGINWIDTH=0 NORESIZE>
        </FRAMESET>

</FRAMESET>
</HTML>

Details.htm
<HTML>
<BODY BGCOLOR=FFFFFF>
```

```
<! This page temporarily houses a document before the first query is made.>

<P>

<CENTER>

<font size=5><STRONG>JavaScript Programming Reference</strong></font>

</CENTER>

</BODY>
</HTML>
```

```
Model.htm
```

```
<HTML>

<! This defines the top left frame. Individual images are used so that they
can be replaced with another image with a different color, and to target
the main window.>

<SCRIPT>


function MakeArray(n)
{
this.length = n;
for(var i = 1; i <= n; i++)
   {
   this[i] = 0
   }
return this
}

function ThisFunction(num) {
var itop=0;
var inf_t = new MakeArray(3);

inf_t[0]="p";
inf_t[1]="m";
inf_t[2]="e";
```

```
top.frames[1].document.forms[0].num.value=num;
last=parseInt(top.frames[1].document.forms[0].last.value,10);

for(var i=0;i<3;i++)
  {
  if(top.frames[1].document.forms[0].elements[i].checked)
    {
    break;
    }
  }
itop=i;
var urll=document.images[parseInt(num,10)].src.substring(0,
document.images[parseInt(num,10)].src.lastIndexOf("."))+inf_t[itop]+".htm";
if(urll.charAt(urll.lastIndexOf(".")-2)=="b")
  urll=urll.substring(0,(urll.lastIndexOf(".")-2))+inf_t[itop]+".htm";

if(last!=0)
  {
  document.images[last].src=document.images[last].src.substring(0,
document.images[last].src.lastIndexOf("b"))+".gif";
  }
else
  {
  document.images[last].src="01.gif"
  }

document.images[parseInt(num,10)].src=document.images[parseInt(num,10)].src.substring(0,
document.images[parseInt(num,10)].src.lastIndexOf("."))+"b.gif";
top.frames[1].document.forms[0].last.value=num;
top.selections.location=urll;
}


</SCRIPT>

<BODY>
<A HREF=# onClick="ThisFunction('0')"
onMouseOver="window.status='window';return true">
<IMG SRC="01.gif" HSPACE=0 WIDTH=150 HEIGHT=15 VSPACE=0 BORDER=0
ALT="window"></A><BR>
<A HREF=# onClick="ThisFunction('1')"
onMouseOver="window.status='frame';return true">
<IMG SRC="02.gif" HSPACE=0 WIDTH=150 HEIGHT=15 VSPACE=0 BORDER=0
```

```
ALT="frame"></A><BR>
<A HREF=# onClick="ThisFunction('2')"
onMouseOver="window.status='location';return true">
<IMG SRC="03.gif" HSPACE=0 WIDTH=150 HEIGHT=15 VSPACE=0 BORDER=0
ALT="location"></A><BR>
<A HREF=# onClick="ThisFunction('3')"
onMouseOver="window.status='history';return true">
<IMG SRC="04.gif" HSPACE=0 WIDTH=150 HEIGHT=15 VSPACE=0 BORDER=0
ALT="history"></A><BR>
<A HREF=# onClick="ThisFunction('4')"
onMouseOver="window.status='navigator';return true">
<IMG SRC="05.gif" HSPACE=0 WIDTH=150 HEIGHT=15 VSPACE=0 BORDER=0
ALT="navigator"></A><BR>
<A HREF=# onClick="ThisFunction('5')"
onMouseOver="window.status='mimeType';return true">
<IMG SRC="06.gif" HSPACE=0 WIDTH=150 HEIGHT=15 VSPACE=0 BORDER=0
ALT="mimeType"></A><BR>
<A HREF=# onClick="ThisFunction('6')"
onMouseOver="window.status='plugins';return true">
<IMG SRC="07.gif" HSPACE=0 WIDTH=150 HEIGHT=15 VSPACE=0 BORDER=0
ALT="plugins"></A><BR>
<A HREF=# onClick="ThisFunction('7')"
onMouseOver="window.status='mimeTypes';return true">
<IMG SRC="08.gif" HSPACE=0 WIDTH=150 HEIGHT=15 VSPACE=0 BORDER=0
ALT="mimeTypes"></A><BR>
<A HREF=# onClick="ThisFunction('8')"
onMouseOver="window.status='document';return true">
<IMG SRC="09.gif" HSPACE=0 WIDTH=150 HEIGHT=15 VSPACE=0 BORDER=0
ALT="document"></A><BR>
<A HREF=# onClick="ThisFunction('9')"
onMouseOver="window.status='applet';return true">
<IMG SRC="10.gif" HSPACE=0 WIDTH=150 HEIGHT=15 VSPACE=0 BORDER=0
ALT="applet"></A><BR>
<A HREF=# onClick="ThisFunction('10')"
onMouseOver="window.status='image';return true">
<IMG SRC="11.gif" HSPACE=0 WIDTH=150 HEIGHT=15 VSPACE=0 BORDER=0
ALT="image"></A><BR>
<A HREF=# onClick="ThisFunction('11')"
onMouseOver="window.status='anchor';return true">
<IMG SRC="12.gif" HSPACE=0 WIDTH=150 HEIGHT=15 VSPACE=0 BORDER=0
ALT="anchor"></A><BR>
<A HREF=# onClick="ThisFunction('12')"
onMouseOver="window.status='link';return true">
<IMG SRC="13.gif" HSPACE=0 WIDTH=150 HEIGHT=15 VSPACE=0 BORDER=0
```

```
ALT="link"></A><BR>
<A HREF=# onClick="ThisFunction('13')"
onMouseOver="window.status='form';return true">
<IMG SRC="14.gif" HSPACE=0 WIDTH=150 HEIGHT=15 VSPACE=0 BORDER=0
ALT="form"></A><BR>
<A HREF=# onClick="ThisFunction('14')"
onMouseOver="window.status='button';return true">
<IMG SRC="15.gif" HSPACE=0 WIDTH=150 HEIGHT=15 VSPACE=0 BORDER=0
ALT="button"></A><BR>
<A HREF=# onClick="ThisFunction('15')"
onMouseOver="window.status='checkbox';return true">
<IMG SRC="16.gif" HSPACE=0 WIDTH=150 HEIGHT=15 VSPACE=0 BORDER=0
ALT="checkbox"></A><BR>
<A HREF=# onClick="ThisFunction('16')"
onMouseOver="window.status='hidden';return true">
<IMG SRC="17.gif" HSPACE=0 WIDTH=150 HEIGHT=15 VSPACE=0 BORDER=0
ALT="hidden"></A><BR>
<A HREF=# onClick="ThisFunction('17')"
onMouseOver="window.status='password';return true">
<IMG SRC="18.gif" HSPACE=0 WIDTH=150 HEIGHT=15 VSPACE=0 BORDER=0
ALT="password"></A><BR>
<A HREF=# onClick="ThisFunction('18')"
onMouseOver="window.status='radio';return true">
<IMG SRC="19.gif" HSPACE=0 WIDTH=150 HEIGHT=15 VSPACE=0 BORDER=0
ALT="radio"></A><BR>
<A HREF=# onClick="ThisFunction('19')"
onMouseOver="window.status='reset';return true">
<IMG SRC="20.gif" HSPACE=0 WIDTH=150 HEIGHT=15 VSPACE=0 BORDER=0
ALT="reset"></A><BR>
<A HREF=# onClick="ThisFunction('20')"
onMouseOver="window.status='select';return true">
<IMG SRC="21.gif" HSPACE=0 WIDTH=150 HEIGHT=15 VSPACE=0 BORDER=0
ALT="select"></A><BR>
<A HREF=# onClick="ThisFunction('21')"
onMouseOver="window.status='options';return true">
<IMG SRC="22.gif" HSPACE=0 WIDTH=150 HEIGHT=15 VSPACE=0 BORDER=0
ALT="options"></A><BR>
<A HREF=# onClick="ThisFunction('22')"
onMouseOver="window.status='submit';return true">
<IMG SRC="23.gif" HSPACE=0 WIDTH=150 HEIGHT=15 VSPACE=0 BORDER=0
ALT="submit"></A><BR>
<A HREF=# onClick="ThisFunction('23')"
onMouseOver="window.status='text';return true">
<IMG SRC="24.gif" HSPACE=0 WIDTH=150 HEIGHT=15 VSPACE=0 BORDER=0
```

```
ALT="text"></A><BR>
<A HREF=# onClick="ThisFunction('24')"
onMouseOver="window.status='textarea';return true">
<IMG SRC="25.gif" HSPACE=0 WIDTH=150 HEIGHT=15 VSPACE=0 BORDER=0
ALT="textarea"></A><BR>
<A HREF=# onClick="ThisFunction('25')"
onMouseOver="window.status='Array';return true">
<IMG SRC="26.gif" HSPACE=0 WIDTH=150 HEIGHT=15 VSPACE=0 BORDER=0
ALT="Array"></A><BR>
<A HREF=# onClick="ThisFunction('26')"
onMouseOver="window.status='Date';return true">
<IMG SRC="27.gif" HSPACE=0 WIDTH=150 HEIGHT=15 VSPACE=0 BORDER=0
ALT="Date"></A><BR>
<A HREF=# onClick="ThisFunction('27')"
onMouseOver="window.status='Math';return true">
<IMG SRC="28.gif" HSPACE=0 WIDTH=150 HEIGHT=15 VSPACE=0 BORDER=0
ALT="Math"></A><BR>
<A HREF=# onClick="ThisFunction('28')"
onMouseOver="window.status='String';return true">
<IMG SRC="29.gif" HSPACE=0 WIDTH=150 HEIGHT=15 VSPACE=0 BORDER=0
ALT="String"></A><BR>

</BODY>

</HTML>
```

Option.htm

```
<HTML>
<HEAD>

<! This is used in conjunction with the Model.htm document to target the
main window, which contains the bodytext.htm document.>

<SCRIPT>
function UpDateWindow()
{
alert(top.infoff.document.test.elements[0]);
}
</SCRIPT>
</HEAD>
<BODY onLoad="document.opt.elements[0].checked=true;" BGCOLOR=FFFFFF>

<FORM name=opt>
```

```
<INPUT TYPE="radio" NAME="SelectInput"
onClick=top.frames[0].ThisFunction(document.opt.num.value)>Properties<BR>

<INPUT TYPE="radio" NAME="SelectInput"
onClick=top.frames[0].ThisFunction(document.opt.num.value)>Methods<BR>

<INPUT TYPE="radio" NAME="SelectInput"
onClick=top.frames[0].ThisFunction(document.opt.num.value)>Event
Handlers<BR>

<INPUT TYPE=hidden name=num>
<INPUT TYPE=hidden name=last value="0">

</FORM>

</BODY>

</HTML>
```

Also, check out the bodytext.htm file on the CD-ROM and some of the individual examples. The files are numbered from 1 through 29, and they are broken into event handlers (*e.htm), methods (*m.htm), and properties (*p.htm). For number 1, the window object, there is 1e.htm, which lists its event handlers; 1m.htm, which lists its methods; and 1p.htm, which lists its properties.

Figure 6.5

Online JavaScript Reference Source using frames

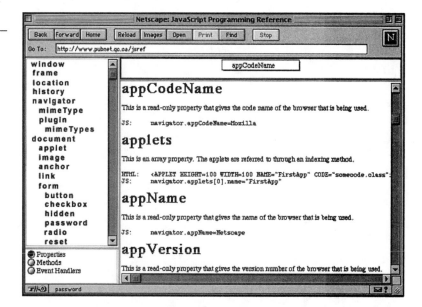

Figure 6.6

*Online Reference
after selection*

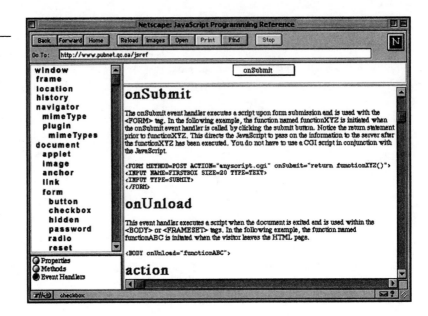

Cookie for Number of Visits

The Cookie for Number of Visits script creates a cookie on the client's machine that tracks the number of times the particular HTML file has been visited.

Cookies are text files that are written onto the client's computer when they access a particular site. These files are then stored on the computer and accessed by a server-side script, or JavaScript, to retrieve information. Cookies are generally used to trace a visitor's number of accesses, preferences, and so on. Cookies can be used commercially to gather information about the client computer's interaction with the Web site. The following script writes a cookie to your hard disk and accesses it to determine the number of times the page has been accessed. A button is provided to clear the cookie counter.

⚠ Warning

> This script does not work on the Macintosh platform.

HTML code for Cookie for number of visits JavaScript:

```
<HTML>
<HEAD>
<TITLE>Cookie Counter</TITLE>
<SCRIPT language="JavaScript">
<!-- begin script

function FixCookieDate (date) {
  var base = new Date(0);
  var skew = base.getTime();
  if (skew > 0)
    date.setTime (date.getTime() - skew);
}

function getCookieVal (offset) {
  var endstr = document.cookie.indexOf (";", offset);
  if (endstr == -1)
    endstr = document.cookie.length;
  return unescape(document.cookie.substring(offset, endstr));
}
```

```javascript
function GetCookie (name) {
  var arg = name + "=";
  var alen = arg.length;
  var clen = document.cookie.length;
  var i = 0;
  while (i < clen) {
    var j = i + alen;
    if (document.cookie.substring(i, j) == arg)
      return getCookieVal (j);
    i = document.cookie.indexOf(" ", i) + 1;
    if (i == 0) break;
  }
  return null;
}


function SetCookie (name, value) {
  var argv = SetCookie.arguments;
  var argc = SetCookie.arguments.length;
  var expires = (argc > 2) ? argv[2] : null;
  var path = (argc > 3) ? argv[3] : null;
  var domain = (argc > 4) ? argv[4] : null;
  var secure = (argc > 5) ? argv[5] : false;
if (expires!=null) FixCookieDate(expires);
  document.cookie = name + "=" + escape (value) +
    ((expires == null) ? "" : ("; expires=" + expires.toGMTString())) +
    ((path == null) ? "" : ("; path=" + path)) +
    ((domain == null) ? "" : ("; domain=" + domain)) +
    ((secure == true) ? "; secure" : "");
}


function DeleteCookie (name) {
  var exp = new Date();
  FixCookieDate (exp);
  exp.setTime (exp.getTime() - 1);
  var cval = GetCookie (name);
  if (cval != null)
    document.cookie = name + "=" + cval + "; expires=" + exp.toGMTString();
}

var countC=parseInt(GetCookie("counter"),10);

if(countC==0) countC=0;
```

```
//date of cookie expiration
var expdate = new Date ();

// 7 days from now the cookie will expire
expdate.setTime (expdate.getTime() + (7*24 * 60 * 60 * 1000));

++countC;

SetCookie ("counter", countC, expdate);

document.writeln("<center>");
document.writeln("    <font color=0000ff size=5>");
document.writeln("       You have accessed this page "+(1+countC)+"
times!");
document.writeln("    </font>");
document.writeln("  <form name=f>");
document.writeln("    <input type=button value='click here to clear the
counter'");
document.writeln("    onClick='DeleteCookie(\"counter\");'>");
document.writeln("  </form>");
document.writeln("  </center>");
// end script —>
</SCRIPT>
</HEAD>
<BODY>
</BODY>
</HTML>
```

Terminology

object: *date*-page 206

method: *getTime()*-page 237

method: *setTime()*-page 238

method: *substring()*-page 252

property: *indexof()*-page 250

property: *length*-page 204, 213-215

property: *cookie*-page 207

function: *unescape*-page 257

method: *toGMTString()*-page 239

Figure 6.7

*Recording Web page
visits with Cookie
counters*

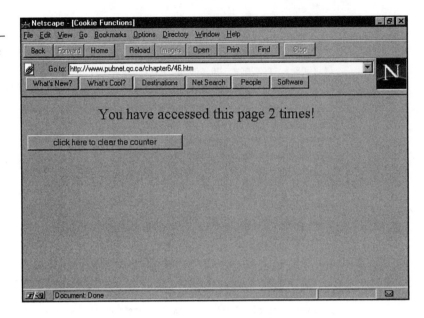

LiveAudio and JavaScript

47.htm

The LiveAudio and JavaScript example enables the playing and controlling of sound files via JavaScript.

Navigator 3.0 and later versions incorporate built-in sound functionality with the LiveAudio plug-in from Netscape. LiveAudio enables the inclusion of sound files through the <EMBED> tag. This plug-in also enables the inclusion of a small library of graphical consoles to change the parameters of the sound being played. Navigator 3.0 adds some new JavaScript functions via LiveConnect to control the sound files accessed via the LiveAudio plug-in. This script calls up the standard LiveAudio control console, and the JavaScript controls the sound. Web sites needing to incorporate sound files with JavaScript functionality will benefit from this script.

The following functions are included in this script that pertain specifically to LiveAudio plug-in data:

> play(): Uses the arguments true or false
>
> pause()
>
> stop()
>
> setvol(): Enables the inclusion of a number from 1 to 100 indicating the volume level

HTML code for the LiveAudio and JavaScript script:

```
<HTML>
<HEAD>
<TITLE>LiveAudio</title>
</HEAD>
<BODY BGCOLOR = FFFFFF>
<CENTER>
<embed name="sound1" SRC="nirvana.aif" HEIGHT=60 WIDTH=144 volume=50
autostart=false controls=console>
<P>
<A HREF="#" onClick = "document.sound1.play(true)">Play Sound</A>
<P>
<A HREF="#" onClick = "document.sound1.pause()">Pause</A>
<P>
<A HREF="#" onClick = "document.sound1.stop()">Stop</A>
<P>
```

```
<A HREF="#" onClick ="document.sound1.setvol(80)">Play Loud</A>
<P>
<A HREF="#" onClick = "document.sound1.setvol(50)">Play Medium</A>
<P>
<A HREF="#" onClick = "document.sound1.setvol(15)">Play Soft</A>
</CENTER>
</BODY>
</HTML>
```

Figure 6.8

LiveAudio provides built-in consoles and JavaScript controls

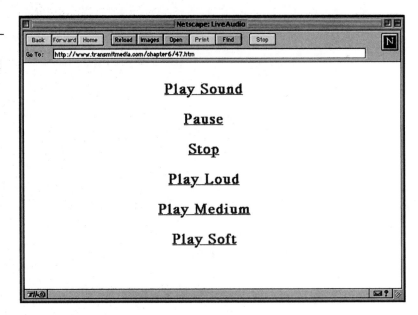

Java and JavaScript

The Java and JavaScript script enables you to pass a variable between JavaScript and a Java applet.

With the release of Navigator 3.0, JavaScript is able to pass variables to a Java applet. This enables programmers to relay information entered in form boxes directly to a Java applet. In the example here, a text string is passed to the applet, which animates the text in a manner defined by Java.

⚠️ **Warning**

> Only public variables can be accessed in Java. Public variables are preceded with the keyword **public** as in the following example:
>
> ```
> public String myVariable
> ```

To run this on a PC, you may need to set the variable NS_ENABLE_MOJA=1 in your autoexec.bat file. This is a temporary situation, and it may not be an issue by the time that Navigator 3 ships.

HTML code for the Java and JavaScript script:

```
<HTML>
<HEAD>
<TITLE>nervous</TITLE>

<SCRIPT>
function ch_text()
{
document.controltext.s=document.textf.n_text.value;
}

</SCRIPT>

</HEAD>
<BODY>
<APPLET code=NervousText.class name="controltext" width=320 height=100>
   <param name="text" value="enter a new text">
</applet>

<FORM name=textf>
  <INPUT TYPE=text name=n_text>
```

```
<INPUT TYPE=button value="click here to change the nervous text"
        onClick="ch_text()">
</FORM>
</BODY>
</HTML>
```

Applet Documentation

```
/*  Daniel Wyszynski
    Center for Applied Large-Scale Computing (CALC)
    04-12-95

    Test of text animation.

    kwalrath: Changed string; added thread suspension. 5-9-95
*/
import java.awt.Graphics;
import java.awt.Font;

public class NervousText extends java.applet.Applet implements Runnable {

        char separated[];
        public String s = null;
        Thread killme = null;
        int i;
        int x_coord = 0, y_coord = 0;
        String num;
        int speed=35;
        int counter =0;
        boolean threadSuspended = false; //added by kwalrath

public void init() {
        resize(150,50);
        setFont(new Font("TimesRoman",Font.BOLD,36));
        s = getParameter("text");
        if (s == null) {
            s = "HotJava";
        }

        separated =  new char [s.length()];
        s.getChars(0,s.length(),separated,0);
    }
```

```
public void start() {
      if(killme == null)
      {
      killme = new Thread(this);
      killme.start();
      }
 }

public void stop() {
      killme = null;
 }

public void run() {
      while (killme != null) {
      try {Thread.sleep(100);} catch (InterruptedException e){}
      repaint();
      }
      killme = null;
 }

public void paint(Graphics g) {
      for(i=0;i<s.length();i++)
      {
      separated =  new char [s.length()];
    s.getChars(0,s.length(),separated,0);
      x_coord = (int) (Math.random()*10+15*i);
      y_coord = (int) (Math.random()*10+36);
      g.drawChars(separated, i,1,x_coord,y_coord);
      }
 }

/* Added by kwalrath. */
public boolean mouseDown(java.awt.Event evt, int x, int y) {
      if (threadSuspended) {
          killme.resume();
      }
      else {
          killme.suspend();
      }
      threadSuspended = !threadSuspended;
    return true;
    }
}
```

Figure 6.9

Java and JavaScript can now work together on a page

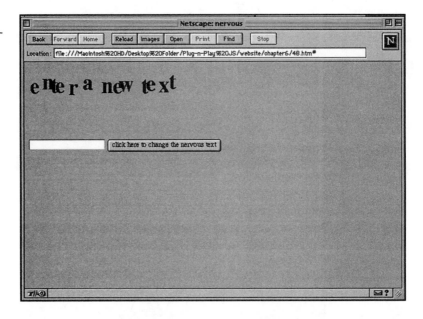

Figure 6.10

Java and JavaScript can now work together on a page

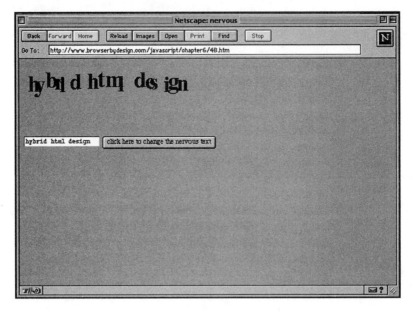

JavaScript and Plug-ins

The JavaScript and Plug-ins script demonstrates how to work with the Navigator 3.0 plug-ins object.

In this example, you see how JavaScript determines which plug-ins are installed on the client computer. This feature verifies that a computer has a specific plug-in. If it does not, you can direct the person to a site where they can download the plug-in.

HTML code for the Java and Plug-ins JavaScript:

```html
<HTML>
<HEAD>
<TITLE>Plugin Functions</TITLE>
<SCRIPT language="javascript">
<!-- begin script
document.writeln("<body bgcolor=ffffff>");
document.writeln("<table border=3><tr>");
document.writeln("<tr><td colspan=3 align=center><font size=5
color=ff0000>Installed Plug-In Objects</font></td></tr><tr>");
document.writeln("<td align=center><font size=4 color=0000ff>Name</font></
td>");
document.writeln("<td align=center><font size=4 color=0000ff>Filename</
font></td>");
document.writeln("<td align=center><font size=4 color=0000ff>description</
font></td>");
document.writeln("</tr><tr>");

//type all available plugin
for(var i=0;i<navigator.plugins.length;i++)
   {
   document.writeln("<td>"+navigator.plugins[i].name+"</td>");
   document.writeln("<td>"+navigator.plugins[i].filename +"</td>");
   document.writeln("<td>"+navigator.plugins[i].description +"</td>");
   //this should print the associate mime type (but it doesn't seem to work)
   document.writeln("<td>");
   //for(var j=0;navigator.mimeTypes.length;j++)
   //   document.writeln(navigator.plugins[i].mimeTypes[j]);
   document.writeln("</td>");
   document.writeln("</tr><tr>");
   }
document.writeln("</tr></table>");
```

```
// end script -->
</SCRIPT>
</HEAD>

</HTML>
```

Figure 6.11

Determining installed plug-ins with JavaScript

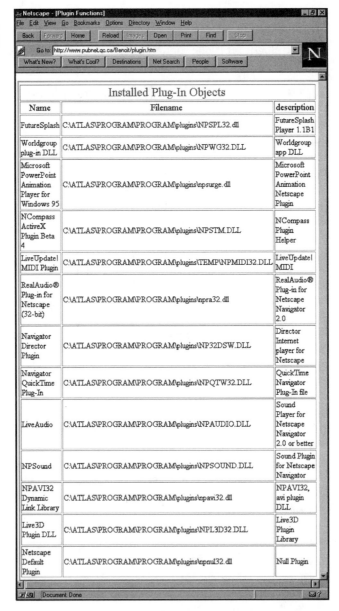

Summary

This chapter introduced many complex implementations of JavaScript. The scripts provided here are primarily for programmers wishing to take advantage of the higher end functionality possible with JavaScript. While the majority of the book has been designed specifically for cut-and-paste implementation, this chapter demonstrates more sophisticated uses of the language. Studying the examples in the chapter while viewing them from the CD will help.

Much of the functionality promised in Navigator 3.0 was not realized by the time this book went to press. Integration with the VRML environment, more extensive interaction with plug-ins, and more should be on the short-term horizon. Explorer 3.0 and later versions are also supporting JavaScript.

Using the examples in this chapter, you can now read and write cookies to a client browser, control multiple frames through triggering event handlers, and share variables with a Java applet.

PART VII

Appendices

Appendix

The JavaScript Programming Reference

This appendix defines all of the JavaScript programming elements available in browser versions up to and including Navigator 3.0. If you are looking for a description of event handlers, objects, properties, methods, operators, and other syntactical elements, they are all contained here.

Event Handlers

Events are user-triggered actions such as button clicking, image loading, mouseover, or other user-initiated actions that can invoke a JavaScript. An event handler, thus, is a JavaScript command that triggers a script when an event occurs as illustrated below:

```
<A HREF="http://www.malicepalace.com" onClick="alert('This could be
dangerous')">Click me/A>
```

For the HTML programmer, event handlers appear as attributes in tag definitions. That is to say that they are included within existing HTML tags, such as <A> (as shown above), in the same way that attributes are included in a tag definition. Event handlers were chosen as the element around which to write this book.

By directing your attention to event handlers, your existing knowledge of HTML and Web page design is leveraged by using familiar actions (like entering or exiting a text box) to sensibly design JavaScripts. In other words, when you design a JavaScript, you want it to begin in response to a certain event—button click, text entry, page loading, or other event. This book leads you through the event handlers available in JavaScript with relevant examples provided for each of them. The event handlers are described in detail in the following sections

onAbort

onAbort is a new event handler that is designed to work with the image object from Navigator 3.0 and later. The event handler intiates a script when you abort loading an image. You can abort loading an image by selecting another URL, clicking the Stop button, and by other means. In the following example, the *alert()* method displays an alert box when the loading of the image named *"image.gif"* is aborted.

```
<IMG SRC="image.gif" onAbort="alert('Are you really too busy to wait?')">
```

If your image contained information that was really critical for the viewer to see, you can alert them using this event handler if they abort loading the image.

onBlur

The *onBlur* event handler is used with the <SELECT>, <TEXTAREA>, and the text TYPE <INPUT> tags. With Navigator 3, this handler is also available for the <BODY> and <FRAMESET> tags. With these tags, the event handler is activated when the window or frame loses the focus of the mouse or cursor. With form elements, the *onBlur* event handler initiates a script when a form field is exited. In the following example, the form element is a text box that contains the *onBlur* event handler. The event handler calls a function named *functionx* when the text box is exited.

```
<FORM>
<INPUT NAME=FIRSTBOX SIZE=20 TYPE=TEXT onBlur="functionx()">
</FORM>
```

onChange

The *onChange* event handler is used with the <SELECT>, <TEXTAREA>, and the text TYPE <INPUT> tag. This event handler initiates a script when the contents of the form field are changed, again valuable for initiating a script when a user modifies an input field. In the following example, the form element is a select list that uses the *onChange* event handler. Once you select an option, the event handler calls a function named *functionA* when the selection has been changed.

```
<FORM>
<SELECT NAME=select onChange="functionA()">
<OPTION VALUE="LA">Los Angeles
<OPTION VALUE="NY">New York
<OPTION VALUE="CH">Chicago
</SELECT>
</FORM>
```

onClick

The *onClick* event handler can be used with submit, reset, button, checkbox, and radio <INPUT> tag types and the <A> tag. In response to a mouse click, the script specified by this event handler will be executed. In the following example, the anchor contains the *onClick* event handler. Clicking on the anchored image calls the function named *functionB*. In JavaScript, the <A> tag is referred to as a link object when it contains the *HREF* attribute. The anchor object itself does not use the event handler. It is the link object that responds to the *onClick* event handler.

```
<A HREF=#TopofDocument onClick="functionB()">
<IMG SRC="picture.gif">
</A>
```

onError

The *onError* event handler is new to Navigator 3. It is used with the <IMG> tag, or image object, and is activated when an image tag's attributes produce an error, such as trying to access an image file that doesn't exist. In the following example, the event handler is used for a clothing catalog that looks for a certain color and feature combination in its inventory. When no clothing fitting the *"Red44OS.gif"* source file is found, the event handler generates an alert box saying that the store is out of stock of that item. The HTML document will likely be generated, at least in part, in conjunction with a database backend that could use the presence or absence of specific image files on the server to generate appropriate messages.

```
<IMG SRC="Red44OS.gif" onError="alert('We have no more red 44 from
OceanSail in stock. Please select another')">
```

In this example, you can have someone fill in the size and color information. After they fill in the information, all of the calculations can be done in the browser.

onFocus

The *onFocus* event handler is used with the <SELECT>, <TEXTAREA>, and text TYPE <INPUT> tags. As with the *onBlur* event handler, *onFocus* is also being made available for the <BODY> and <FRAMESET> tags; however, it was still under development at the time of this writing. The *onFocus* event handler is the opposite of *onBlur* and activates a script when the form field is entered. In the following example, the event handler calls the *functionZ* function when the textarea is entered with either a mouse click or through tabbing.

```
<FORM>
<TEXTAREA ROWS=10 COLS=50 onFocus="functionZ()">
</FORM>
```

onLoad

The *onLoad* event handler is used with the <BODY>, <FRAMESET>, and <IMG> tags. There are two distinct uses of the *onLoad* event handler. The first (which has been enabled since Navigator 2) executes a script once the window or all frames are loaded. In the following example, the *functionY* function is called by the event handler. This means that when the page is opened the first time, the script will be executed.

```
<BODY onLoad="functionY()">
```

The second use of the *onLoad* event handler is associated with images. Specifically, when an image has finished loading, the event handler is activated. This does not work with looping animated GIF files. This usage has only been enabled since Navigator 3.0 and later versions.

```
<IMG SRC="some.gif" onLoad="function999()">
```

In this example, *function999* is initiated by the *onLoad* event handler after the picture has loaded.

onMouseOut

The *onMouseOut* event handler is activated when the mouse passes outside of text or images contained within <A> anchor tags. This works the opposite of *onMouseOver*. One use of the tag could be for children's sites, where you want to have different functions occur based on the mouse's screen position. This event handler is available for Navigator 3.0 and later versions. In the following example, *functionR* is initiated once the mouse leaves the text "Function R".

```
<A HREF="http://www.3pdesign.com" onMouseOut="functionR()">Function R</A>
```

onMouseOver

The *onMouseOver* event handler is used with the <A> tag and is activated when the mouse passes over an anchored reference. A popular implementation of this works in conjunction with a window status function to make specified text appear in the status bar. In the following example, the *functionK* function is called by the event handler when the mouse is dragged over the text "Function K".

```
<A HREF="http://www.3pdesign.com" onMouseOver="functionK()">Function K</A>
```

onReset

The *onReset* event handler is activated when the <INPUT TYPE="reset"> tag is selected within a form. The event handler itself is contained within the <FORM> tag. This handler is available for Navigator 3 and later versions. In the following example, an alert box displays when the Reset button is selected.

```
<FORM onReset="alert('The form has been reset.')">
<INPUT NAME=FIRSTBOX SIZE=20 TYPE=TEXT>
<INPUT NAME=Resat TYPE=RESET>
</FORM>
```

onSelect

The *onSelect* event handler is used with the <TEXTAREA> and the text TYPE <INPUT> tag. This event handler initiates a script when the text is selected within a text box. In the following example, the event handler initiates the *functionQ* function when any text is selected within the text box. It is easy to confuse this event handler with the *onFocus* event handler. In the case of *onFocus*, the script is executed when the element is first entered, or selected in the traditional sense (e.g., being clicked with a mouse or entered using the tab key). In the case of onSelect, it is activated when text within a form element is selected by highlighting the characters using the mouse or the shift and arrow keys.

```
<FORM>
<INPUT NAME=FIRSTBOX SIZE=20 TYPE=TEXT onSelect="functionQ()">
</FORM>
```

onSubmit

The *onSubmit* event handler executes a script upon form submission and is used with the <FORM> tag. It can be used to provide functionality without relying on traditional CGI programming. In the following example, the *functionXYZ* function is initiated when the *onSubmit* event handler is called by clicking the submit button. Notice the `return` statement prior to *functionXYZ*. This directs the JavaScript to pass the information on to the server after *functionXYZ* has been executed. You must return true in the event handler for the form to be submitted; return false prevents the form from being submitted. You do not have to use a CGI script in conjunction with the JavaScript.

```
<FORM METHOD=POST ACTION="anyscript.cgi"
     onSubmit="return functionXYZ()">
<INPUT NAME=FIRSTBOX SIZE=20 TYPE=TEXT>
<INPUT TYPE=SUBMIT>
</FORM>
```

onUnload

The onUnload event handler executes a script when the document is exited and is used within the <BODY> or <FRAMESET> tags. In the following example, the *functionABC* function is initiated when the visitor leaves the HTML page. You may want to include a sound or an alert message for your visitors when they leave your page.

```
<BODY onUnload="functionABC()">
```

Event Handler Overview

Well, the first mystery of JavaScript is solved. How do the scripts actually get put in motion? Without an event handler, no JavaScript will be executed. Chapters 2 through 5 introduce each of the event handlers in situations that you can expect to use them in Web applications. The onClick, onMouseOver, and onMouseOut event handlers are introduced in Chapter 2. Using these will develop your confidence to work with the window event handlers; onLoad and onUnload, in Chapter 3. In Chapter 4, the form event handlers—onBlur, onChange, onFocus, onSelect, and onSubmit are introduced. In Chapter 5, the new image event handlers from Navigator 3; onAbort, onError, and onLoad (the latter is new for the image tag) are presented. Chapter 6 uses all of the event handlers in various implementations. (editor's note: The only event handler not included in the chapter examples is *onReset*, which was introduced as this book was going to press.)

The next part of JavaScript's mystery will be solved by the introduction of objects and statements.

☐ Objects: The elements that you use JavaScript to affect or interpret.

☐ Statements: The elements that direct the flow of the JavaScript.

    ☐ Functions: Special types of statements that contain other statements to perform one or more actions.

    ☐ Methods: Special types of functions that require an object to perform.

Before getting lost in programming soup, you should become familiar with JavaScript objects. Understanding the JavaScript Object Hierarchy will help give order to what may otherwise seem like one more bowl of gobbledy-gook.

Objects

Objects are entities that can be interpreted or affected by using JavaScript. For you to be able to affect or read anything on the HTML page, there must exist a corresponding object in JavaScript. You cannot, for example, reference Bookmarks, because there is no bookmark object in JavaScript. On the other hand, you can go forward or backward using the History object. The primary objects in Navigator are the Window, Document, History, Location, and Navigator objects.

Some of these objects, such as History, can be interpreted by JavaScript. Others have properties that can be interpreted or affected through scripting. The BGCOLOR property of the Document object, for instance, can be interpreted, affected, or changed by JavaScript. Before introducing the objects, their hierarchy and related properties, methods, and event handlers will be presented.

The JavaScript Object Model

When using the JavaScript object model, you are able to refer to distinct programming elements by defining them through parent-child relationships. This means that you can use the object model to refer to an object much like the way that you would use a full directory path to designate a particular file. You can also refer to individual elements by using their name, as given using the NAME attribute. In the following example, a form named *FormName* is created with an element named "*SampleText*". The two statements that follow both refer to the same *Text* element (*SampleText*):

```
<FORM NAME=FormName>
    <INPUT TYPE="Text" NAME="SampleText" SIZE=20>
</FORM>
document.forms[0].SampleText;
document.FormName.SampleText;
```

In the example, the *document.forms[0].SampleText* property belongs to the *forms* array property of the *document* object. The *SampleText* property belongs to the *form* object named *FormName*. *FormName* is a property of the document object.

The object model extends individual objects through controlling properties of their properties. This can seem rather strange at first. Many properties are themselves objects with their own properties. There are also array properties, such as the *forms* property of the document object in the example above. The index number in the brackets following the array determines which object is selected. The first object is numbered zero [0]. If there were two or more forms, you can use the array property to define which form your JavaScript concerns. Using the hierarchical model, you will be able to control objects succinctly and directly. Once you become familiar with the model, the JavaScript examples in the book will be much less intimidating.

In the table on the next few pages, all of the JavaScript objects available in Navigator 2 and Navigator 3, along with their associated properties, methods, and event handlers will be presented. Remember, you can only affect or interpret objects that exist in JavaScript. The built-in objects are listed separately following the table, while all others are presented in their hierarchical position. When an object functions as a property of another object, it is indented.

The way that objects are referred to in JavaScript is *object1.object2.property2*, in which *object1* is the highest level object, *object2* is a property of *object1*, and *property2* is a property of *object2*. An example is *navigator.plugins.name*, in which the *name* of the *plugins* object, which is itself a property of the *navigator* object, is referenced. The sections on properties and methods following will give you the tools you need to begin working with statements and functions.

JavaScript Object Hierarchy

Object	Properties	Methods	Event Handlers
Window	defaultStatus	alert	onLoad
	frames	blur	onUnload
	opener	close	onBlur
	parent	confirm	onFocus
	scroll	focus	
	self	open	
	status	prompt	
	top	clearTimeout	
	window	setTimeout	

continues

Object	Properties	Methods	Event Handlers
Frame	defaultStatus	alert	none (the onLoad and onUnload event handlers belong to the window object)
	frames	blur	
	opener	close	
	parent	confirm	
	scroll	focus	
	self	open	
	status	prompt	
	top	clearTimeout	
	window	setTimeout	
Location	hash	reload	none
	host	replace	
	hostname		
	href		
	pathname		
	port		
	protocol		
	search		
History	length	back	none
		forward	
		go	
Navigator	appCodeName	javaEnabled	none
	appName		
	appVersion		
	mimeTypes		
	plugins		
	userAgent		
mimeTypes	description	none	none

Object	Properties	Methods	Event Handlers
	enabledPlugin		
	type		
	suffixes		
plugins	description	refresh	none
	filename		
	length		
	name		
document	alinkColor	clear	None (the onLoad and onUnload event handlers belong to the window object)
	anchors	close	
	applets	open	
	area	write	
	bgColor	writeln	
	cookie		
	fgColor		
	forms		
	images		
	lastModified		
	linkColor		
	links		
	location		
	referrer		
	title		
	vlinkColor		
applet	dependent on applet	dependent on applet	none
image	border	none	none
	complete		
	height		

continues

Object	Properties	Methods	Event Handlers
	hspace		
	lowsrc		
	name		
	src		
	vspace		
	width		
form	action	submit	onSubmit
	elements	reset	onReset
	encoding		
	FileUpload		
	method		
	name		
	target		
button	name	click	onClick
	type		
	value		
checkbox	checked	click	onClick
	defaultChecked		
	name		
	type		
	value		
FileUpload	name	none	none
	value		
hidden	defaultValue	none	none
	name		
	type		
	value		
password	defaultValue	blur	onBlur
	name	focus	onChange
	type	select	onFocus
	value		onSelect

Object	Properties	Methods	Event Handlers
radio	checked	click	onClick
	defaultChecked		
	name		
	type		
	value		
reset	name	click	onClick
	type		
	value		
select	length	none	onBlur
	name		onChange
	options		onSelect
	selectedIndex		
	type		
options	defaultSelected	none	none
	index		
	length		
	name		
	selected		
	text		
	value		
submit	name	click	onClick
	type		
	value		
text	defaultValue	focus	onBlur
	name	blur	onChange
	type	select	onFocus
	value		onSelect
textarea	defaultValue	focus	onBlur
	name	blur	onChange
	type	select	onFocus

continues

Object	Properties	Methods	Event Handlers
	value		onSelect
link	hash	none	onClick
	host		onMouseOut
	hostname		onMouseOver
	href		
	pathname		
	port		
	protocol		
	search		
	target		
area	hash	none	onClick
	host		onMouseOut
	hostname		onMouseOver
	href		
	pathname		
	port		
	protocol		
	search		
	target		
anchor	none	none	none

Built-in Objects

In addition to the objects that are extensible from the object hierarchy, JavaScript contains several built-in objects that exist independently of the hierarchy. These objects enable you to work with object types that are not otherwise defined. The *Date* object, for example, gives you the ability to work with date-type data that is not possible with the value types that JavaScript supports (which are *numbers, logical, strings*). To make a new object that is based on the Array, Date, or String objects, use the following syntax:

```
var MyDate = New Date();
```

Object	Properties	Methods	Event Handlers
Array	length	join	none
		reverse	
		sort	
Date	none	getDate	none
		getDay	
		getHours	
		getMinutes	
		getMonth	
		getSeconds	
		getTime	
		getTimeZoneoffset	
		getYear	
		parse	
		prototype	
		setDate	
		setHours	
		setMinutes	
		setMonth	
		setSeconds	
		setTime	
		setYear	
		toGMTString	
		toLocaleString	
		UTC	
Math	E	abs	none
	LN10	acos	
	LN2	asin	
	PI	atan	
	SQRT1_2	atan2	
	SQRT2	ceil	

continues

Object	Properties	Methods	Event Handlers
		cos	
		exp	
		floor	
		log	
		max	
		min	
		pow	
		random	
		round	
		sin	
		sqrt	
		tan	
		toString	
String	length	anchor	none
	prototype	big	
		blink	
		bold	
		charAt	
		fixed	
		fontColor	
		fontSize	
		indexOf	
		italics	
		lastIndexOf	
		link	
		small	
		split	
		strike	
		sub	
		substring	
		sup	

Object	Properties	Methods	Event Handlers
String		toLowerCase	
		toUpperCase	

User-Defined Objects

In addition to the objects available to you in JavaScript, you are also able to create your own objects with properties and methods. To do this, you need to write a function that has the name of the object you wish to create. Functions, discussed later in this appendix, are necessary here to define an object. Notice that the object's properties are referenced in the function's arguments.

```
function invoiceObject (custname, address, amount, duedate, custno) {
        this.custname = custname;
        this.address = address;
        this.amount = amount;
        this.duedate = duedate;
        this.custno = custno;
}
function OraclesUnpaidInvoice() {
        var OraclesUnpaidInvoice = new invoiceObject ("Oracle", "Redwood
Shores, CA", 5000, "April 25", "666Oracle");
}
```

In the preceding example, the *invoiceObject* object is defined by the *invoiceObject()* function. Once the object, along with its parameters, has been defined, the function OraclesUnpaidInvoice() creates a new invoice object with its own parameter values. In the example, the parameters for objects based on the *invoiceObject* are custname, address, amount, and custno. For OraclesUnpaidInvoice, the specific parameters are implemented and are associated with that particular *invoiceObject (e.g., Oracle, Redwood Shores, CA; 5000; etc.)*. The keyword *this*, which will be seen later in the appendix, is an extremely useful keyword that describes the current object.

Properties

Now that you have been introduced to the objects available in JavaScript, you will see how to affect and interpret their properties. Following is an example of the syntax used to work with objects and their properties:

```
document.bgColor="FF00FF";
location.href evaluates to "http://www.browserbydesign.com";
```

Properties will be presented alphabetically within an alphabetical list of objects. The HTML and JavaScript (JS) examples follow each of the properties.

Area Object Properties

The area object is the JavaScript representation of the area tag used in client-side image maps. It uses the same properties as the link object.

hash

This property specifies the part of the URL address to the right of the hash mark (#). In the address *http://www.x.com:80/doc.htm#test*, the hash property returns "*#test*". There is no corresponding HTML. It indicates an anchored reference within a document.

```
JS:      areaname.hash="#test";
```

host

This property specifies the domain name and port of the URL. In the address *http://www.x.com:80/some.htm#test*, the host property returns "*www.x.com:80*". There is no corresponding HTML.

```
JS:      areaname.host="www.x.com:80";
```

hostname

This property specifies the domain name of the URL. In the address *http://www.x.com:80/some.htm#test*, the hostname property returns "*www.x.com*". There is no corresponding HTML.

```
JS:      areaname.hostname="www.x.com";
```

href

This property specifies the entire URL. In the address *http://www.x.com:80/some.htm#test*, the href property returns "http://www.x.com:80/some.htm#test ". There is no corresponding HTML.

```
JS:      areaname.href="http://www.x.com:80/some.htm#test"
```

pathname

This property specifies the pathname of the URL. In the address *http://www.x.com:80/test/some.htm#test*, the pathname property returns "*/test/some.htm*". There is no corresponding HTML.

```
JS:      areaname.pathname="/test/some.htm"
```

port

This property specifies the domain name of the URL. In the address *http://www.x.com:80/some.htm#test*, the port property returns "*:80*". There is no corresponding HTML.

```
JS:      areaname.port=":80"
```

protocol

This property specifies the protocol of the URL. In the address *http://www.x.com:80/some.htm#test*, the *protocol* property returns "*http:*". There is no corresponding HTML.

```
JS:      areaname.protocol="http:"
```

search

This property is a string beginning with a question mark (?) that specifies query information in the URL. The query information follows the question mark and its syntax is determined by the CGI program on the server where the query is directed.

```
HTML:    <AREA COORDS="10,10,50,50" HREF="http:/www.xyx.com/
quiz?q=12&a=blue" NAME=firstLink>
JS:      firstLink.search="?q=12&a=blue";
```

target

This property designates the window or frame whose contents you wish to change in response to a link or form request.

```
HTML:    <AREA COORDS="10,10,50,50" HREF="1.htm" TARGET="MainFrame"
NAME="MyArea">
JS:      MyArea.target evaluates to "MainFrame"
```

Array Object Properties

The Array object is new to Navigator 3.0. It is used to refer to more than one instance of a specific object. This can be used in conjunction with existing Navigator objects, such as images and links, as well as with user-defined objects (see the preceding example).

length

This property indicates the number of elements in an array. This could refer to anchors, links, or other elements that are referred to using Array definition.

```
JS:     Arrays.length
```

Button Object Properties

The button object is the JavaScript representation of the button type form input tag.

name

This is used to reference the button object. Using the name property enables you to refer to an object by name, rather than using the full JavaScript hierarchy to refer to it.

```
HTML:   <INPUT TYPE=BUTTON NAME=FirstButton>
JS:     button.name evaluates to FirstButton
```

type

This property reflects the type attribute of the input tag. For buttons, the type attribute is button.

```
HTML:   <INPUT TYPE=BUTTON NAME=FirstButton>
JS:     FirstButton.type evaluates to BUTTON
```

value

This property reflects the value attribute of the input tag. For buttons, this refers to the text that appears on the button when displayed in the HTML page.

```
HTML:   <INPUT TYPE=BUTTON NAME=FirstButton VALUE="Click Me">
JS:     FirstButton.value evaluates to "Click Me"
```

Checkbox Object Properties

The Checkbox object is the JavaScript representation of the checkbox type form input tag.

checked

This is used with radio buttons and checkboxes. It indicates whether or not an option is selected. Unlike defaultChecked, this property refers to the state of the button at any moment, not just when the document is first opened.

```
HTML:    <INPUT NAME=CheckMe TYPE=RADIO CHECKED>
JS:      CheckMe.checked evaluates to True
```

defaultChecked

This is used with radio or checkbox form elements. It indicates that the form element has been checked or selected. The difference between this attribute and the *checked* attribute is that this determines the initial state of the form element. The default state for elements without this attribute is deselected.

```
HTML:    <INPUT NAME=CheckMe TYPE=RADIO CHECKED>
JS:      CheckMe.defaultChecked evaluates to True
```

name

This is used to reference the checkbox object. Using the name property enables you to refer to an object by name, rather than using the full JavaScript hierarchy to refer to it.

```
HTML:    <INPUT TYPE=CHECKBOX NAME=CheckMe>
JS:      checkbox.name evaluates to CheckMe
```

type

This property reflects the type attribute of the input tag. For the checkbox object, the type attribute is checkbox.

```
HTML:    <INPUT TYPE=CHECKBOX NAME=CheckMe>
JS:      CheckMe.type evaluates to CHECKBOX
```

value

This property reflects the value attribute of the input tag. For the checkbox object, this refers to the information passed to the server based on the checkbox being selected.

```
HTML:    <INPUT TYPE=CHECKBOX NAME=CheckMe VALUE="Selection A">
JS:      CheckMe.value evaluates to "Selection A"
```

Date Object Properties

The Date object is used to work with Date-type data.

prototype

This property is used to add properties to a Date object. There is no HTML equivalent.

```
JS:      MyDateObject.prototype.propertyName
```

Document Object Properties

The Document object is the JavaScript representation of the contents of the body tag.

alinkColor

This property determines the color of the text and borders of linked references while the mouse is clicked down on them. It accepts defined color names and hexadecimal numbers as valid values.

```
HTML:    <BODY ALINK=FF0000>
JS:      document.alinkColor="FF0000";
```

anchors

The anchors array property specifies a named location that can be linked to by another document. This is an array property that uses an indexing method to refer to array elements on the page. As seen in the example, the indexing method defines the referenced element by referring to it. This is different from the link object that contains the HREF attribute. Both use the <A> tag.

```
HTML:    <A NAME="AnchorText">Anchored Text</A>
JS:      document.anchors[0].name  evaluates to "AnchorText"
```

In examples where array objects are used, such as the anchors array property of the document object, the first indexed item is used as a reference. In this case, the first anchor tag in the document is named "*AnchorText.*" The first indexed item in any array is referred to within the brackets following the array as number 0. The anchors array object has one property, length, which defines the number of anchors within a document.

applets

This is an array property that reflects the inclusion of Java applets within a document. The applets are referred to through the indexing method associated with array objects. The applets array object has one property, length, which defines the number of applets within a document.

```
HTML:    <APPLET HEIGHT=100 WIDTH=100 NAME="FirstApp" CODE="somecode.class">
JS:      document.applets[0].name evaluates to "FirstApp"
```

area

This is an array property that reflects the inclusion of Java applets within a document. The applets are referred to through the indexing method associated with array objects. The applets array object has one property, length, which defines the number of applets within a document.

```
HTML:    <AREA COORDS="10,10,50,50" HREF="http:/www.onthemap.com">
JS:      document.;
```

bgcolor

This property reflects the background color of the HTML document. It accepts defined color names and hexadecimal numbers as valid values.

```
HTML:<BODY BGCOLOR=000000>
JS:      document.bgcolor="000000";
```

cookie

This property is used to read or write cookies on the client hard disk. Cookies are small text files that record information for future reference. This could include user preferences and other information for the server to use in future interaction with the user. There is no HTML equivalent.

```
JS:      document.cookie = "MyCookie=Large44D";
```

fgColor

This property defines the text color in the HTML document. It uses hexadecimal or special color names.

```
HTML:    <BODY TEXT=000000>
JS:      document.fgColor=000000;
```

forms

This property is used to define forms within an HTML page. It uses either an indexed argument or the form name as an argument. The forms array object has one property, length, which defines the number of forms within a document. There is no corresponding HTML.

```
JS:      document.forms[0].element1.value="sometext";
```

images

This property is used to define images within an HTML page. It uses either an indexed argument or the image name as an argument. The images array object has one property, length, which defines the number of images within a document. There is no corresponding HTML.

```
JS:      document.images[0].src="http://www.browserbydesign.com/image.gif";
```

lastModified

This property represents the date that the document was last modified. It is read-only and has no HTML equivalent.

```
JS:      document.lastModified evaluates to July 31 12:00:00 1996
```

linkColor

This determines the color of linked text in the body of the HTML document for URLs that have not yet been visited.

```
HTML:    <BODY LINK=FF0000>
JS:      document.linkColor="FF0000";
```

links

This is an array property that reflects the number of links in the document. There is no HTML equivalent. The links array object has one property, length, which defines the number of links within a document.

```
JS:      document.links[0]
```

location

This property is a string that specifies the complete URL of the document. This is a specific property of the document object, as opposed to the location object, which has its own properties. There is no corresponding HTML.

```
JS:      document.location evaluates to "http://www.pubnet.qc.ca/ben"
```

referrer

This property specifies the URL of the document that called the present document. There is no corresponding HTML equivalent.

```
JS:      document.referrer evaluates to "http://www.3pdesign.com"
```

title

This property represents the title of a document and is available to read only.

```
HTML:    <TITLE>My Title</TITLE>
JS       document.title evaluates to "My Title"
```

vlinkColor

This property determines the text and border color of visited linked references within the HTML document. It accepts defined color names and hexadecimal numbers as valid values.

```
HTML:    <BODY VLINK="#FF0000">
JS:      document.vlinkColor evaluates to "FF0000"
```

Form Object Properties

The form object is the JavaScript representation of the form tag from HTML.

action

This property references a specified URL that form contents will be sent to. This is usually a CGI program.

```
HTML:    <FORM ACTION="http://domainname.com/cgi-bin">
JS: document.formName.action = "http://domainname.com/cgi-bin/myCgi";
```

elements

This array object is used with the form object to describe form elements in a page. All input types are considered to be form elements. The individual form element is referred to by its indexed position or as a named object.

```
JS:      FirstForm.elements[0].value;
```

encoding

This property is used with forms or form elements. It indicates the type of encoding being used.

```
HTML:    <FORM NAME=FirstForm ENCTYPE="multipart/form-data">
JS:      FirstForm.encoding evaluates to "multipart/form-data"
```

fileUpload

This property is used to enable the user to specify a file to load. It is new to Navigator 3.0. The file name to upload is provided by the user at runtime. The name parameter that is used with fileUpload is used for referencing the element, *not* for specifying the file to be uploaded.

```
HTML:    <INPUT TYPE="file" NAME="UploadFile">
JS:      UploadFile.type evaluates to "file"
```

method

This determines how form field input information is processed. Possible values are get or post. Get is used to retrieve information, Post is used to send information.

```
HTML:    <FORM NAME="TheForm" METHOD=POST>
JS:      TheForm.method="POST"
```

name

This property defines the name of the form.

```
HTML:    <FORM NAME="FirstForm">
JS:       document.forms[0].name evaluates to "FirstForm"
```

target

This property designates the window or frame whose contents you wish to change in response to a link or form request.

```
HTML:    <FORM TARGET="MainFrame" NAME="FirstForm">
JS:      FirstForm.target evaluates to "MainFrame"
```

Frame Object Properties

From a JavaScript perspective, frames are windows. They share all the properties and methods of the window object. They do not have any event handlers associated with them. To include event handler functionality in a frame, the event handler would be included in the <BODY> tag of the document that is referred to by the SRC attribute of the <FRAME> tag.

defaultStatus

This indicates the message that appears in the status bar of the window when the document is first opened. There is no HTML equivalent.

```
JS:     window.defaultStatus = "Some text...";
```

frames

This array object property is used to define frames within an HTML page. The frame can be referenced by using the indexed number of its named reference. The frames array object has one property, length, which defines the number of child frames within a window. There is no corresponding HTML. A child frame is a frame contained within a frameset. The frameset document is considered the parent document.

JS: window.frames.length evaluates to the number of frames within the window

opener

This property is new to Navigator 3. It refers to the window name of the calling document when a window is opened using the open method. There is no HTML equivalent.

```
JS:     window.opener="http://www.browserbydesign.com"
```

parent

This property is used to describe a parent window within a framed page. The parent window is the one containing the frameset definition of the child window. There is no HTML equivalent.

JS: window.parent evaluates to the parent window

scroll

The scroll property is new to Navigator 3.0. It scrolls a window a specific number of pixels. Its arguments are the number of pixels along the x and y axis.

JS: window1.scroll(10,100) results in the window being scrolled 10 pixels to the right and 100 pixels down

self

This property refers to the current window or frame. It is used to reduce ambiguity in code. There is no HTML equivalent.

```
JS:     self.status="Welcome to my Home Page.";
```

status

This determines the text to display at the bottom of the Navigator window. There is no HTML equiavalent.

```
JS:     window.status="Welcome to my home page"
```

top

This property corresponds to the topmost ancestor window, which is its own parent. The property has three properties of its own: defaultStatus, status, and length. There is no HTML equivalent.

```
JS:     top.frameName evaluates to FrameName which is a child of the top
most window
```

window

This property, which makes clear reference to the current window, is virtually synonymous in usage to *self*. It does not have a corresponding element in HTML.

```
JS:     window
```

Hidden Object Properties

The hidden object is the JavaScript representation of the hidden type form input tag.

defaultValue

This property determines the value of the form element when the document is first opened.

```
HTML:   <INPUT TYPE=HIDDEN NAME=HideMe VALUE="some text">
JS:     HideMe.defaultValue evaluates to "some text"
```

name

This is used to reference the hidden object. Using the name property enables you to refer to an object by name, rather than using the full JavaScript hierarchy to refer to it.

```
HTML:    <INPUT TYPE=HIDDEN NAME=HideMe>
JS:      hidden.name evaluates to HideMe
```

type

This property reflects the type attribute of the input tag. For hidden objects, the type attribute is hidden.

```
HTML:    <INPUT TYPE=HIDDEN NAME=HideMe VALUE="some text">
JS:      HideMe.type evaluates to HIDDEN
```

value

This property reflects the value attribute of the input tag. For hidden objects, this refers to the text value assigned to the element using the VALUE attribute.

```
HTML:    <INPUT TYPE=HIDDEN NAME=HideMe VALUE="some text">
JS:      HideMe.value evaluates to "some text"
```

History Object Properties

This object reflects the contents of the Go menu in Navigator.

length

This property reflects the number of sites in the history object that are visible under the Go menu.

```
JS:      history.length evaluates to an integer defining the number of pages
visited.
```

Image Object Properties

The image object is new to Navigator 3.0. It is the JavaScript representation of the image tag <IMG>. The image object is a property of the document object, like the images object. The primary difference between the images object, which is an array object, and the image object, is that the former uses indexing methods that are available to array objects. This can be seen in the following example:

```
document.images[0].src="somegif.gif"
```

If you were to do the same using the image object, you would probably use the name of the image object that you had used to define it, as seen here:

```
MyNamedImage = new Image([width],[height])
MyNamedImage.src = "somegif.gif"
```

The images object, like all array objects, has one property, length, which reflects the number of images in the document.

The preloading of images before they are actually needed for display is a particularly useful implementation of image creation and manipulation. For instance, if you wanted to design a page that had an image with multiple source files based on user interaction, you could make them load very quickly by creating a new image object and then placing it into your HTML page.

First, a function that contains statements that create the object and give it a source file needs to be executed. This can be done in the <BODY> tag using the onLoad event handler:

```
function onLoader() {
MyNamedImage = new Image(160,120)
MyNamedImage.src = "http://www.construct.net/deepBlueWorld.jpg"
}
```

Then, you include a second script that is associated with the event that you want to initiate the changing of the image. The image file will load very quickly because it had already been loaded into cache:

```
function ReplaceImage() {
document.images[0].src = MyNamedImage
}
```

If the above function was called by a mouse click or other event, the first image in the HTML document would be changed to the image defined by MyNamedImage.

border

This property determines the border width, as measured in pixels, that surrounds an image.

```
HTML:    <IMG BORDER=5 SRC="some.gif">
JS:      image.border = 5;
```

complete

This property determines whether an image is completely loaded or not. It is a read-only property and there is no HTML equivalent.

```
JS:      imagename.complete
```

height

This property specifies the height of an image either in exact pixels or a percentage of the window height.

```
HTML:    <IMG SRC="imageA.gif" NAME="imageA" HEIGHT=40>
JS:      imageA.height evaluates to 40
```

hspace

This property specifies the horizontal space that surrounds an image and is measured in pixels.

```
HTML:    <IMG SRC="imageA.gif" NAME="imageA" HSPACE=10>
JS:      imageA.hspace evaluates to 10
```

length

This property belongs to the images object, not the image object. It reflects the number of images in a document. There is no HTML equivalent.

```
JS:      document.images.length evaluates to the integer number of images in
the document.
```

lowsrc

This property is used to define a low-resolution image that is displayed in the page before the document specified by src is loaded.

```
HTML:    <IMG SRC="some.gif" LOWSRC="someLowRes.gif" NAME="MyHiLoRes">
JS:      MyHiLoRes.lowsrc="someLowRes.gif"
```

src

This property is used to define the source file for a displayed image.

```
HTML:    <IMG SRC="some.gif" LOWSRC="someLowRes.gif" NAME="MyHiLoRes">
JS:      MyHiLoRes.src="some.gif"
```

vspace

This property specifies the vertical space that surrounds an image and is measured in pixels.

```
HTML:    <IMG SRC="imageA.gif" NAME="imageA" VSPACE=10>
JS:      imageA.vspace evaluates to 10
```

width

This property specifies the width of an image either in exact pixels or a percentage of the window width.

```
HTML:    <IMG SRC="imageA.gif" NAME="imageA" WIDTH=40>
JS:      imageA.width evaluates to 40
```

Link Object Properties

The link object, as contrasted to the anchor object, includes an HREF attribute in the <A> tag definition. There is also a links array object, like the images and forms array objects, which has only one property, length, which reflects the number of links in the document. See the image object description for more information.

hash

This property specifies the part of the URL address to the right of the hash mark (#). In the address *http://www.x.com:80/doc.htm#test*, the hash property returns "*#test*". There is no corresponding HTML. It indicates an anchored reference within a document.

```
JS:      linkName.hash="#test";
```

host

This property specifies the domain name and port of the URL. In the address *http://www.x.com:80/some.htm#test*, the host property returns "*www.x.com:80*". There is no corresponding HTML.

```
JS:      linkName.host="www.x.com:80";
```

hostname

This property specifies the domain name of the URL. In the address *http://www.x.com:80/some.htm#test*, the hostname property returns "*www.x.com*". There is no corresponding HTML.

```
JS:      linkName.hostname="www.x.com";
```

href

This property specifies the entire URL. In the address *http://www.x.com:80/some.htm#test*", the href property returns "*http://www.x.com:80/some.htm#test*". There is no corresponding HTML.

```
JS:     linkName.href="http://www.x.com:80/some.htm#test"
```

length

This property belongs to the links object, not the link object. It reflects the number of links in a document. There is no HTML equivalent.

```
JS:     document.links.length evaluates to the integer number of links in
the document.
```

pathname

This property specifies the pathname of the URL. In the address *http://www.x.com:80/test/some.htm#test*, the pathname property returns "*/test/some.htm*". There is no corresponding HTML.

```
JS:     linkName.pathname="/test/some.htm"
```

port

This property specifies the domain name of the URL. In the address *http://www.x.com:80/some.htm#test*, the *port* property returns "*:80*". There is no corresponding HTML.

```
JS:     linkName.port=":80"
```

protocol

This property specifies the protocol of the URL. In the address *http://www.x.com:80/some.htm#test*, the *protocol* property returns "*http:*". There is no corresponding HTML.

```
JS:     linkName.protocol="http:"
```

target

This property designates the window or frame whose contents you wish to change in response to a link or form request.

```
HTML:    <A HREF="1.htm" TARGET="MainFrame" NAME="First">
JS:      First.target evaluates to "MainFrame"
```

Location Object Properties

The location object is used to describe the URL of the window. It is a property of the window object.

hash

This property specifies the part of the URL address to the right of the hash mark (#). In the address *http://www.x.com:80/doc.htm#test*, the hash property returns "*#test*". There is no corresponding HTML.

```
JS:     location.hash="#test";
```

host

This property specifies the domain name and port of the URL. In the address *http://www.x.com:80/some.htm#test*, the host property returns "*www.x.com:80*". There is no corresponding HTML.

```
JS:     location.host="www.x.com:80";
```

hostname

This property specifies the domain name of the URL. In the address *http://www.x.com:80/some.htm#test*, the hostname property returns "*www.x.com*". There is no corresponding HTML.

```
JS:     location.hostname="www.x.com";
```

href

This property specifies the entire URL. In the address *http://www.x.com:80/some.htm#test*, the href property returns "*http://www.x.com:80/some.htm#test* ". There is no corresponding HTML.

```
JS:     location.href="http://www.x.com:80/some.htm#test"
```

pathname

This property specifies the pathname of the URL. In the address *http://www.x.com:80/test/some.htm#test*, the pathname property returns "*/test/some.htm*". There is no corresponding HTML.

```
JS:     location.pathname="/test/some.htm"
```

port

This property specifies the domain name of the URL. In the address *http://www.x.com:80/some.htm#test*, the *port* property returns ":80". There is no corresponding HTML.

```
JS:     location.port=":80"
```

protocol

This property specifies the protocol of the URL. In the address *http://www.x.com:80/some.htm#test*, the *protocol* property returns "*http:*". There is no corresponding HTML.

```
JS:     location.protocol="http:"
```

search

This property is a string beginning with a question mark (?) that specifies query information in the URL.

```
HTML:   <A HREF="http:/www.xyx.com/quiz?q=12&a=blue" NAME=firstLink>
JS:     firstLink.search="?q=12&a=blue";
```

Math Object Properties

The Math Object extends the JavaScript language by providing constant values, in the form of properties, and conversion processes, in the form of methods. Constant values, such as pi, provide a shorthand way for engineers and other technical professionals to refer to important, often used mathematical values. Conversion processes, such as determining a square root, are performed by methods, which are featured later in this appendix.

E

This property gives Euler's constant as a value. This constant is used in differential calculus equations and is represented in math formulas as E. There is no HTML equivalent.

```
JS:     Math.E evaluates to 2.718282
```

LN2

This value corresponds to the natural logarithm of two, which is approximately 0.693. There is no HTML equivalent.

```
JS:     Math.LN2 evaluates to 0.693
```

LN10

This value corresponds to the natural logarithm of ten, which is approximately 2.302. There is no HTML equivalent.

```
JS:    Math.LN2 evaluates to 2.302
```

PI

This references the constant number that is equal to the ratio of the circumference of a circle compared to its diameter. There is no corresponding HTML.

```
JS:    Math.PI evaluates to 3.1416
```

SQRT1_2

This property represents the square root of one-half, approximately 0.707. There is no HTML equivalent.

```
JS:Math.SQRT1_2 evaluates to 0.707
```

SQRT2

This property represents the square root of two, approximately 1.414. There is no HTML equivalent.

```
JS:Math.SQRT2 evaluates to 1.414
```

mimeTypes Object Properties

The mimeTypes object is a property of the navigator object. It is used to determine whether a certain file type is supported.

description

The description property describes the file format type of the referenced MIME type.

```
JS:    navigator.mimeTypes[image/jpeg].description evaluates to "JPEG
Image plug"
```

enabledPlugins

The enabledPlugins property reflects the plugin that will display a file type. This was still being implemented as this book went to press.

type

This property provides the MIME type name of a specific file format, such as application/director or image/jpeg.

JS: `navigator.mimeTypes[4].type` evaluates to `"image/jpeg"` (the number of the mimeTypes element is arbitrary)

suffixes

The suffixes property lists the various suffixes of file names that will be recognized as being a specific MIME type.

JS: `navigator.mimeTypes[image/jpeg].suffixes` evaluates to `"jpeg, jpg, jpe, jfif, pjpeg, pjp"`

Navigator Object Properties

The navigator object is used by JavaScript to determine characteristics about the browser itself. Information such as the operating system and version number are associated with this object.

appCodeName

This is a read-only property that gives the code name of the browser that is being used.

JS: `navigator.appCodeName` evaluates to `Mozilla`

appName

This is a read-only property that gives the name of the browser that is being used.

JS: `navigator.appName` evaluates to `Netscape`

appVersion

This is a read-only property that gives the version number of the browser that is being used.

JS: `navigator.appVersion` evaluates to `3.0b4`

javaEnabled

This is a read-only property that is new to Navigator 3.0 and later. It returns true if the browser is Java-enabled. If the browser supports Java, but has been switched off by the user, the property returns false.

```
JS:    navigator.javaEnabled evaluates to True (or 1)
```

mimeTypes

The mimeTypes property is a read-only property that is new to Navigator 3.0 and later. It is an array property that reflects all the file formats supported by the browser. It also has one property, length, which gives the number of mimeTypes that are available to the browser.

```
JS:    navigator.mimeTypes.length evaluates to the number of MIME types
supported by the browser.
```

plugins

The plugins property is a read-only property that is new to Navigator 3.0 and later. It is an array property that reflects all the plugins presently installed for the browser. It also has one property, length, which gives the number of plugins that are available to the browser.

```
JS:    navigator.plugins.length evaluates to the number of plugins
available to the browser.
```

userAgent

This property is a string value that identifies the client browser to the host server. It is a read-only property and has no HTML equivalent. It includes the appCodeName, appVersion, and operating system information.

```
JS:    navigator.userAgent evaluates to Mozilla/3.0b5 (Win32;I)
```

Options Object Properties

The options object is the JavaScript representation of an option tag occurring within a select tag.

defaultSelected

This property determines the default state of an option object. It indicates that the option is selected when the document is first opened. Without this, the default is unselected.

```
HTML:    <OPTION VALUE="Moderate" SELECTED NAME="optionname">
JS:      optionname.defaultSelected
```

index

This property reflects the index of an option within a select group. There is no corresponding HTML.

```
JS:      selectGroupName.options[indexNumber].
```

length

This property reflects the number of options within a select group. There is no HTML equivalent.

```
JS:      selectName.options.length evaluates to the number of options in the
select group
```

name

This property names the option. It is not displayed in the browser.

```
HTML:    <OPTION NAME="MyOption">
JS:      selectName.options[0].name evaluates to "MyOption"
```

selected

This property determines whether an option in a select object has been selected.

```
HTML:    <OPTION SELECTED VALUE="Blue">Blue
JS:      options[0].selected evaluates to TRUE
```

selectedIndex

This property represents the option selected in a select object. It can be used with either the select object or the options array property of the select object. There is no HTML equivalent.

```
JS:      selectObject.options.selectedIndex evaluates to the selected option
```

text

This property designates the text value of a selected option that is displayed in the browser.

```
HTML:    <OPTION SELECTED VALUE="TheBest">My Selection
JS:      FormName.options[0].text evaluates to "My Selection"
```

value

This property designates the value of a selected option. This value is used for the server and is not displayed in the browser.

```
HTML:    <OPTION SELECTED VALUE="TheBest">My Selection
JS:      FormName.options[0].text evaluates to "TheBest"
```

Password Object Properties

The password object is the JavaScript representation of the password type form input tag.

defaultValue

This property determines the value of the form element when the document is first opened.

```
HTML:    <INPUT TYPE=PASSWORD NAME=MyPass VALUE="some text">
JS:      MyPass.defaultValue evaluates to "some text"
```

name

This is used to reference the password object. Using the name property enables you to refer to an object by name, rather than using the full JavaScript hierarchy to refer to it.

```
HTML:    <INPUT TYPE=PASSWORD NAME=MyPass>
JS:      password.name evaluates to MyPass
```

type

This property reflects the type attribute of the input tag. For password objects, the type attribute is password.

```
HTML:    <INPUT TYPE=PASSWORD NAME=MyPass VALUE="some text">
JS:      MyPass.type evaluates to PASSWORD
```

value

This property reflects the value attribute of the input tag. For password objects, this refers to the text value assigned to the element using the VALUE attribute.

```
HTML:    <INPUT TYPE=PASSWORD NAME=MyPass VALUE="some text">
JS:      MyPass.value evaluates to "some text"
```

Plugin Object Properties

The plugin object is new to Navigator 3.0. It is a property of the navigator object.

description

The description property is provided by the plugin to the browser. It describes the plugin.

JS: navigator.plugins[0].description evaluates to "Live3D Plugin
Library"

fileName

This property reflects the plugin file that interprets a MIME type. This is not the file that is being viewed, but the file that permits the file to be viewed.

JS: navigator.plugins[0].filename evaluates to
"c:\atlas\program\program\plugins\npl3d32.dll"

length

This property is a read-only property that gives the number of plugins available to the browser.

JS: navigator.plugins.length evaluates to the number of plugins
installed

mimeTypes

This property is used to tell whether or not a plugin supports a specific MIME type. It returns true if the MIME type is supported by the plugin.

JS: navigator.plugins[0].mimeTypes[application/director] evaluates to
FALSE

name

This property is a read-only property that reflects the name of the selected plugin.

JS: navigator.plugins[0].name evaluates to "Live3D Plugin DLL"

Radio Object Properties

The radio object is the JavaScript representation of the radio type form input tag.

checked

This is used with radio buttons and checkboxes. It indicates whether or not an option is selected. Unlike defaultChecked, this property refers to the state of the button at any moment, not just when the document is first opened.

```
HTML:    <INPUT TYPE=RADIO CHECKED>
JS:      radiobuttonname.checked
```

defaultChecked

This is used with radio or checkbox form elements. It indicates that the form element has been checked or selected. The difference between this attribute and the *checked* attribute is that this determines the initial state of the form element. The default state for elements without this attribute is deselected.

```
HTML:    <INPUT TYPE=RADIO CHECKED>
JS:      radiobuttonname.defaultChecked
```

name

This property names the radio button. It is not displayed in the browser.

```
HTML:    <FORM>
           <INPUT TYPE="RADIO" NAME="option1">
           ...
         </FORM>
JS:      formName.elements[0].name evaluates to "option1"
```

type

This property reflects the type attribute of the input tag. For radio objects, the type attribute is radio.

```
HTML:    <INPUT TYPE=RADIO NAME=MyRadio VALUE="some text">
JS:      MyRadio.type evaluates to RADIO
```

value

This property defines the value of radio form elements. This is a reflection of the VALUE attribute. It is displayed in the browser.

```
HTML:    <INPUT TYPE=RADIO NAME=MyRadio VALUE="some text">
JS:      MyRadio.value evaluates to "some text"
```

Reset Object Properties

The reset object is the JavaScript representation of the reset type form input tag.

name

This property names the reset button. It is not displayed in the browser.

```
HTML:    <INPUT TYPE="RESET" VALUE="Click to Refresh" NAME="ResetMe">
JS:      formName.elements[0].name evaluates to "ResetMe"
```

type

This property reflects the type attribute of the input tag. For reset objects, the type attribute is reset.

```
HTML:    <INPUT TYPE="RESET" VALUE="Click to Refresh" NAME="ResetMe">
JS:      ResetMe.type evaluates to RESET
```

value

This property defines the text that appears on the reset button. This is a reflection of the VALUE attribute. It is displayed in the browser.

```
HTML:    <INPUT TYPE="RESET" VALUE="Click to Refresh" NAME="ResetMe">
JS:      ResetMe.value evaluates to "Click to Refresh"
```

Select Object Properties

The select object is the JavaScript representation of the select tag. It appears in the browser as either a pulldown menu or as a list with a scroll bar (if necessary).

length

This property reflects the number of options within a select group. There is no HTML equivalent.

```
JS:      selectName.length evaluates to the number of options in the select
group
```

name

This property names the select group. It is not displayed in the browser.

```
HTML:    <SELECT NAME="MyGroup">
JS:      formName.elements[0].name evaluates to "MyGroup"
```

options

This is an array property that contains an entry for each option in a select object. It has the following properties: defaultSelected, index, length, name, selected, selectedIndex, text, and value.

```
HTML:    <OPTION NAME="anyName" VALUE="None of the above">
JS:      selectName.options[0].value="None of the above"
```

selectedIndex

This property represents the option selected in a select object. It can be used with either the select object or the options array property of the select object. There is no HTML equivalent.

```
JS:      selectObject.options.selectedIndex evaluates to the selected option
```

type

This property is used if you need to use the MULTIPLE attribute of the <SELECT> tag.

```
HTML:    <SELECT TYPE=MULTIPLE NAME=MultiSelect>

JS:      MultiSelect.type evaluates to MULTIPLE
```

String Object Properties

The String object is a built-in object that enables JavaScript to use text, or string, variables.

length

This property indicates the number of characters in a string object. There is no HTML equivalent.

```
JS:      string.length evaluates to the number of characters in the string
```

prototype

This property is used to add properties and methods to the String, Date, and User-Defined objects. There is no HTML equivalent.

```
JS:      StringObjectName.prototype.proporMethName = nameofExistingFunction
```

In this case, the function named nameofExistingFunction was created to give definition to the prototype property. All objects of the type StringObjectName will now have a property or method titled proporMethName associated with them that is based on the function nameofExistingFunction.

Submit Object Properties

The submit object is the JavaScript representation of the submit type form input tag.

name

This property names the submit button. It is not displayed in the browser.

```
HTML:    <INPUT TYPE="SUBMIT" VALUE="Submission Time"
NAME="TheSubmitButton">
JS:      formName.elements[0].name evaluates to "TheSubmitButton"
```

type

This property reflects the type attribute of the input tag. For submit objects, the type attribute is submit.

```
HTML:    <INPUT TYPE="SUBMIT" VALUE="Submission Time"
NAME="TheSubmitButton">
JS:      TheSubmitButton.type evaluates to SUBMIT
```

value

This property defines the text that appears on the submit button. This is a reflection of the VALUE attribute. It is displayed in the browser.

```
HTML:    <INPUT TYPE="SUBMIT" VALUE="Submission Time"
NAME="TheSubmitButton">
JS:      TheSubmitButton.value evaluates to "Submission Time"
```

Text Object Properties

The text object is the JavaScript representation of the text type form input tag.

defaultValue

The defaultValue property defines the value of a text object as the page is first loaded. This is determined by the VALUE attribute of the <INPUT> tag. The difference between this attribute and the *value* attribute is that this determines the initial state of the form element. The default state for elements without this attribute is blank text.

```
HTML:    <INPUT TYPE="TEXT" VALUE="Text to appear" NAME="MyText">
JS:      MyText.defaultValue evaluates to "Text to appear"
```

name

This property names the text object. It is not displayed in the browser.

```
HTML:    <INPUT TYPE="TEXT" VALUE="Text to appear" NAME="MyText">
JS:      formName.elements[0].name evaluates to "MyText"
```

type

This property reflects the type attribute of the input tag. For text objects, the type attribute is text.

```
HTML:    <INPUT TYPE="TEXT" VALUE="Text to appear" NAME="MyText">
JS:      MyText.type evaluates to TEXT
```

value

This property defines the text that appears in the text box. Unlike defaultValue, this property refers to the text that appears in the text box at any time, including when it is first loaded and any time that the text is changed.

```
HTML:    <INPUT TYPE="TEXT" VALUE="Text to appear" NAME="MyText">
JS:      MyText.value evaluates to "Text to appear"
```

Textarea Object Properties

The textarea object is the JavaScript representation of the textarea tag.

defaultValue

The defaultValue property defines the value of a textarea object as the page is first loaded. This is determined by the VALUE attribute of the <INPUT> tag. The difference between this attribute and the *value* attribute is that this determines the initial state of the form element. The default state for elements without this attribute is blank text.

```
HTML:    <TEXTAREA VALUE="Text to appear" NAME="MyTextArea">
JS:      MyTextArea.defaultValue evaluates to "Text to appear"
```

name

This property names the text object. It is not displayed in the browser.

```
HTML:    <TEXTAREA VALUE="Text to appear" NAME="MyTextArea">
JS:      formName.elements[0].name evaluates to "MyTextArea"
```

type

This property reflects the type attribute of the input tag. For text objects, the type attribute is text.

```
HTML:    <TEXTAREA VALUE="Text to appear" NAME="MyTextArea">
JS:      MyTextArea.type evaluates to TEXTAREA
```

value

This property defines the text that appears in the textarea box. Unlike defaultValue, this property refers to the text that appears in the textarea box at any time, including when it is first loaded and any time that the text is changed.

```
HTML:    <TEXTAREA VALUE="Text to appear" NAME="MyTextArea">
JS:      MyTextArea.value evaluates to "Text to appear"
```

User-Defined Object Properties

prototype

This property is used to add properties and methods to the String, Date, and User-Defined objects. There is no HTML equivalent.

```
JS:      UserDefinedObjectName.prototype.proporMethName =
nameofExistingFunction
```

In this case, the function named nameofExistingFunction was created to give definition to the prototype property. All objects of the type UserDefinedObjectName will now have a property or method titled proporMethName associated with them that is based on the function nameofExistingFunction.

Window Object Properties

defaultStatus

This indicates the message that appears in the status bar of the window when the document is first opened. There is no HTML equivalent.

```
JS:     window.defaultStatus = "Some text...";
```

frames

This array object property is used to define frames within an HTML page. The frame can be referenced by using the indexed number of its named reference. The frames array object has one property, length, which defines the number of child frames within a window. There is no corresponding HTML. A child frame is a frame contained within a frameset. The frameset document is considered the parent document.

JS: window.frames.length evaluates to the number of frames within the window

opener

This property is new to Navigator 3. It refers to the window name of the calling document when a window is opened using the open method. There is no HTML equivalent.

```
JS:     window.opener="http://www.browserbydesign.com"
```

parent

This property is used to describe a parent window within a framed page. The parent window is the one containing the frameset definition of the child window. There is no HTML equivalent.

JS: window.parent evaluates to the parent window

scroll

The scroll property is new to Navigator 3.0. It scrolls a window a specific number of pixels. Its arguments are the number of pixels along the x and y axis.

JS: **window1.scroll(10,100) results in the window being scrolled 10 pixels to the right and 100 pixels down**

self

This property refers to the current window or frame. It is used to reduce ambiguity in code. There is no HTML equivalent.

```
JS:     self.status="Welcome to my Home Page.";
```

status

This determines the text to display at the bottom of the Navigator window. There is no HTML equivalent.

```
JS:     window.status="Welcome to my home page"
```

top

This property corresponds to the topmost ancestor window, which is its own parent. The property has three properties of its own: defaultStatus, status, and length. There is no HTML equivalent.

```
JS:     top.frameName evaluates to FrameName which is a child of the top
most window
```

window

This property, which makes clear reference to the current window, is virtually synonymous in usage to *self*. It does not have a corresponding element in HTML.

```
JS:     window.status="This appears in the status bar"
```

Methods and Built-in Functions

Methods, unlike properties, act as modifiers to objects. Where properties describe objects, methods and objects have an adverbial relationship. Functions are used to designate additional properties, which will apply to the object(s) with which they are associated in the function. Using an English parts of speech metaphor, the method takes the place of the verb; the object takes the place of the subject; the argument (which is contained within parentheses) takes the place of the direct or indirect object. An example is the alert() method of the window object. Its argument displays as text in a window created by the method. Consider the following contrast between speech and JavaScript:

The Math object calculates the square root of x.

```
Math.sqrt(x)
```

Here, the Math object is the subject, the sqrt() method performs the verb function, while x is used as the indirect object. Technically, methods are functions, and functions are statements. In usage; however, they perform very differently:

Statements: Direct the flow of the JavaScript.

Functions: Group statements together into units that can be regularly called without having to rewrite the statements you wish performed.

Methods and built-in functions: Special functions that do not require statements within braces ({}). Because the function they perform is understood by JavaScript, all that is needed for the method to activate is an argument.

In the following example, the argument 16 is treated in a predefined manner to determine its square root:

```
Math.sqrt(16) evaluates to 4
```

Compare this to the PI property of the math object that, as seen here, functions as an object itself.

```
Math.PI*3 evaluates to 9.425
```

Objects and properties can often be thought of interchangeably, although at the end of the object chain, properties perform a task similar to adjectives in human languages. For example, the document object has the form property. Form is also considered an object with its own set of properties, some of which also have their own properties. At the furthest link of the chain, properties define their object with names, numeric values, or other expression types.

The following methods and built-in functions are available in JavaScript. They are listed alphabetically under the objects to which they belong.

Array Object Methods

join

This is a new property to Navigator 3. It is used to join the elements in an array into a single string. It uses a separator as an argument that is used to divide the strings into logical entities. If no character is entered, a comma (,) is used by default. There is no HTML equivalent. In the example below, the ArrayofNoise object was created, which has three elements. The join() method using the argument "and " results in the joining of the three using the argument to separate the elements.

```
JS:     ArrayofNoise = new Array("Loud","Heated","Electric")
JS:     ArrayofNoise.join("and ")evaluates to "Loud and Heated and Electric"
```

reverse

This method reverses the order of elements in an array. For example, if you have five elements, the fifth element becomes number zero, the first becomes number four (remember that indexing results in the first number starting at zero). There is no HTML equivalent.

```
JS:     MyArray = new Array("x","y","z")
JS:     MyArray.reverse() evaluates to "z","y","x"
JS:     MyArray evaluates to {"z", "y", "x"}
```

sort

This method sorts elements in an array as determined by its argument, which is generally a function. If no argument is given, the elements are sorted alphabetically. There is no HTML equivalent.

```
JS:     MyArray = new Array("a", "m", "b");
JS:     MyArray.sort();
JS:     MyArray evaluates to {"a", "b", "m"}
```

Button Object Methods

click

This method performs the same action as if you clicked the button. There is no HTML equivalent.

```
JS:     NoiseForm.Button1.click();
```

Checkbox Object Methods

click

This method toggles between being selected and deselected. There is no HTML equivalent.

```
JS:     NoiseForm.Checkbox1.click();
```

Date Object Methods

getDate

This method returns the day of the month for the specified date. Its value is between 1 and 31. There is no HTML equivalent.

```
JS:     MyDate=new Date("November 5, 1996 11:15:00")
JS:     DateObject.getDate(MyDate) evaluates to 5;
```

getDay

This method returns the day of the week for the specified date. Its value is between 0 to 6, representing Sunday through Saturday. There is no HTML equivalent. November 5November 5 is on a Tuesday, which is represented by the number 2.

```
JS:     MyDate=new Date("November 5 November 5, 1996 11:15:00");
JS:     DateObject.getDay(MyDate) evaluates to 2;
```

getHours

This method returns the hour using the 24-hour clock of an event on a specified date. Its value is between 0 to 23, representing 12:00 AM to 11:00 PM. There is no HTML equivalent.

```
JS:     MyDate=new Date("November 5, 1996 11:15:00");
JS:     DateObject.getHours(MyDate) evaluates to 11;
```

getMinutes

This method returns the minutes of an event on a specified date. Its value is between 0 and 59. There is no HTML equivalent.

```
JS:     MyDate=new Date("November 5, 1996 11:15:00")
JS:     DateObject.getMinutes(MyDate) evaluates to 15
```

getMonth

This method returns the month of the year for the specified date. Its value is between 0 to 11, representing January through December. There is no HTML equivalent.

```
JS:     MyDate=new Date("November 5, 1996 11:15:00")
JS:     DateObject.getMonth(MyDate) evaluates to 10
```

getSeconds

This method returns the seconds of an event on a specified date. Its value is between 0 and 59. There is no HTML equivalent.

```
JS:     MyDate=new Date("November 5, 1996 11:15:00")
JS:     DateObject.getSeconds(MyDate) evaluates to 0
```

getTime

This method returns the number of milliseconds that have passed since January 1, 1970 00:00:00. It is often used to assign relative relationships between date objects.

```
JS:     MyDate=new Date("November 5, 1996 11:15:00");
JS:     mydate.getTime() evaluates to 847224900000
```

getTimezoneOffset

This method returns the time zone offset in minutes for the current locale. This regards daylight savings time, and is generally between +60 and -60.

```
JS:     mydate.getTimezoneOffset() evaluates to 0
```

getYear

This method returns the year for the specified date. You subtract 1900 from the value it returns to calcluate the year. Due to limitations, it cannot calculate years prior to 1904 or after 2037. There is no HTML equivalent.

```
JS:     MyDate=new Date("November 5, 1996 11:15:00")
JS:     DateObject.getYear(MyDate) evaluates to 96
```

parse

This built-in function returns the number of milliseconds since January 1, 1970 00:00:00 GMT for its string argument. It uses the built-in Date object, not a user-defined Date object. This is often used in conjunction wth the setTime method to establish comparative date values. There is no HTML equivalent.

```
JS:     MyDateObj.setTime(Date.parse("Jan 1, 1997"));
```

setDate

This method sets or resets the day of the month for a specified date. Valid values are between 1 and 31. There is no HTML equivalent.

```
JS:     DateObject.setDate(13);
```

setHours

This method sets or resets the hour using the 24-hour clock for an event on a specified date. Valid values are between 0 to 23, representing 12:00 AM to 11:00 PM. There is no HTML equivalent.

```
JS:     DateObject.setHours(10);
```

setMinutes

This method sets or resets the minutes for an event on a specified date. Valid values are between 0 and 59. There is no HTML equivalent.

```
JS:     DateObject.setMinutes(15);
```

setMonth

This method sets or resets the month of the year for a specified event. Valid values are between 0 to 11, representing January through December. There is no HTML equivalent.

```
JS:     DateObject.setMonth(8);
```

setSeconds

This method sets or resets the seconds for an event on a specified date. Valid values are between 0 and 59. There is no HTML equivalent.

```
JS:     DateObject.setSeconds(30);
```

setTime

This method sets or resets the number of milliseconds that have passed since January 1, 1970 00:00:00 for a particular event. It is generally used to assign relative relationships between date objects.

```
JS:     MyFuturePlan=new Date("December 31, 1999");
JS:     MyFriendsPlan=new Date();
JS:     MyFriendsPlan.setTime(MyFuturePlan.getTime());
```

setYear

This method sets or resets the year for a specified event. You subtract 1900 from the value it returns to calclute the year. Due to limitations, it cannot calculate years prior to 1904 or after 2037. There is no HTML equivalent.

```
JS:     DateObject.setYear(97);
```

toGMTString

This method converts a Date object into a String object using the Internet GMT conventions. There is no HTML equivalent.

```
JS:     MyDate.toGMTString() evaluates to Tue, 05 Nov 1996 20:15:00 (Notice
that the book was written in California during daylight savings time. This
explains the 8 hour difference between the time selected and the time
revealed by this method.)
```

toLocaleString

This method converts a Date object into a String object using the current locale's conventions. The date format varies depending on the operating system. There is no HTML equivalent.

```
JS:     MyDate.toLocaleString();
```

UTC

This method returns the number of milliseconds that have passed since January 1, 1970 00:00:00 and its argument. The UTC method takes comma-delimited date parameters for its argument. There is no HTML equivalent.

```
JS:     MyDate = new Date(Date.UTC(97, 10, 1, 0, 0, 0));
JS:     MyDate evaluates to "October 1, 1997 00:00:00"
```

Document Object Methods

clear

This method clears the contents of a window. There is no HTML equivalent.

```
JS:     windowName.document.clear();
```

close

This method stops incoming data and forces data already received to be displayed. **Document: Done** is displayed in the status bar when this method is enacted. There is no HTML equivalent. In Navigator 3.0 and later, the user is asked to confirm when the window is closed.

```
JS:     MyString="Some Text.";
JS:     MyNamedWindow.document.open();
JS:     MyNamedWindow.document.write(MyString);
JS:     MyNamedWindow.document.close();
```

open

This method opens a stream for collecting the output of write and writeln methods. The method uses a two part MIME type as its argument. If none are provided, it assumes it is text/html. Valid arguments for this method are text/html; text/plain; image/gif; image/jpeg; image/x-bitmap; and two part plug-in descriptions, such as application/x-director. There is no corresponding HTML.

```
JS:     MyString="Some Text.";
JS:     MyNamedWindow=window.open();
JS:     MyNamedWindow.document.open();
JS:     MyNamedWindow.document.write(MyString);
JS:     MyNamedWindow.document.close();
```

write

This method is used to write HTML expressions in a specified window. For event handlers, you must use the writeln method. There is no HTML equivalent.

```
JS:     MyString="face";
JS:     document.write("In your ", Mystring) evaluates to "In your face"
```

writeln

This method writes HTML expressions in a specified window. The difference between write and writeln is that the latter inserts a carriage return after the text. There is no HTML equivalent.

```
JS:     MyString="face";
JS:     document.writeln("In your ", Mystring)evaluates to "In your face";
```

Form Object Methods

reset

This method performs the same action as if you clicked on the reset button. There is no HTML equivalent.

```
JS:     Mydocument.CheatSheetForm.reset();
```

submit

This method performs the same action as if you clicked on the submit button. It is generally used to send information to and from the server. There is no HTML equivalent.

```
JS:      Mydocument.CheatSheetForm.submit();
```

Frame Object Methods

Technically speaking, the frame object is a window object. It therefore shares the properties and methods of the window object. Unlike the window object, the frame object cannot access event handlers. For this reason, event handlers such as onLoad are not available to the <FRAME> tag. They are contained within the <BODY> tag of the HTML document that occupies the frame.

alert

This method displays an Alert dialog box with a text message and an OK button. There is no HTML equivalent.

```
JS:      alert("I have something to say.");
```

blur

This method in Navigator 3.0 now applies to the *frame* and *window* objects, as well as form *elements*. Blurring a form element or window refers to removing it from the "*focus*". In the case of a textbox, it would be when you clicked into another form element or the HTML page itself. In the case of a window, it would be when you directed your computer to display the screen from another application. The browser no longer has the "*focus*" of the computer. There is no HTML equivalent.

```
JS:      formElementName.blur();
```

clearTimeout

This method cancels a timeout that was set using the setTimeout method. There is no HTML equivalent.

```
JS:      clearTimeout(aNamedTimer);
```

close

This method for closes the active window. There is no HTML equivalent.

```
JS:      frameName.close();
```

confirm

This method displays a Confirm dialog box with a text message and OK and Cancel buttons. It uses a string object as its argument. If OK is selected, the method returns *true*; if Cancel is selected, it returns *false*. There is no HTML equivalent.

```
JS:    confirm("Are you sure you want to leave the Web site already?");
```

focus

This method in Navigator 3.0 now applies to the *frame* and *window* objects, as well as form *elements*. Focusing a form element or window means bringing the cursor or the window itself into an active state. In the case of a window, it would be when you directed your computer to display the browser after having viewed another application. The browser then has the "*focus*" of the computer. There is no HTML equivalent.

```
JS:    formElementName.focus();
```

open

This method opens a new browser window. It is able to control several features in the new window. Each of the parameters in its argument control a different feature. If you want to display a toolbar or hide one, you would set the window display "toolbars=yes" or "toolbars=no", respectively. Notice that no spaces are placed between the parameters. The first two parameters, URL, which gives the HREF, and the name of the window, are required arguments. If you want to open a window that is not associated with an URL, use empty quotation marks (" "). Naming the window enables you to target it from another window or frame. Values for each of the additional parameters can be set to yes or no, 1 or 0. They are not required arguments. There is no HTML equivalent. The method and its arguments are presented in the following example.

```
JS:    MyWindow=window.open("URL", "Window
Name",["toolbars=yes","location=yes","directories=yes","status=yes","menubar=yes",
"scrollbars=yes","resizable=yes","width=PixelValue","height=PixelValue"]);
```

prompt

This method is used to prompt a visitor to your Web page to enter a response. It uses two arguments: the message you wish displayed, and an initial value for the prompt box. The initial value, if blank, should be indicated by using empty quotation marks (" "). There is no HTML equivalent.

```
JS:    prompt("What name will you be using?", "");
```

setTimeout

This method evaluates an expression after a specified number of milliseconds have passed. In the following example, MyTimer identifies the timer in order for the clearTimeout method to cancel it.

```
JS:     MyTimer=setTimeout("alert('Time up!');",10000);
```

History Object Methods

back

This method performs the same function as history.go(-1). It reloads the previous URL in the history object (the page you were just at). There is no HTML equivalent.

```
JS:     history.back();
```

forward

This method advances to the next URL in the history list. It performs the same act as the forward button in the browser. There is no HTML equivalent. Both methods in the following examples do the same thing.

```
JS:     history.forward();
JS:     history.go(1);
```

go

This method is used to navigate through the browser's current history. It uses an integer or an URL as its argument. The current page is numbered zero (0); positive numbers go forward in history, negative numbers go backward in history. If the location argument is a string, *go* loads the nearest history entry whose URL contains the location as a substring. URL matching is not case-sensitive. There is no HTML equivalent.

```
JS:     history.go(-1);
JS:     history.go("http://www.browserbydesign.com");
```

Location Object Methods

reload

This method is new to Navigator 3.0. It reloads the window's current document. There is no HTML equivalent.

```
JS:     location.reload();
```

replace

This method is new to Navigator 3.0. It replaces the present document with the one referred to as a parameter. There is no HTML equivalent.

```
JS:    location.replace("http://www.typo.com/");
```

Math Object Methods

abs

This method returns the absolute value of a number. The absolute value of a number is the distance between the number and zero. There is no HTML equivalent.

```
JS:    Math.abs(-23) evaluates to 23
```

acos

This method returns the arc cosine of a number in radians. There is no HTML equivalent.

```
JS:    Math.acos(.3) evaluates to 1.266
```

asin

This method returns the arc sine of a number in radians. There is no HTML equivalent.

```
JS:    Math.asin(.3) evaluates to 0.3047
```

atan

This method returns the arc tangent of a number in radians. There is no HTML equivalent.

```
JS:    Math.atan(.3) evaluates to 0.3093
```

atan2

This method is new to Navigator 3.0. It returns the angle (theta component) of the polar coordinate (r,theta) that corresponds to its argument: a specific cartesian coordinate. There is no HTML equivalent.

```
JS:    Math.atan2(4,3) evaluates to 0.9273
```

ceil

This method returns the least integer greater than or equal to a number. For numbers less than zero, it would be the next integer closer to zero, for those greater than zero, the next integer further from zero. There is no HTML equivalent.

```
JS:     ceil(93.4) evaluates to 94
```

cos

This method returns the cosine of a number. Its argument is a value that represents the size of an angle in radians. The number it generates is a value between -1 and 1. There is no HTML equivalent.

```
JS:     Math.cos(1.266) evaluates to 0.300
```

exp

This method returns the numeric value e^x, where e is Euler's constant, and x is its argument.

```
JS:     exp(1) evaluates to 2.7183
```

floor

This method returns the greatest integer less than or equal to a number. For numbers less than zero, it would be the next integer further from zero, for those greater than zero, the next integer closer to zero. There is no HTML equivalent.

```
JS:     Math.floor(-93.4) evaluates to -94
```

log

This method returns the natural logarithm for a number. Its argument is any positive numeric value. There is no HTML equivalent.

```
JS:     Math.log(10) evaluates to 2.3026;
```

max

This method returns the greater of two numbers. There is no HTML equivalent.

```
JS:     Math.max(10,15) evaluates to 15;
```

min

This method returns the lesser of two numbers. There is no HTML equivalent.

```
JS:     Math.min(10,15) evaluates to 10;
```

pow

This method returns a number that uses a base number and an exponent. The base number is then raised to the power of the exponent (this is the number of times that you multiply a number by itself—2 raised to the power of 3 (the third power) equals 2 x 2 x 2). There is no HTML equivalent.

```
JS:     Math.pow(2,3) evaluates to 8
JS:     Math.pow(5,3) evaluates to 125
```

random

This method returns a random number between 0 and 1. There is no HTML equivalent.

```
JS:     Math.random() evaluates to 0.4829
```

round

This method returns the closest integer to a numeric expression. There is no HTML equivalent.

```
JS:     Math.round(45.49999) evaluates to 45
JS:     Math.round(45.50000) evaluates to 46
```

sin

This method returns the sine of a number. Its argument is a value that represents the size of an angle in radians. The number it generates is a value between -1 and 1. There is no HTML equivalent.

```
JS:     Math.sin(Math.PI/2) evaluates to 1
```

sqrt

This method returns the square root of its argument. There is no HMTL equivalent.

```
JS:     Math.sqrt(256) evaluates to 16
```

tan

This method returns the tangent of a number. Its argument is a value that represents the size of an angle in radians. The number it generates is a value between -1 and 1. There is no HTML equivalent.

```
JS:     Math.sin(Math.PI/4) evaluates to 0.9999
```

Password Object Methods

blur

The blur method refers to the instant when a form element is exited by the mouse or cursor. It is the opposite of the focus method which refers to the instant that a form element is first entered. There is no HTML equivalent.

```
JS:     PasswordName.blur();
```

focus

Focusing a form element refers to the moment when you enter the element using the mouse or tab key. There is no HTML equivalent.

```
JS:     PasswordName.blur();
```

select

This method is used to select the contents of a form element. In the following example, the password input box named "MyPassword" has its contents selected with the JavaScript. There is no HTML equivalent.

```
HTML:   <INPUT TYPE=password NAME="MyPassword">
JS:     MyPassword.select();
```

Plugins Object Methods

refresh

The refresh method is new to Navigator 3.0. It enables you to update a browser to recognize a file format supported by a plugin that has been downloaded while the browser is open. In this manner, the browser does not need to be closed and reopened to recognize a file format type. If you use the parameter, true, Navigator will update any file formats of that type that are in the document.

```
JS:     navigator.plugins.refresh(true)
```

Radio Object Methods

click

This method toggles between being selected and deselected. There is no HTML equivalent.

```
JS:     NoiseForm.RadioButton.click();
```

Reset Object Methods

click

This method performs the same action as if you clicked the reset button. There is no HTML equivalent.

```
JS:     NoiseForm.ResetButton.click();
```

String Object Methods

The methods for the *string* object are used primarily with the write() and writeln() methods of the document object. They enable you to specify the HTML text formatting associated with the text that is the method's argument.

anchor

This method is used in conjunction with the *write* or *writeln* methods. It enables you to specify an anchor within a document that you are creating with JavaScript. The first line in the example below is added to create a *string* object for the method in the second line. The third line shows how it would appear in the HTML source code.

```
JS:     MyString="SomeText";
JS:     document.writeln(MyString.anchor("Anchored"));
evaluates to
HTML:   <A NAME="SomeText">Anchored</A>
```

big

This method is used in conjunction with the *write* or *writeln* methods. It renders its string object argument in a big font. In the following example, the first line defines a *string* object for the method in the following line. The third line shows how it would appear in the HTML source code.

```
JS:     MyString="Twisted Conversation";
JS:     document.writeln(MyString.big());
evaluates to
HTML:   <BIG>Twisted Conversation</BIG>
```

blink

This method is used in conjunction with the *write* or *writeln* methods. It renders its string object argument in blinking text. In the following example, the first line defines a *string* object for the method in the following line. The third line shows how it would appear in the HTML source code.

```
JS:     MyString="Blinking Mania";
JS:     document.writeln(MyString.blink());
evaluates to
HTML:   <BLINK>Blinking Mania</BLINK>
```

bold

This method is used in conjunction with the *write* or *writeln* methods. It renders its *string* object argument in a bolded typeface. In the example, the first line defines a *string* object for the method in the following line. The third line shows how it would appear in the HTML source code.

```
JS:     MyString="Bold and Brash";
JS:     document.writeln(MyString.bold());
evaluates to
HTML:   <BOLD>Bold and Brash</BOLD>
```

charAt

This method designates a character within a string object. Its argument is indexed starting from 0 and defines the character in relation to its distance from the first character in the string. There is no HTML equivalent. In the example below, the third character, indicated by the argument (2), is selected (z). In the second example, the ninth character is selected. Remember to subtract 1 from the number to refer to its indexed position, because the first position is zero, not one.

```
JS:     MyString="Lazy Brown Dog.";
JS:     MyString.charAt(2) evaluates to "z"
JS:     MyString.charAt(8) evaluates to "w"
```

fixed

This method is used in conjunction with the *write* or *writeln* methods. It renders its string object argument in a fixed-pitch font. In the following example, the first line defines a string object for the method in the following line. The third line shows how it would appear in the HTML source code.

```
JS:     MyString="Fix this broken String";
JS:     document.writeln(MyString.fixed());
evaluates to
HTML:   <TT>Fix this broken String</TT>
```

fontcolor

This method is used to affect the color of the font and is used in conjunction with the *write* or *writeln* methods. It renders its *string* object with a hexadecimal color or special color name as its argument. In the following example, the first line defines a string object for the method in the following line. The third line shows how it would appear in the HTML source code.

```
JS:     MyString="What color is your umbrella?";
JS:     document.writeln(MyString.fontcolor("00FF00"));
evaluates to
HTML:   <FONT COLOR=00FF00>What color is your umbrella?</FONT>
```

fontsize

This method is used to affect the size of the font and is used in conjunction with the *write* or *writeln* methods. It renders its string object at a relative font size using an integer value between 1 and 7. In the example, the first line defines a *string* object for the method in the following line. The third line shows how it would appear in the HTML source code.

```
JS:     MyString="This font sure is big!";
JS:     document.writeln(MyString.fontsize(7));
evaluates to
HTML:   <FONT SIZE=7> This font sure is big!</FONT>
```

indexOf

This method returns the distance in characters that a character is from the first character in a string object. Its argument is indexed starting from 0 and defines the first character that meets the argument criteria. There is no HTML equivalent.

```
JS:     MyString="Lazy Brown Dog.";
JS:     MyString.indexOf("B") evaluates to 5
JS:     MyString.indexOf("L") evaluates to 0
```

italics

This method is used in conjunction with the *write* or *writeln* methods. It renders its string object argument in an italicized typeface. In the following example, the first line defines a string object for the method in the following line. The third line shows how it would appear in the HTML source code.

```
JS:      MyString="Italics provide emphasis";
JS:      document.writeln(MyString.italics());
evaluates to
HTML:    <I>Italics provide emphasis</I>
```

lastIndexOf

This method returns the distance that the last character that meets the argument criteria is from the first character in a string object. Its argument is indexed starting from 0. There is no HTML equivalent.

```
JS:      MyString="Lazy Brown Dog.";
JS:      MyString.lastIndexOf("o") evaluates to 12
```

link

This method is used in conjunction with the *write* or *writeln* methods. It enables you to specify a hyperlink within a document that you are creating with JavaScript. The first line in the following example is added to create a string object for the method in the second line. The third line shows how it would appear in the HTML source code.

```
JS:      MyString="SomeText";
JS:      MyURL="http://www.3pdesign.com";
JS:      document.writeln(MyString.link(MyURL));
evaluates to
HTML:    <A HREF="http://www.3pdesign.com" NAME="SomeText">Linked Text</A>
```

small

This method is used in conjunction with the *write* or *writeln* methods. It renders its string object argument in a small font. In the following example, the first line defines a string object for the method in the following line. The third line shows how it would appear in the HTML source code.

```
JS:      MyString="My little mouth";
JS:      document.writeln(MyString.small());
evaluates to
HTML:    <SMALL>My little mouth</SMALL>
```

strike

This method is used in conjunction with the *write* or *writeln* methods. It renders its string object argument with a strike placed through the center of it. In the example, the first line defines a string object for the method in the following line. The third line shows how it would appear in the HTML source code.

```
JS:     MyString="Smoking in Public";
JS:     document.writeln(MyString.strike());
evaluates to
HTML:   <STRIKE>My little mouth</STRIKE>
```

sub

This method is used in conjunction with the *write* or *writeln* methods. It renders its string object argument in a subscript font. In the example, the first line defines a string object for the method in the following line. The third line shows how it would appear in the HTML source code.

```
JS:     MyString="Subbing it";
JS:     document.writeln(MyString.sub());
evaluates to
HTML:   <SUB>My little mouth</SUB>
```

substring

This method is used to display a portion of a string object. It uses two arguments: the first one determines which indexed character the substring begins with; the second one determines which indexed character it ends with. The first character is number 0, the second is number 1, and so on. There is no HTML equivalent.

```
JS:     MyString="Fargo to Hellington";
JS:     MyString.substring(3,12) evaluates to "go to Hell"
```

sup

This method is used in conjunction with the *write* or *writeln* methods. It renders its string object argument in a superscript font. In the example, the first line defines a string object for the method in the following line. The third line shows how it would appear in the HTML source code.

```
JS:     MyString="superscripting";
JS:     document.writeln(MyString.sup());
evaluates to
HTML:   <SUP>superscripting</SUP>
```

toLowerCase

This method returns the string value to lowercase. There is no HTML equivalent.

```
JS:      MyString="HTML"
JS:      MyString.toLowerCase() evaluates to "html"
```

toUpperCase

This method returns the string value to uppercase. There is no HTML equivalent.

```
JS:      MyString="html"
JS:      MyString.toUpperCase() evaluates to "HTML"
```

Submit Object Methods

click

This method performs the same action as if you clicked the submit button. There is no HTML equivalent.

```
JS:      NoiseForm.SubmitButton.click();
```

Text Object Methods

blur

The blur method refers to the instant when a form element is exited by the mouse or cursor. It is the opposite of the focus method which refers to the instant that a form element is first entered. There is no HTML equivalent.

```
JS:      TextObjectName.blur();focus
```

Focusing a form element refers to the moment when you enter the element using the mouse or tab key. There is no HTML equivalent.

```
JS:      TextObjectName.blur();
```

select

This method is used to select the contents of a form element. In the following example, the text object named "TextObjectName" has its contents selected with the JavaScript. There is no HTML equivalent.

```
HTML:    <INPUT TYPE=password NAME="TextObjectName">
JS:      TextObjectName.select();
```

Textarea Object Methods

blur

The blur method refers to the instant when a form element is exited by the mouse or cursor. It is the opposite of the focus method which refers to the instant that a form element is first entered. There is no HTML equivalent.

```
JS:     TextAreaObject.blur();
```

focus

Focusing a form element refers to the moment when you enter the element using the mouse or tab key. There is no HTML equivalent.

```
JS:     TextAreaObject.blur();
```

select

This method is used to select the contents of a form element. In the following example, the textarea object named "TextObjectName" has its contents selected with the JavaScript. There is no HTML equivalent.

```
HTML:   <TEXTAREA NAME="TextAreaObject">
JS:     TextAreaObject.select();
```

Window Object Methods

alert

This method displays an Alert dialog box with a text message and an OK button. There is no HTML equivalent.

```
JS:     alert("I have something to say.");
```

blur

This method in Navigator 3.0 now applies to the *frame* and *window* objects, as well as form *elements*. Blurring a form element or window refers to removing it from the "*focus*". In the case of a window, it would be when you directed your computer to display the screen from another application. The browser no longer has the "*focus*" of the computer. There is no HTML equivalent.

```
JS:     formElementName.blur();
```

clearTimeout

This method cancels a timeout that was set using the setTimeout method. There is no HTML equivalent.

```
JS:     clearTimeout(aNamedTimer);
```

close

This method for closes the active window. There is no HTML equivalent.

```
JS:     windowName.close();
```

confirm

This method displays a Confirm dialog box with a text message and OK and Cancel buttons. It uses a string object as its argument. If OK is selected, the method returns *true*; if Cancel is selected, it returns *false*. There is no HTML equivalent.

```
JS:     confirm("Are you sure you want to leave the Web site already?");
```

focus

This method in Navigator 3.0 now applies to the *frame* and *window* objects, as well as form *elements*. Focusing a form element or window refers to bringing the cursor or the window itself into an active state. In the case of a window, it would be when you directed your computer to display the browser after having viewed another application. The browser then has the *"focus"* of the computer. There is no HTML equivalent.

```
JS:     formElementName.focus();
```

open

This method opens a new browser window. It is able to control several features in the new window. Each of the parameters in its argument control a different feature. If you want to display a toolbar or hide one, you would set the window display "toolbars=yes" or "toolbars=no", respectively. Notice that no spaces are placed between the parameters. The first two parameters, URL, which gives the HREF, and the name of the window, are required arguments. If you want to open a window that is not associated with an URL, use empty quotation marks (""). Naming the window enables you to target it from another window or frame. Values for each of the additional parameters can be set to yes or no, 1 or 0. They are not required arguments.

There is no HTML equivalent. The method and its arguments are presented in the following example.

```
JS:     MyWindow=window.open("URL", "Window
Name",["toolbars=yes","location=yes","directories=yes","status=yes","menubar=yes",
"scrollbars=yes","resizable=yes","width=PixelValue","height=PixelValue"]);
```

prompt

This method is used to prompt a visitor to your Web page to enter a response. It uses two arguments: the message you wish displayed, and an initial value for the prompt box. The initial value, if blank, should be indicated by using empty quotation marks (""). There is no HTML equivalent.

```
JS:     prompt("What name will you be using?", "");
```

setTimeout

This method evaluates an expression after a specified number of milliseconds have passed. In the following example, MyTimer identifies the timer in order for the clearTimeout method to cancel it.

```
JS:     MyTimer=setTimeout("alert('Time up!');",10000);
```

Built-in Functions

escape

This built-in function encodes non-alphanumeric characters, such as spaces, using hexadecimal ASCII values. The most typical instance is the encoding for the space character (%20). There is no HTML equivalent.

```
JS:     escape("the end") evaluates to "the&20end"
```

eval

This built-in function evaluates a string and returns a value. There is no HTML equivalent.

```
JS:     x=10; y=20; z=30;
JS:     eval("x + y + z +900") evaluates to 960
```

isNaN

This method is only available for UNIX platforms. It evaluates an argument to determine if it is Not a Number(NaN). Its returned value is either true or false. There is no HTML equivalent.

```
JS:   var va = Math.sqrt(2);
JS:      isNan(va) evaluates to True

JS:   var va="a";
JS:      isNan(va) evaluates to False
```

parseFloat

This built-in function returns a floating point number from a string object. If the function encounters any characters that are not numerals, decimal points, positive or negative signs, or exponents, it returns a floating point number based on the characters up until that point in the string. This is a very useful method for converting string values into numeric values. There is no HTML equivalent.

```
JS:      MyString="3.14";
JS:      parseFloat(MyString) evaluates to 3.14;
JS:      parseFloat("3.14") evaluates to 3.14;
```

parseInt

This built-in function returns an integer in a specified base from a string object. A specified base would be base 2, base 16 (hexadecimal), or the default, base 10. If the input string begins with "0x", the method returns a base 16 integer; if the input string begins with "0", it returns a base 8 (octal) integer. All other non-specified input strings return base 10 integers. If the function encounters any characters that are not numerals, decimal points, positive or negative signs, or exponents, it returns the number based on the characters up until that point in the string. Notice in the example, that if the base cannot interpret the number (e.g., the number 9 in base 8), it and all the characters following it are ignored. Use this function to perform hexadecimal conversions and other conversions as necessary. There is no HTML equivalent.

```
JS:      MyString="1079";
JS:      parseInt(MyString, 16) evaluates to 4217
JS:      parseInt(MyString, 8) evaluates to 71
JS:      parseInt(MyString, 7) evaluates to 7
JS:      parseInt(MyString) evaluates to 1079
```

unescape

This built-in function decodes hexadecimal ASCII values into alphanumeric characters. There is no HTML equivalent.

```
JS:      unescape("the&20end") evaluates to "the end"
```

Values, Variables, and Literals

Values

After being introduced to the *objects*, *properties*, and *methods* in JavaScript, the next thing to become familiar with are values, variables, and literals. When working with any programming language, it is important to remember to use appropriate value types for their syntactical usage. If you don't, you will have errors when calculations are attempted to be performed (consider 99 + "Melonhead" for instance, or 84 * "My Fair Lady"). In JavaScript, there are four types of value types available:

1. Numbers: Many languages have different types of number values. Integers and floating point number values (those requiring a decimal point) are often separated into different groups. In JavaScript, all real numbers belong to a single value type.

2. Logical: Like most programming languages, JavaScript is able to use logical, or Boolean values. Logical values are either true or false.

3. Strings: The string value enables you to store text in reusable variables. It also enables you to treat a string object in a concise manner that would not otherwise be possible.

4. Null: The null value accesses a special keyword of JavaScript that denotes a null value. This is equal to zero or no returned answer.

Different functions and methods require different value types for their arguments. It is not difficult to convert between the various value types. JavaScript is flexible enough to allow the changing of value types for variables within <SCRIPT> and </SCRIPT> tags. In other words, a variable named MyVariable could be a string value at one point, then changed to another value type merely with another declaration. Consider the following code:

```
MyVariable="Some text";
MyVariable=59;
```

In the first example, a string value is given, and MyVariable is operationalized as a string object. In the second line of code, MyVariable was operationalized as a numeric value. To convert a variable; however, takes an additional line or two of code. The methods to convert were introduced in the section on methods. These are:

```
Number to String:      Var MyVariable = "999";
String to Number:      Var MyString = "FF00AA";
        Var MyNumber = parseInt(Mystring, 16);
```

Logical values are constructed from either string or number values by making them equal to True or False, respectively. To see more about data type conversions, refer to the description for the *eval*, *parseInt*, and *parseFloat* built-in functions. These are each used to convert strings to numbers.

Variables

Closely related to values are variables. Variables are names that are used to hold values. Variables can be named using uppercase and lowercase alphabetic characters, digits 0-9, and the underscore character (_). The first character in a variable name must be a letter or the underscore character. JavaScript is case sensitive, which means that if a letter is in upper case or lower case, it must always be referred to using the uppercase or lowercase letter as appropriate. In other words, JavaScript distinguishes between x and X.

Variables can be either global or local in scope. Global means that all functions can use the same variable as a particular value. A global variable is declared before the first function definition in the <SCRIPT> tag. A local variable is only available to the function that contains it, and it is declared within a function definition. The following example illustrates the difference in the structural position of the two variable types.

```
<SCRIPT>
var globalvar1=5;
function fivetimestwo() {
        var localvar1 = 2  * globalvar1;
        alert ("Five times two is" + localvar1);
}

function fivetimesten() {
        var localvar2 = localvar1  * globalvar1;
        alert ("Five times ten is" + localvar2);
}
</SCRIPT>
```

In the preceding example, the *globalvar1* global variable is declared before any functions are defined. The *localvar1* local variable is declared within the *fivetimestwo()* function. The first function is capable of being executed because it is able to use the global variable and the local variable that is declared within the function. The *localvar2* local variable is declared within the *fivetimesten()* function. In the second function, an attempt is made to use the *localvar1* variable. This is not possible because it is declared locally within the first function. If the variable *localvar1* had been declared before the function *fivetimestwo()*, the function *fivetimesten()* could have used the value to return a value. As it is, the function does not execute because of the function's inability to recognize the *localvar1* variable.

Literals

The last of the elements to describe that you will be working with to supply information to functions and expressions are literals. There are several types of literals:

☐ Integer literals: Whole numbers such as 3 or 7;

☐ Floating point literals: Numbers expressed with a decimal point, such as 0.2 or 99.9999;

☐ Boolean literals: "True" or "false"

☐ String literals: Zero or more characters contained within single (') or double("") quotation marks;

☐ Special characters which include:

    ☐ \b: Indicates a backspace

    ☐ \f: Indicates a form feed

    ☐ \n: Indicates a new line

    ☐ \r: Indicates a carriage return

    ☐ \t: Indicates a tab character

    ☐ \": Indicates a quotation mark enclosed within a string, as in the following example:

```
JavaScript:      MyQuote="He said don\'t go home."
Result:   He said don't go home.
```

Expressions and Operators

Now that you have been introduced to values, variables, and literals, expressions and operators will enable you to assign, affect, and determine their values. Expressions are sets of literals, variables, operators, and expressions that evaluate to a single string. That is to say, expressions return a single value: there is no ambiguity in an expression's result. $X=7$ is a perfect example of such an unambiguous expression. There are three kinds of expressions available in JavaScript:

☐ Arithmetic: Evaluates to a number

☐ String: Evaluates to a character string

☐ Logical: Evaluates to either true or false

In addition to these three expression types, there are also conditional expressions (also called ternary operators). Conditional expressions use the Question mark (?) and use the following syntax:

```
(condition) ? value1: value2
```

If the condition is true, the expression has the value of *value1*, if not, it has the value of *value2*. All expression types use operators to work with *operands*. Operands are the values, variables, or literals used with operators to form an expression. Operators are generally separated into two main groups: assignment operators and standard operators. The first group of operators assign values to the left hand side of the operator; standard operators are used to otherwise affect a value. Within standard operators, there are arithmetic, string, and logical operators.

The assignment operators are:

Operator	Value
x=y	x=y
x+=y	x=x+y
x-=y	x=x-y
x*=y	x=x*y
x/=y	x=x/y
x%=y	x=x%y

There are additional assignment operators available for bitwise operators that will be presented in the following section. Each of the operator types that are not used for assignment are broken into two categories: binary and unary. The former requires two operands, the latter requires a single operand.

Arithmetic Operators

The arithmetic operators include the standard operators, addition (+), subtraction (–), multiplication (*), and division (/). In addition to the standard arithmetic operators, the following operators are available in JavaScript.

Modulus (%) Operators

Modulus operators return the integer remainder from a division equation between two numbers. In other words, 10 divided by 3 equals 3, remainder 1. The equation *10 % 3*, therefore, returns 1.

Increment (++) Operators

Increment operators increase the value of a variable by 1. It is generally placed after the number, but is sometimes placed before. To increase a number, use *x++* syntax. In working with two numbers, the placement of the increment operator affects how the equation is performed. If it is placed before the operand, the left operand uses the value of the number after it has been incremented; if it is placed after the operand, it uses the unincremented value to perform the calculation. In the following examples, the default value of b is 5.

```
a=++b    (a=6, b=6)
a=b++    (a=5, b=6)
```

Decrement (—) Operators

Decrement operators decrease the value of a variable by 1. To make a number decrease, use *x—* syntax. In working with two numbers, the placement of the increment operator affects how the equation is performed. If it is before the operand, the left operand uses the value of the number after it has been incremented; if it is placed after the operand, it uses the unincremented value to perform the calculation. In the following examples, the default value of b is 5.

```
a=—b     (a=4, b=4)
a=b—     (a=5, b=4)
```

Negation (-) Operators

Negation operators reverse the polarity of a numeric value. It is placed before the value (X=-X).

Bitwise Operators

The bitwise operators support binary equations. Binary numbers use the base two numbering system, and are made up of the numbers one and zero. There are several types of bitwise operators: logical, shift, and assignment types.

Logical Operators

Before performing logical calculations, these operators convert the numeric values into binary numbers. When the number has been converted, comparisons are made between the numbers to see how they pass individual logical tests.

The three logical bitwise operators are **AND (&)**, **OR (|)**, and **XOR (^)**. The AND operator returns a 1 for each bit if both operands are ones; the OR operator returns a one if either operand is a one; and the XOR operator returns a one if one, but not both, of the operands is a one. These work as follows:

> 13 & 10 returns 8 (1101 & 1010 = 1000)
>
> 13 | 10 returns 15   (1101 | 1010 = 1111)
>
> 13 ^ 10 returns 7   (1101 ^ 1010 = 0111)

Shift Operators

Shift operators move the first operand in a binary number a specified number of positions left or right. Each position left or right will increase or decrease the number by a power of two. There are three shift operators:

- ☐ Left Shift (<<)
- ☐ Sign-Propogating Right Shift (>>)
- ☐ Zero-fill Right Shift (>>>)

The latter two function the same for positive values. The shift operators take two arguments, the numeric value to be shifted and the number of bit positions by which the first operand is to be shifted. These work as follows:

> 13 << 2 returns 52 (1101 becomes 110100)
>
> 13 >> 2 returns 3 (1101 becomes 11)
>
> 13 >>> 2 returns 3 (1101 becomes 11)

Assignment Operators

The bitwise assignment operators function the same way as the other assignment operators, described above. These are:

Operator	Value
a <<= b	a = a<<b
a >>= b	a = a>>b
a >>> = b	a = a>>>b
a&=b	a=a&b
a|=b	a=a|b
a^=b	a=a^b

Comparison Operators

The comparison operators are used to compare two values and return a true or false logical value. They are often used with conditional statements to test for values. The six available comparison operators are:

Operator	Description
Equal (==)	This operator returns true if its operands are equal. if(x==y) {statements...}
Not Equal (!=)	This operator returns true if its operands are not equal. if(x!=y) {statements...}
Greater Than (>)	This operator returns true if the left operand is greater than the right operand. if(x>y) {statements...}
Greater Than or Equal to (>=)	This operator returns true if the left operand is greater than or equal to the right operand. if(x>=y) {statements...}
Lesser Than (<)	This operator returns true if the left operands is lesser than the right operand. if(x<y) {statements...}
Lesser Than or Equal to (<=)	This operator returns true if the left operands is lesser than the right operand. if(x<=y) {statements...}

Logical Operators

Logical operators return Boolean values (e.g., True or False). The logical operators available in JavaScript are:

AND (&&): This operator returns a true if both of its operands, which are logical expressions, are true.

Expresssion1 && Expresssion2

OR (| |): This operator returns a true if either of its operands, which are logical expressions, are true.

Expresssion1 | | Expresssion2

NOT (!): This is a unary operator that reverses the condition of the expression with which it is used. In other words, if the expression was true, it becomes false; if false, it becomes true.

!Expression1

String Operators

String values can be used with the comparison operators above, as well as with two arithmetic operators. These concatenate strings as demonstrated:

```
"Ringling "+"Brothers" evaluates to "Ringling Brothers";
MyString="This is";
MyString+=" "+ Math.cos(0) +" strange example.";
MyString evaluates to "This is 1 strange example."
```

typeof Operator

The typeof operator is new to Navigator 3.0. It is used to determine the value type of a programming element or reserved word. This can be seen in the example below:

```
typeof parse == "function"
typeof "typed text" == "string"
typeof Date == "object"
typeof true == "boolean"
```

Operator Precedence

When more than one operator are used in an expression, the order in which the individual operators are executed can affect the outcome of the expression. Consider the following:

```
17 = 5 + 4 * 3
```

When no parentheses are present, the operators follow a predetermined order of execution. As seen in the example, the multiplication operator has a higher level of precedence than the addition operator. From highest to lowest precedence, operators are executed as follows:

Operator Precedence	
Operator Name	Operator
call, member	() []
negation/increment	! - ++ —
multiply/divide	* /
addition/subtraction	+ -
bitwise shift	<< >> >>>
relational	< <= > >=
equality	== !=
bitwise-and	&
bitwise-xor	^
bitwise-or	|
logical-and	&&
logical-or	||
conditional	?
assignment	= += -= *= /= %= <<= >>= >>>= &= |= ^=
comma	,

Now that you have been introduced to operators, you can begin to create expressions utilizing values, variables, and operators. The final piece of the JavaScript puzzle to look into are statements and the flow control they provide.

Statements

Statements direct the flow of JavaScripts. Much of the power in JavaScript lies in its ability to perform complex functions through loop statements, object manipulation statements, and conditional statements. Many of the more complex JavaScripts make extensive use of statements. Using statements effectively will help you reduce the lines of code that you use, assist you in advanced applications such as designing animations, and give you a much higher degree of control over your JavaScript than otherwise possible.

In designing loop statements, a simple differentiation between loop types is extremely helpful. You use *if…else* statements principally when testing conditions that are either true or false. In other words, there are only two possible conditions, such as *if(x>y)*. The value *x* is either greater than the value *y*, or not greater.

You use *for* statements to declare an initial condition of a variable, a test condition for the statement to be executed, and a statement that updates the value of the variable's condition. The loop then iterates a block of statements for the tested range of values. All values that meet the defined criteria will process the series of statements that follow the *for* statement.

The *while* loop is similar to the *for* statement in that all values that meet your defined criteria will process the series of statements that follow the *while* statement. The *while* loop, however, does not declare a variable's value. It merely tests a variable until a condition becomes true, then breaks out of the loop.

The following sections discuss the statements currently available in JavaScript.

Break Statements

Break statements interrupt *while* or *for* loops. When setting up loops to perform repeated actions, the break statement prevents the loop from being endless. Once a condition has been met, the loop is interrupted, or broken. The code remaining after the interrupted loop statement is then processed normally.

```
function breakme() {
        while (x>0) {
                if (x>3)
                        break;
```

```
            x++;
        }
        return x;
}
```

In the preceding example, the while loop is interrupted by the break when x becomes greater than 3. This enables you to interrupt a loop from becoming endless through selecting the criteria that enables values to pass.

Comment Statements

Every language has its own way of commenting text that you do not want to be executed. JavaScript uses the forward slash character (/) for this purpose. There are two ways to use the comment marks:

```
// single line comment
/* multiple line comment*/
```

The top statement is used for a single line of commented text; the bottom statement is generally used for two or more lines of commented text.

Continue Statements

Continue statements terminate while or for loops differently from the break statement, which stops them completely. In the case of the while loop, the test condition is returned to; in the case of the for loop, the updated value or expression is passed.

```
while(x<10) {
        x++;
        if (x==8)
                continue;
        a+=x;
}
```

In the preceding example, the while loop repeats while x is less than 10. When x is equal to 8, the continue statement breaks the while loop, and continues to execute any statements that were waiting for the while loop to close.

For Loops

For loops consist of three optional expressions (separated by semicolons and contained within parentheses) and a block of statements. For loop syntax is:

```
    for  ([initial expression]; [condition]; [update expression])
{statements}
```

The initial expression can use the var statement to declare a variable if necessary.

```
for (x=5; x<10; x++) {statements}
```

For...In Statements

For...In statements treat a specified variable for each property of an object. For each property, JavaScript executes the specified statements.

```
for (var in obj)  {statements}
```

Functions

Functions are the statments that contain other statements for execution and are called by event handlers or other functions. Every function has a name, parameter(s) enclosed in parentheses, and a body of statement definition(s), as shown below:

```
function myFunction () {
        alert("Go home, now!")
}
```

If...Else Statements

The *if...then* format for JavaScript actually uses an *if...else* phrasing as follows:

```
        if (condition) {
                statements
        }  [else  {
                else statements
        } ]
```

If a test condition is true, the statements are executed; if they are false, the else statements are executed. If statements may include nested if statements.

New Statements

New statements enable you to define a new instance of a defined object type. These objects are either built-in objects or user-defined objects. To create a new object you first have to define it. After being defined, you use the following syntax:

```
new myObject(parameter1,parameter2, ...)
```

Objects are defined using functions. See the discussion on user-defined objects earlier in this appendix.

Return Statements

Specifies the value to be returned by a function.

This Keyword

This keyword is not really a statement. It is often grouped with statements for lack of a better classification. It is very useful for describing objects in JavaScript with a shorthand method. Consider the following two lines of code.

```
document.MusicForm.elements[0].value="True";
this.value="True";
```

Both examples may refer to the same form element. Using *this* enables you to use shorthand when defining the object within which the function call is made. In other words, if your form element has an *onChange* event handler, and the value changes, you can use *this.value* to test for field entry.

Var Statements

Var statements declare variables. Variables may be declared by using the var statement or simply by assigning them a value. Consider the following:

```
var varname[=varvalue]          or          varname=varvalue
```

Both declarations do the same thing. It is considered good practice to include the *var* statement with variable declarations, although it is not generally required.

While Statements

Similar to the *for* loop, this statement evaluates an expression condition, and if true, executes statements. It repeats this process as long as the condition is true.

```
while (condition)   {statements}
```

With Statements

With statements establish an object as the default object for multiple statements.

```
with (object)  {statements}
```

Consider the following example:

```
with (MyWindow.document) {
        open();
        write("Not so much code used");
        close();
}
```

Using the with statement enables the code to take much less space than would otherwise have been the case.

Reserved Words

There are some words that JavaScript will not permit you to use except for specific purposes. The reserved words in this list cannot be used as JavaScript variables, functions, methods, or object names. Some of the reserved words are keywords used in JavaScript; others are reserved for future use. It is generally a good idea in programming to avoid names that could conceivably be reserved by the system.

abstract	double	import
boolean	else	in
break	extends	instanceof
byte	false	int
case	final	interface
catch	finally	long
char	float	native
class	for	new
const	function	null
continue	goto	package
default	if	private
do	implements	protected

public	synchronized	try
return	this	var
short	throw	void
static	throws	while
super	transient	with
switch	true	

Appendix

Multiple Browser Capability

When developing pages that incorporate JavaScript, it is important to remember that many browsers will not recognize the scripts. For this reason, you may wish to build in some reverse compatibility to accommodate a wider browser audience. This is also true of differences in JavaScript as recognized by Navigator 2.0 and Navigator 3.0 (as well as with other browsers that interpret JavaScript). The following scripts will show you how to integrate JavaScript across various Navigator versions and for browsers that do not recognize JavaScript.

JavaScript for non-JavaScript browsers

For browsers that do not recognize the <SCRIPT> contents, the <NOSCRIPT> tag is available to avoid conflicts with JavaScript-enabled browsers. The contents of this tag will be ignored by Navigator, but interpreted by other browsers.

Example:

```
<noscript>
  <META HTTP-EQUIV=REFRESH CONTENT="0; URL=page2.htm">
</noscript>
```

In this example, page2.htm is loaded by browsers that do not support JavaScript.

Identifying the operating system

JavaScript provides several properties to identify which operating system the client is using. One option is to implement the appVersion property of the navigator object. The following example shows you how to use this property in order to perform a different action to accommodate the operating system.

```
if(navigator.appVersion.charAt(navigator.appVersion.indexOf("(")+1) == "W")
{
    document.writeln("<center>");
    document.writeln("<h1>You are using your browser under Windows</h1>");
    document.writeln("</center>");
    }
else if(navigator.appVersion.charAt(navigator.appVersion.indexOf("(")+1) ==
➡"M") {
    document.writeln("<center>");
    document.writeln("<h1>You are using your browser under Macintosh</
➡h1>");
    document.writeln("</center>");
    }
else {
    document.writeln("<center>");
    document.writeln("<h1>You are not using your browser under window or
➡mac</h1>");
    document.writeln("<h1>You are under "+navigator.appVersion+"!</h1>");
    document.writeln("</center>");
    }
```

Identifying the version number

JavaScript also provides several properties to identify which version of the browser the client is using.

Some of the functionality shown in this book is only available in the Navigator 3 and later versions. So it is useful to know which version of Navigator the client is using in order to design a workaround for previous browser versions.

Example:

```
if(parseInt(navigator.appVersion.charAt(0),10) >= 3) {
    document.writeln("<center><h1>Your using the version 3 or higher</h1></
➥center>");
    }
else {
    document.writeln("<center><h1>Your using the version
"+navigator.appVersion+"</h1></center>");
    }
```

Identifying the browser

To identify the client's browser you have to use the appName property of the navigator object. The navigator.appVersion property is a string that displays "Netscape."

You can also identify the browser name by testing the first letter in the browser name.

Example:

```
if(navigator.appVersion.charAt(0)=="N") {
  //do something for netscape
  }
else {
  // do something for the other JavaScript browser
  }
```

A Real life example (the new 41.htm)

This page is the example #41 extended for multiple browser environment.

This script can be used as a basic layout for a multiple browser environment.

It is an example that utilizes slightly different functionality for Navigator 3.0, 2.0 and a non-JavaScript compatible browser.

```
<HTML><HEAD><TITLE>Change image using source attribute</TITLE></HEAD>
<BODY BGCOLOR="#FFFFFF">
<SCRIPT>
  imageURL="clock.jpg"
  function changeImage() {
    if(imageURL=="cup.jpg") {
      imageURL = "clock.jpg";
    } else {
      imageURL = "cup.jpg";
    }
    if(parseInt(navigator.appVersion.charAt(0),10) >= 3) {
      document.images[0].src =imageURL;
    } else {
      window.open(imageURL.substring(0,imageURL.indexOf("."))+".htm",
"NewWindow",
"toolbar=no,directories=no,menubar=no,scrollbars=no,width=200,height=400");
    }
  }
</SCRIPT>
  <P>
  <CENTER>
  <H2>Changing an Image Using the onClick Event Handler</H2>
  <FORM>
  <INPUT TYPE=Button VALUE="Change the image source"
onClick="changeImage()">
  </FORM>
  <P>
  <IMG SRC="clock.jpg" width=180 height=180 NAME="myImage">
  </CENTER>
<noscript>
<META HTTP-EQUIV=REFRESH CONTENT="0; URL=41b1.htm">
</noscript>
</BODY>
</HTML>
```

Additional pages for non-scripting browsers

The following pages are added for non-scripting browsers to load. For browsers that read JavaScript, these are unnecessary.

41b1.htm:

```
<HTML><HEAD><TITLE>Change image using source attribute</TITLE></HEAD>
<BODY BGCOLOR="#FFFFFF">
  <P>
  <CENTER>
  <H2>Changing an Image Using URL</H2>
  <a href=41b2.htm>click here</a>
  <P>
  <IMG SRC="clock.jpg" width=180 height=180 NAME="myImage">
  </CENTER>
</body>
</html>
```

41b2.htm:

```
<HTML><HEAD><TITLE>Change image using source attribute</TITLE></HEAD>
<BODY BGCOLOR="#FFFFFF">
  <P>
  <CENTER>
  <H2>Changing an Image Using URL</H2>
  <a href=41b1.htm>click here</a>
  <P>
  <IMG SRC="cup.jpg" width=180 height=180 NAME="myImage">
  </CENTER>
</body>
</html>
```

In the case of Navigator 3.0, the statement:
```
if(parseInt(navigator.appVersion.charAt(0),10) >= 3)
```
directs Navigator versions 3.0 and later to use the new src property of the image array object to change the source of the image in the page (see Chapter 5 for more information).

In the case of Navigator 2.0 the browser executes the statement within the else clause:

```
window.open(imageURL.substring(0,imageURL.indexOf("."))+".htm",
➥"NewWindow",
"toolbar=no,directories=no,menubar=no,scrollbars=no,width=200,height=400");
```

In the case of other browsers, the `<META HTTP-EQUIV="Refresh">` statement loads a page that has a link built into it that operates functionally in roughly the same way as the JavaScript examples.

When designing pages with JavaScript, it is a good idea to be inclusive of other browsers. Building in reverse compatibility as defined in this Appendix can help ensure that other browsers can still get the information they need from the Web page.

C

A p p e n d i x

Using JavaScript with LiveWire

JavaScript is the scripting language for application development with LiveWire. It can be executed on the server or on the client. This appendix discusses JavaScript as it relates to LiveWire.

Using Client and Server Scripts

In general, a LiveWire application can contain JavaScript that is interpreted by the server (with the LiveWire runtime interpreter) and by the client, Netscape Navigator.

In source code HTML, client-side JavaScript is delimited by the SCRIPT tag and server-side JavaScript by the SERVER tag. LiveWire compiles the source code HTML into platform-independent bytecodes, parsing and compiling server-side JavaScript statements. At runtime, the Netscape server translates the bytecodes into HTML statements (possibly including client JavaScript) and sends them across the network to the client. Navigator interprets client JavaScript and performs standard HTML layout.

This process is illustrated the following figure.

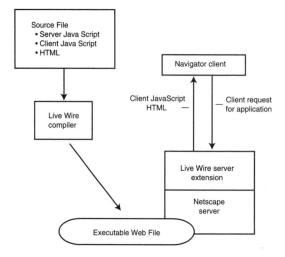

Client and Server JavaScript Processes

When you run a complex LiveWire application, a variety of things occur, some on the server and some on the client. Although the end-user does not need to know the details, it is important for you, the application developer, to understand what happens "under the hood."

In an application that contains both client and server JavaScript

☐ You create an HTML page containing server and client JavaScript statements, compile it to a LiveWire Web file, and install it on the server.

☐ A user accesses the application URL with the Navigator.

☐ LiveWire dynamically creates HTML based on server JavaScript statements, sending HTML and client JavaScript statements to the client.

☐ Navigator interprets client JavaScript statements, formats HTML output, and displays results to the user. Of course, if a user is not using Netscape Navigator (or some other JavaScript-capable client), then the client will not interpret JavaScript statements. Likewise, if you create a page containing server JavaScript, it must be installed on a Netscape server to operate properly.

Partitioning Client and Server JavaScripts

There are usually a variety of ways to partition an application between client and server. Some tasks can be performed only on the client or on the server; others can be performed on either. Although there is no definitive way to know "what to do where," you can follow these general guidelines:

As a rule of thumb, employ client scripts for the following tasks:

☐ Validating user input; that is, checking that values entered in forms are valid.

☐ Prompting a user for confirmation.

☐ Displaying error or informational popups.

☐ Performing aggregate calculations (such as sums or averages) or other processing on data retrieved from the server.

☐ Conditionalizing HTML.

☐ Performing other functions that do not require information from the server.

Use server scripts for

☐ Maintaining information through a series of client accesses.

☐ Maintaining data shared among several clients or applications.

☐ Accessing a database.

☐ Accessing files on the server.

☐ Calling C libraries on the server.

☐ Dynamically customizing Java applets; for example, visualizing data using a Java applet.

Using LiveWire Functions

There are a number of JavaScript functions that are built-in to LiveWire. These functions are defined only for server JavaScript.

The write Function

The write function displays the values of JavaScript expressions in HTML. For example, the statement

```
write("<P>Customer Name is:" + project.custname)
```

causes LiveWire to generate HTML that is sent to the client. In this case, the HTML includes a paragraph tag and some text, concatenated with the value of the custname property of the project object, which, for example, might be "Fred's software company." The client would then receive the following HTML:

```
<P>Customer Name is: Fred's software company.
```

As far as the client is concerned, this is static HTML. However, it is actually generated dynamically by LiveWire.

The writeURL Function

The writeURL function generates a URL compatible with the URL encoding methods of maintaining the client object. You do not need to use this function unless the application is using either client URL encoding or short URL encoding to maintain the client object.

Suppose your application has a variable, nextPage, that you set to a string identifying the page to link to, based on actions by the user. If you want to dynamically generate a hyperlink using this named property, you could do it like this

```
<A HREF='nextPage'>
```

Assuming the value of nextPage is set to be the appropriate URL, this would work fine. However, if you are using an URL-encoding method to preserve the client object, this URL would not contain the neccessary parameters to maintain client properties. To do this, you must use writeURL as follows:

```
<A HREF='writeURL(nextPage)'>
```

You do not need to use writeURL for a normal static URL, because LiveWire will automatically append any parameters neccessary to the URL; however, you must use writeURL any time an application generates an URL dynamically, if the application uses an URL encoding technique to maintain the client object.

 Note

> Even though an application is initially installed to use one technique to maintain client, it may be modified later to use an URL encoding technique. If the application generates dynamic URLs, it would not work properly. Therefore, it is good practice always to use writeURL to generate dynamic URLs.

The redirect Function

The redirect function redirects the client to the specified URL. For example,

```
redirect("http://www.terrapin.com/lw/apps/page2.html")
```

sends the client to the indicated URL. The client immediately loads the indicated page. Any previous content is discarded. The client will not display any HTML or perform any JavaScript statements in the page following the redirect statement.

The debug Function

The debug function outputs its argument to the Trace facility. Use this function to display the value of an expression for debugging purposes.

The flush Function

To improve performance, LiveWire buffers write output and sends it to the client in 64Kbyte blocks. The flush function sends data resulting from write functions from the internal buffer to the client. If you do not explicitly perform a flush, LiveWire will flush data after each 64Kbytes of generated content in a document.

You can use flush to control when data is sent to the client, for example, before an operation that will create a delay, such as a database query. Also, if a database query retrieves a large number of rows, flushing the buffer after displaying a certain number of rows prevents long delays in displaying data. Don't confuse the flush function with the flush method of File.

Note   Any changes to the client object should be done before flushing the buffer if the application is using a client-side technique for maintaining the client object.

The following script is an example of using flush. This code fragment iterates through a text file and emits output for each line in the file, preceded by a line number and five spaces. Then flush causes the output to be displayed to the client.

```
while (!In.eof()) {
        AscLine = In.readln()
        if (!In.eof())
                write(LPad(LineCount + ": ", 5), AscLine, "\n")
        LineCount++
        flush()
}
```

For information on performing file input and output, refer to the section, "Using Files on the Server," later in this chapter.

Communicating Between Client and Server

In developing a client-server application, keep in mind the strengths and weaknesses of client and server platforms. Servers are usually (though not always) high-performance workstations with lots of processor speed and large storage capacities. Clients are often (though not always) desktop systems with less processor power and storage capacity. However, servers can become overloaded when accessed by thousands of clients, so it can be advantageous to offload processing to the client. Preprocessing data on the client can also reduce bandwidth requirements, if the client application can aggregate data.

The LiveWire object framework preserves information over time, but client JavaScript is more ephemeral. Navigator objects exist only as the user accesses a page. Also, servers can aggregate information from many clients and many applications, and can store large amounts of data in databases. It is important to keep these characteristics in mind when partitioning functionality between client and server.

In developing applications, you might want to communicate between client and server JavaScript. In particular, you might want to do the following:

☐ Send information from scripts on the Navigator client to LiveWire applications on the server. Typically, this information is based on user input that may be processed first by client JavaScript functions.

☐ Send information from a LiveWire application on the server to client JavaScript functions in the Navigator.

With JavaScript, both of these tasks can be accomplished easily.

Sending Values from Client to Server

In HTML, you send values to the server using form elements such as text fields and radio buttons. When the user clicks a submit button, the Navigator submits the values entered in the form to the server for processing. The ACTION attribute of the <FORM> tag determines the application to which the values are submitted. For example

```
<FORM NAME="myform" ACTION="http://www.myserver.com/app/page.html">
```

If you want to send user-entered values to a LiveWire application, you need do nothing special. Each form element corresponds to a request property.

If you want to process data on the client first, you have to create a client-JavaScript function to perform processing on the form-element values and then assign the output of the client function to a form element. The element can be hidden, so it is not displayed to the user. This enables you to perform client preprocessing.

For example, say you have a client-JavaScript function named calc that performs some calculations based on the user's input. You want to pass the result of this function to your LiveWire application for further processing. You first need to define a hidden form element for the result, as follows:

```
<INPUT TYPE="hidden" NAME="result" SIZE=5>
```

You then need to create an onClick event handler for the submit button that assigns the output of the function to the hidden element:

```
<INPUT TYPE="submit" VALUE="Submit"
onClick="this.form.result.value=calc(this.form)">
```

The value of result will be submitted along with any other form-element values. This value will be referenced as request.result in the LiveWire application.

Sending Values from Server to Client

A LiveWire application communicates to the client through HTML and client-based JavaScript. If you simply want to display information to the user, then there is no subtlety: you create the dynamic HTML to format the information as you want it displayed. However, you may want to send values to client scripts directly. You can accomplish this by implementing a variety of methods such as:

☐ Default form values

☐ Hidden form elements

☐ Direct substitution in client SCRIPT statements or event handlers

To display an HTML form with default values set in the form elements, use the INPUT tag to create the desired form element, substituting a server-side JavaScript expression for the VALUE attribute. For example, say you want to display a text element and set the default value based on the value of client.custname. You can do this with the following statement:

```
<INPUT TYPE="text" NAME="customerName" SIZE="30" VALUE='client.custname'>
```

The initial value of this text field is set to the value of the LiveWire client.custname variable.

You can use a similar technique with hidden form elements if you do not want to display the value to the user. For example,

```
<INPUT TYPE="hidden" NAME="custID" SIZE=5 VALUE='client.custID'>
```

In both cases, these values are reflected in client-side JavaScript in property values of Navigator objects. If these two elements are in a form named "entryForm," then these values are reflected into JavaScript properties document.entryForm.customerName and document.entryForm.custID, respectively. You can then perform client processing on these values in Navigator scripts, but only if the scripts occur after the definition of the form elements in the page.

You can also use LiveWire to generate client-side scripts. This is the most straightforward way of sending values from the server to client JavaScript. These values can be used in subsequent statements on the client. As a simple example, you can initialize a client-side variable named budget based on the value of client.amount as follows:

```
<SERVER>
write("<SCRIPT>var budget = " + client.amount + "</SCRIPT>")
</SERVER>
```

Using Cookies for Client-server Communication

Cookies are a mechanism used by Navigator to maintain information between requests using a file called cookie.txt (the cookie file). The contents of the cookie file is available through the client JavaScript document.cookie property. If an application is using client cookies to maintain the client object, you can use the cookie file to communicate between client and server scripts.

The advantage of using cookies for client-server communication is that it provides a uniform mechanism for passing values between client and server and enables you to maintain persistent values on the client.

When using client cookies for client object maintenance, LiveWire adds the following entry for each property value:

```
NETSCAPE_LIVEWIRE.propName=propValue;
```

where propName is the name of the property and propValue is its value. Special characters in propValue are encoded in the cookie file.

You can use the built-in JavaScript function escape to encode characters and unescape to decode them; however, these functions do not handle spaces. As a result, you must manually encode and decode space, forward slash (/), and the at-sign (@).

The following are examples of functions for getting and setting cookie values. These functions assume the use of some helper functions called encode and decode that perform the proper character encoding.

```
function getCookie(Name) {
        var search = "NETSCAPE_LIVEWIRE." + Name + "="
        var RetStr = ""
        var offset = 0
        var end    = 0
        if (document.cookie.length > 0) {
                offset = document.cookie.indexOf(search)
                if (offset != -1) {
                        offset += search.length
                        end = document.cookie.indexOf(";", offset)
```

```
                        if (end == -1)
                                end = document.cookie.length
                RetStr = decode(document.cookie.substring(offset, end))
                        }
                }
        return (RetStr);
}
function setCookie(Name, Value, Expire) {
        document.cookie = "NETSCAPE_LIVEWIRE." + Name + "="
        + encode(Value)
        + ((Expire == null) ? "" : ("; expires=" + Expire.toGMTString()))
}
```

These functions could be called in client JavaScript to get and set values of the client object, for example as follows

```
var Kill = new Date()
Kill.setDate(Kill.getDate() + 7)
var value = getCookie("answer")
if (value == "")
        setCookie("answer", "42", Kill)
else
        document.write("The answer is ", value)
```

These statements check if there is a client property called answer. If there is not, it creates it and sets its value to 42; if there is, it displays its value.

Using Files on the Server

LiveWire provides a File object that enables applications to write to the server's file system. This is useful for generating persistent HTML files and for storing information without using a database server. One of the main advantages of storing information in a file instead of LiveWire objects is that the information is preserved even if the server goes down.

Exercise caution when using the File object. An application can write files anywhere the operating system allows. If you create an application that writes or modifies files on the server, you should ensure that users cannot misuse this capability.

For security reasons, LiveWire does not provide automatic access to the file system of client machines. If needed, the user can save information directly to the client file system by making appropriate menu choices in Navigator.

Creating a File Object

To create a File object, use the standard JavaScript syntax for object creation:

```
fileObjectName = new File("path")
```

where fileObjectName is the JavaScript object name by which you will refer to the file, and path is the file path, relative to the application directory (the directory in which the Web file resides). The path should be in the format of the server's file system, not an URL path.

Opening and Closing a File

Once you have created a File object, you must open the file with the open method to read from it or write to it. The open method has the following syntax:

```
result = fileObjectName.open("mode")
```

This method will return true if the operation is a success and false if the operation is a failure. If the file is already open, the operation will fail and the original file will remain open.

The parameter mode is a string that specifies the mode in which to open the file. The following table describes how the file is opened for each mode.

File Access Modes	
Mode	Description
r	Opens the file, if it exists, as a text file for reading and returns true. If the file does not exist, returns false.
w	Opens the file as a text file for writing. Creates a new (initially empty) text file whether or not the file exists.
a	Opens the file as a text file for appending (writing at the end of the file). Creates the file if it does not already exist.
r+	Opens the file as a text file for reading and writing. Reading and writing commence at the beginning of the file. If the file exists, returns true. If the file does not exist, returns false.
w+	Opens the file as a text file for reading and writing. Creates a new (initially empty) file whether or not the file already exists.

continues

File Access Modes, continued	
Mode	Description
a+	Opens the file as a text file for reading and writing. Reading and writing commence at the end of the file. Creates the file if it does not already exist.
b	Append to any of these modes to open the file as binary rather than text. Only applicable on Windows operating systems.

When an application is finished with a file, it should close the file by calling the close method. If the file is not open, close will fail. This method returns true if successful, false otherwise.

You can output the name of a file simply by using the write method. For example, the following statement displays the filename:

```
x = new File("/path/file.txt")
write(x)
```

Locking Files

Most applications can be accessed by many users simultaneously, but in general it is not recommended for more than one user to access the same file simultaneously, because this can lead to unexpected errors. For example, one user of an application could move the pointer to the end of the file when another user expected the pointer to be at the beginning of the file.

To prevent multiple users from accessing the same file at one time, use the locking facility of the project and server objects. Use the lock method of project to ensure that no other user can access the file when one user has it locked. If more than one application will access the same file, use the lock method of server. In general, this means you should precede all file operations with lock and follow them with unlock.

Working with Files

The file object has a number of methods that you can use once a file is opened:

☐ Positioning: setPosition, getPosition, eof. Use these methods to set and get the current pointer position in the file and determine if it is at the end of the file.

☐ Reading from a file: read, readln, readByte.

☐ Writing to a file: write, writeln, writeByte.

☐ Converting between binary and text formats: byteToString, stringToByte. Use these methods to convert a single number to a character and vice versa.

☐ Informational methods: getLength, exists, error, clearError. Use these methods to get information on a file, and to get and clear error status.

Positioning Within a File

A file object has a pointer that indicates the current position in the file. When you open a file, the pointer is positioned at either the beginning or the end of the file, depending on the mode you used to open it. In an empty file, the beginning and end of the file are the same.

The setPosition method positions the pointer within the file, returning true if successful; false otherwise. The syntax is

```
fileObj.setPosition(position [,reference])
```

fileObj is a file object, position is an integer indicating where to position the pointer, and reference indicates the reference point for position, as follows:

0: relative to beginning of file

1: relative to current position

2: relative to end of file

Other (or unspecified): relative to beginning of file

The getPosition method returns the current position in the file, where the first byte in the file is byte 0. This method returns -1 if there is an error. The syntax is

```
fileObj.getPosition()
```

The eof method returns true if the pointer is at the end of the file, and false otherwise. This method will return true after the first read operation that attempts to read past the end of file.

```
fileObj.eof()
```

Reading from a File

Use these methods to read from a file: read, readln, and readByte.

The read method reads the specified number of bytes from a file and returns a string. The syntax is

```
fileObj.read(count)
```

fileObj is a file object and count is an integer specifying the number of bytes to read. If count specifies more bytes than are left in the file, then the method reads to the end of the file.

The readln method reads the next line from the file and returns the next line from the file as a string. The syntax is

```
fileObj.readln()
```

fileObj is a file object. The line-separator characters (either \r\n on Windows or just \n on Unix or Macintosh) are not included in the string. The character \r is skipped; \n determines the actual end of the line. This compromise gets reasonable behavior on both Windows and Unix platforms.

The readByte method reads the next byte from the file and returns the numeric value of the next byte, or -1. The syntax is

```
fileObj.readByte()
```

Writing to a File

The methods for writing to a file: write, writeln, and writeByte also include a flush method to flush internal buffers to disk.

The write method writes a string to the file. It returns true if successful; otherwise it returns false. The syntax is

```
fileObj.write(string)
```

where fileObj is a file object and string is a JavaScript string.

The writeln method writes a string to the file, followed by \n (\r\n in text mode on Windows). It returns true if the write was successful; otherwise it returns false. The syntax is

```
fileObj.writeln(string)
```

The writeByte method writes a byte to the file. It returns true if successful; otherwise it returns false. The syntax is

```
fileObj.writeByte(number)
```

where fileObj is a file object and number is a number.

When you use any of the file methods for writing to a file, they are buffered internally. The flush method writes the buffer to the file on disk. This method returns true if successful, and false otherwise. If fileObj is a file object, the syntax is

```
fileObj.flush()
```

Converting Data

There are two primary file formats: ASCII text and binary. The file object has two methods for converting data between these two formats: byteToString and stringToByte.

The byteToString method converts a number into a one-character string. This method is static, so no object is required. The syntax is

```
File.byteToString(number)
```

If the argument is not a number, the method will return the empty string.

The stringToByte method converts the first character of its argument, a string, into a number. This method is static, so no object is required. The syntax is

```
File.stringToByte(string)
```

The method returns a numeric value of the first character, or zero.

Retrieving File Information

There are several file methods you can use to retrieve information on files and to work with the error status.

The getLength method returns the number of bytes (or characters for a text file) in the file, or -1 if there is an error. The syntax is

```
fileObj.getLength()
```

The exists method returns true if the file exists; otherwise it returns false.

```
fileObj.exists()
```

The error method returns the error status or -1 if the file is not open or cannot be opened. The error status will be nonzero if an error occurred, zero otherwise (no error). Error status codes are platform dependent; refer to your operating system documentation. The syntax is

```
fileObj.error()
```

The clearError method clears both the error status (the value of error) and the value of eof:

```
fileObj.clearError()
```

Using File I/O: An Example

The following simple example creates a file object, opens it for reading, and generates HTML that echoes the lines in the file, with a hard line break after each line.

```
x = new File("/tmp/names.txt") // path name is platform dependent
fileIsOpen = x.open("r")
if (fileIsOpen) {
        write("file name: " + x + "<BR>")
        while (!x.eof()) {
                line = x.readln()
        if (!x.eof())
        write(line+"<br>")
        }
        if (x.error() != 0)
                write("error reading file" + "<BR>")
        x.close()
}
```

Using External Libraries

A LiveWire application can call functions written in languages such as C, C++, or Pascal and compiled into libraries on the server. Such functions are called external functions. Libraries are DLLs (dynamic link libraries) on Windows operating systems and SOs (shared objects) on Unix operating systems.

Using external functions in an application is useful if

☐ you already have complex functions written in native code that you can use in your application.

☐ the application requires some computation-intensive functions. In general, functions written in native code will run faster than those written in JavaScript.

☐ the application requires some other task that you cannot do in JavaScript.

To use an external library in a LiveWire application:

1. Write and compile the library (DLL or SO) in a form compatible with LiveWire.

2. With Application Manager, identify the library to be used by installing a new application or modifying installation parameters for an existing application. Once you identify an external library using Application Manager, all applications on the server can call external functions in that library.

3. Restart the server to load the library with your application. The functions in the external library are now available to all applications on the server.

4. In your application, use the JavaScript function RegisterCFunction to identify the functions in the library to be called, and callC to call the functions.

5. Recompile and restart your application to make all the changes take effect.

 Warning

You must restart your server to install a library to use with an application. You must restart the server any time you add new library files or change the names of the library files used by an application.

Guidelines for Writing C Functions

Although you can write external libraries in any language, the calling conventions that LiveWire uses are C calling conventions.

Your C code must include the header file lwccall.h. Functions to be called from JavaScript must be exported, and must conform to this typdef:

```
typedef void (*LivewireUserCFunction)
        ( int argc, struct LivewireCCallData argv[],
        struct LivewireCCallData *result);
```

The header file lwccall.h is provided in \livewire\samples\ccallapp. This directory also includes the source code for a sample application that calls a C function defined in lwccall.c. Refer to these files for more specific guidelines on writing C functions for use with LiveWire.

Identifying Library Files

Before you can run an application that uses external libraries, you must identify the library files using Application Manager. You can identify libraries when you initially install an application (by clicking Add) or when you modify an application's installation parameters (by clicking Modify).

 Warning

> After you enter the paths of library files in Application Manager, you must restart your server for the changes to take effect. You must then be sure to compile and restart your application.

Once you have identified an external library using Application Manager, all applications running on the server can call functions in the library (by using registerCFunction and callC).

Registering External Functions

Use the JavaScript function registerCFunction to register an external function for use with a LiveWire application, with this syntax:

```
registerCFunction(JSFunctionName, libraryPath, CFunctionName)
```

This function returns true if it registers the function successfully. If it does not register the function successfully, it returns false. This might happen if LiveWire could not find the library at the specified location or the specified function inside the library.

The parameters are as follows:

☐ JSFunctionName is the name of the function as it will be called in JavaScript with the callC function.

☐ libraryPath is the full file path of the library, using the conventions of your operating system. Note: Backslash (\ ) is a special character in JavaScript, so you must use a double backslash (\ \ ) to separate Windows directory and file names in libraryPath.

☐ CFunctionName is the name of the C function as it is defined in the library.

An application must register a function with registerCFunction before it can call it with callC. Once the application registers the function, it may call the function any number of times. A good place to register functions is in an application's initial startup page.

Using External Functions in JavaScript

Once your application has registered a function with registerCFunction, it can call the function with the JavaScript function callC, using this syntax:

```
callC(JSFunctionName, arguments... )
```

This function returns a string value returned by the external function. The callC function can only return string values.

The parameters are as follows:

☐ JSFunctionName is the name of the function as it was identified with RegisterCFunction.

☐ arguments is a comma-delimited list of arguments to the external function. The arguments can be any JavaScript values: strings, numbers, boolean values, or null. The number of arguments must match the number of arguments required by the external function.

Calling External Functions: an Example

The sample application ccallapp, installed in the LiveWire samples directory, includes C source code (in lwccall.c) that defines a C function named mystuff_EchoCCallArguments. This function accepts any number of arguments, and then returns a string that contains HTML listing the arguments. This sample illustrates calling C functions from a LiveWire application and returning values.

To run this sample application, you must compile lwccall.c with your C compiler. Command lines for several common compilers are provided in the comments in the file.

The following JavaScript statements from lwccall.html register the C function echoCCallArguments, call the function with some arguments, and then generate HTML based on the value returned by the function.

```
var isRegistered = registerCFunction("echoCCallArguments",
➥"c:\\livewire\\samples\\ccallapp\\mystuff.dll",
➥"mystuff_EchoCCallArguments")
if (isRegistered == true) {
        var returnValue = callC("echoCCallArguments", "first arg", 42,
➥true, "last arg")
        write(returnValue)
}
```

The call to callC calls the function echoCCallArguments with the indicated arguments. The HTML generated by the write statement is as follows:

```
argc = 4<br>
argv[0].tag: string; value = first arg<br>
argv[1].tag: double; value = 42<br>
argv[2].tag: boolean; value = true<br>
argv[3].tag: string; value = last arg<br>
```

Appendix

HTML Issues with JavaScript

While the JavaScript technology lends itself to those with limited or no programming knowledge at all, there are a number of precautions that should be heeded to ensure a bug-free script. There's nothing worse than an impressive Web page feature ruined by simple human oversight. This appendix will provide insight to help you avoid any possible pitfalls along the way.

JavaScript and HTML Layout

To use JavaScript properly in Navigator, it is important to have a basic understanding of how Netscape Navigator performs layout. Layout refers to transforming the plain text directives of HTML into graphical display on your computer. Generally speaking, layout happens sequentially in Navigator. That is, Navigator starts from the top of the HTML file and works its way down, figuring out how to display output to the screen as it goes. So, it starts with the HEAD of an HTML document, then starts at the top of the BODY and works its way down.

Because of this "top-down" behavior, JavaScript only reflects HTML that it has encountered. For example, suppose you define a form with a couple of text input elments:

```
<FORM NAME="statform">
<input type = "text" name = "username" size = 20>
<input type = "text" name = "userage" size = 3>
```

These form elements are reflected as JavaScript objects *document.statform.username* and *document.statform.userage*, that you can use anywhere after the form is defined. However, you can not use these objects before the form is defined. So, for example, you could display the value of these objects in a script after the form definition:

```
<SCRIPT>
document.write(document.statform.username.value)
document.write(document.statform.userage.value)
</SCRIPT>
```

However, if you tried to do this before the form definition (that is, above it in the HTML page), you would get an error, because the objects don't exist yet in the Navigator.

Likewise, once layout has occured, setting a property value does not affect its value or its appearance. For example, suppose you have a document title defined as follows:

```
<TITLE>My JavaScript Page</TITLE>
```

This is reflected in JavaScript as the value of *document.title*. After Navigator has displayed this in layout (in this case, in the title bar of the Navigator window), you cannot change the value in JavaScript. So, if later in the page, you have the following script:

```
document.title = "The New Improved JavaScript Page"
```

it will not change the value of *document.title*, affect the appearance of the page, or generate an error.

Embedding JavaScript in HTML

JavaScript can be embedded in an HTML document in two ways:

☐ As statements and functions using the <SCRIPT> tag.

☐ As event handlers using HTML tags.

The <SCRIPT> Tag

A script embedded in HTML with the <SCRIPT> tag uses the following format:

```
<SCRIPT>
   JavaScript statements...
</SCRIPT>
```

The optional LANGUAGE attribute specifies the scripting language as follows:

```
<SCRIPT LANGUAGE="JavaScript">
   JavaScript statements...
</SCRIPT>
```

The HMTL tag, <SCRIPT>, and its closing counterpart, </SCRIPT> can enclose any number of JavaScript statements in a document.

 Note Remember that JavaScript is case sensitive; lanGUAge LANguaGE.

The following example shows JavaScript embedded in HTML as a script.

```
<HTML>
<HEAD>
<SCRIPT LANGUAGE="JavaScript">
document.write("Hello net.")
```

```
</SCRIPT>
</HEAD>
<BODY>
That's all, folks.
</BODY>
</HTML>
```

The page display for the preceding example reads as:

Hello net. That's all folks.

Hiding Script Code

Scripts can be placed inside comment fields to ensure that your JavaScript code is not displayed by old browsers that do not recognize JavaScript. The entire script is encased by HTML comment tags:

```
<!-- Begin to hide script contents from old browsers.
// End the hiding here. -->
```

Defining and Calling Functions

Scripts placed within <SCRIPT> tags are evaluated after the page loads. Functions are stored, but not executed. Functions are executed by events in the page.

It's important to understand the difference between defining a function and calling the function. Defining the function simply names the function and specifies what to do when the function is called. Calling the function actually performs the specified actions with the indicated parameters.

The following example shows a script with a function and comments.

```
<HEAD>
<SCRIPT LANGUAGE="JavaScript">
<!-- to hide script contents from old browsers
  function square(i) {
    document.write("The call passed ", i ," to the function.","<BR>")
    return i * i
  }
  document.write("The function returned ",square(5),".")
// end hiding contents from old browsers  -->
</SCRIPT>
</HEAD>
<BODY>
<BR>
```

```
All done.
</BODY>
```

The page display for the preceding example reads as:

We passed 5 to the function.

The function returned 25.

All done.

The HEAD Tag

Generally, you should define the functions for a page in the HEAD portion of a document. Because the HEAD is loaded first, this practice guarantees that functions are loaded before the user has a chance to do anything that might call a function.

The following example shows a script with two functions.

```
<HEAD>
<SCRIPT>
<!-- hide script from old browsers
function bar() {
    document.write("<HR ALIGN='left' WIDTH=25%>")
}
function output(head, level, string) {
    document.write("<H" + level + ">" + head + "</H" + level + "><P>" +
➥string)
}
// end hiding from old browsers -->
</SCRIPT>
</HEAD>
<BODY>
<SCRIPT>
<!-- hide script from old browsers
document.write(bar(),output("Make Me Big",3,"Make me ordinary."))
// end hiding from old browsers -->
</SCRIPT>
<P>
Thanks.
</BODY>
```

Quotes

Use single quotes (') to delimit string literals so that scripts can distinguish the literal from attribute values enclosed in double quotes. In the previous example, function bar contains the literal 'left' within a double-quoted attribute value. Here's another example:

```
<INPUT TYPE="button" VALUE="Press Me" onClick="myfunc('astring')">
```

Embedding JavaScripts as Event Handlers

JavaScript applications in the Navigator are largely event-driven. Events are actions that occur, usually as a result of something the user does. For example, a button click is an event, as is giving focus to a form element. There is a specific set of events that Navigator recognizes. You can define event handlers as scripts that are automatically executed when an event occurs.

Event handlers are embedded in documents as attributes of HTML tags to which you assign JavaScript code to execute. The general syntax is as follows:

```
<TAG eventHandler="JavaScript Code">
```

where TAG is some HTML tag and eventHandler is the name of the event handler.

For example, suppose you have created a JavaScript function called compute. You can cause Navigator to perform this function when the user clicks on a button by assigning the function call to the button's onClick event handler:

```
<INPUT TYPE="button" VALUE="Calculate" onClick="compute(this.form)">
```

You can put any JavaScript statements inside the quotes following onClick. These statements get executed when the user clicks on the button. If you want to include more than one statement, separate statements with a semicolon (;).

Defining Functions for Event Handlers

In general, it is a good idea to define functions for your event handlers for the following reasons:

1. It makes your code modular—you can use the same function as an event handler for many different items.

2. It makes your code easier to read.

Recall from the preceding code example the use of *this.form* to refer to the current form. The keyword *this* refers to the current object—in the preceding example, the button object. The construct *this.form* then refers to the form containing the button. The onClick event handler is a call to the compute() function, with *this.form*, the current form, as the parameter to the function.

Events and Their HTML Element Counterparts

The events that apply to HTML document elements are shown in the following table:

Events	HTML Elements
Focus, Blur, Change events	text fields, textareas, and selections
Click events	buttons, radio buttons, checkboxes, submit buttons, reset buttons, links
Select events	text fields, textareas
MouseOver event	links

If an event applies to an HTML element tag, then you can define an event handler for it. In general, an event handler has the name of the event, preceded by "on." For example, the event handler for the Focus event is onFocus.

Emulating Events with Methods

Many objects also have methods that emulate events. For example, button has a click method that emulates the button being clicked.

 Note

> The event-emulation methods do not trigger event-handlers. So, for example, the click method does not trigger an onClick event-handler. However, you can always call an event-handler directly (for example, you can call onClick explicitly in a script).

Event	Occurs When	Event Handler
blur	User removes input focus from form element	onBlur
click	User clicks on form element or link	onClick
change	User changes value of text, textarea, or select element	onChange
focus	User gives form element input focus	onFocus
load	User loads the page in the Navigator	onLoad
mouseover	User moves mouse pointer over a link or anchor	onMouseOver
select	User selects form element's input field	onSelect
submit	User submits a form	onSubmit
unload	User exits the page	onUnload

Forms and Event Handler Attributes

The following example demonstrates a script with a form and an event handler attribute.

```
<HEAD>
<SCRIPT LANGUAGE="JavaScript">
function compute(form) {
   if (confirm("Are you sure?"))
      form.result.value = eval(form.expr.value)
   else
      alert("Please come back again.")
}
</SCRIPT>
</HEAD>
<BODY>
<FORM>
Enter an expression:
<INPUT TYPE="text" NAME="expr" SIZE=15 >
<INPUT TYPE="button" VALUE="Calculate" ONCLICK="compute(this.form)">
<BR>
Result:
<INPUT TYPE="text" NAME="result" SIZE=15 >
<BR>
</FORM>
</BODY>
```

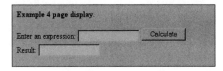

The following example shows a script with a form and event handler attribute within a BODY tag.

```
<HEAD>
<SCRIPT LANGUAGE="JavaScript">
<!-- hide script from old browsers
function checkNum(str, min, max) {
    if (str == "") {
        alert("Enter a number in the field, please.")
        return false
    }
    for (var i = 0; i  "9") {
            alert("Try a number, please.")
            return false
        }
    }
    var val = parseInt(str, 10)
    if ((val  max)) {
        alert("Try a number from 1 to 10.")
        return false
    }
    return true
}
function thanks() {
    alert("Thanks for your input.")
// end hiding from old browsers -->
</SCRIPT>
</HEAD>
<BODY>
<FORM NAME="ex5">
Please enter a small number:
<INPUT NAME="num"
    onChange="if (!checkNum(this.value, 1, 10))
            {this.focus();this.select();} else {thanks()}">
</FORM>
</BODY>
```

The page display for the preceding example is as follows.

Enter a number in the field and then click your mouse anywhere OUTSIDE of the field. Depending on what you enter, you will be prompted to enter another number, or thanked.

Tips and Techniques

The following sections describe various useful scripting techniques that will help you confirm scripting accuracy and avoid major headaches in the long run. Maintaining a JavaScript-enhanced Web site shouldn't extend itself beyond normal site maintenance. Implementing some recommended practical methods for site or page administration can ensure your viewers see what they're supposed to before they get bored and distracted and move on to someone's site that runs like it should.

Updating Pages

JavaScript in Navigator generates its results from the top of the page down. Once something has been formatted, you can't change it without reloading the page. Currently, you cannot update a particular part of a page without updating the entire page. However, you can update a "sub-window" in a frame separately.

Printing

You cannot currently print output created with JavaScript. For example, if you had the following in a page:

```
<P>This is some text.
<SCRIPT>document.write("<P>And some generated text")</SCRIPT>
```

and you printed it, you would get only "This is some text", even though you would see both lines onscreen.

Using Quotes

Be sure to alternate double quotes with single quotes. Because event handlers in HTML must be enclosed in quotes, you must use single quotes to delimit arguments. For example

```
<FORM NAME="myform">
<INPUT TYPE="button" NAME="Button1" VALUE="Open Sesame!"
onClick="window.open('stmtsov.html', 'newWin',
➥'toolbar=no,directories=no')">
</FORM>
```

You can also escape quotes by preceding them by a backslash (\ ).

Defining Functions

It is always a good idea to define all of your functions in the HEAD of your HTML page. This way, all functions will be defined before any content is displayed. Otherwise, the user might perform some action while the page is still loading that triggers an event handler and calls an undefined function, leading to an error.

Creating Arrays

An array is an ordered set of values that you reference through an array name and an index. For example, you could have an array called emp, that contains employees' names indexed by their employee number. So emp[1] would be employee number one, emp[2] employee number two, and so on.

JavaScript does not have an explicit array data type, but because of the intimate relationship between arrays and object properties (see JavaScript Object Model), it is easy to create arrays in JavaScript. You can define an array object type as shown in the following code:

```
function MakeArray(n) {
   this.length = n;
   for (var i = 1; i <= n; i++) {
     this[i] = 0 }
     return this
     }
}
```

This defines an array such that the first property, length, (with index of zero), represents the number of elements in the array. The remaining properties have an integer index of one or greater, and are initialized to zero.

You can then create an array by a call to new with the array name, specifying the number of elements it has. For example:

```
emp = new MakeArray(20);
```

creates an array called emp with 20 elements, and initializes the elements to zero.

Populating Arrays

You can populate an array by simply assigning values to its elements. For example:

```
emp[1] = "Casey Jones"
emp[2] = "Phil Lesh"
emp[3] = "August West"
```

and so on.

You can also create arrays of objects. For example, suppose you define an object type named Employees, as follows:

```
function Employee(empno, name, dept) {
    this.empno = empno;
    this.name = name;
    this.dept = dept;
}
```

Then the following statements define an array of these objects:

```
emp = new MakeArray(3)
emp[1] = new Employee(1, "Casey Jones", "Engineering")
emp[2] = new Employee(2, "Phil Lesh", "Music")
emp[3] = new Employee(3, "August West", "Admin")
```

Then you can easily display the objects in this array using the show_props function (defined in the section on the JavaScript Object Model) as follows:

```
for (var n =1; n <= 3; n++) {
    document.write(show_props(emp[n], "emp") + "
");
}
```

Appendix

Online Resources for JavaScript

The online resources listed here are accessible over the Internet. By directing your browser to the addresses below, you will find additional information to help you in designing pages with JavaScript.

Academy Projects QuickView

Page switcher with frames.

http://www.bergen.gov/AAST/QuickView.html

ATG's Gallery of (Semi) Recent Works

An online gallery created using some of the new features of Netscape 2.0, including frames, tables, backgrounds, and JavaScript. Version 2 uses a Java/CGI/JavaScript package called WinSize0.5b to automatically resize the gallery window relative to the client's screen size.

http://www.mrl.nyu.edu/athomas/artwork.html

The Complete Idiot's Guide to JavaScript

The homesite for the book published by Que/Alpha in March, 1996. Provides source files, links, resources, tips, tricks, and anything else that might come along.

http://www.winternet.com/~sjwalter/javascript/nn/index.html

Experiments in JavaScript

Contains examples and tutorials on using JavaScript.

http://gmccomb.com/javascript/

Follow the block

Requires Netscape 3.0. Shows the power and speed of the new image replacement capability of Navigator.

http://www.lhouse.com/~jbloomberg/colors/

gamelan

Provides a collection of JavaScript examples and documentation maintained by gamelan.com.

http://www.gamelan.com/noframe/
Gamelan.javascript.html

Hybrid HTML Design

JavaScript links mixed with Java resources.

http://www.browserbydesign.com/book/Resource/java.htm

inquiry.com—Ask the Javascript Pro

This is a dicussion group and question answering service forum. inquiry.com is a free service for software developers, providing information on software products, development techniques, and emerging technologies.

http://www.inquiry.com/techtips/js_pro/

JavaScript—Intro by Voodoo

INTRODUCTION TO JAVASCRIPT. Shows how to use different features. This is a good place to start for the JavaScript novice.

http://www.webconn.com/java/javascript/intro/

JavaScript 411 Home Page

This is a good place to begin with JavaScript. Contains tutorial, resources library, and search and faq resources.

http://www.freqgrafx.com/411/

JavaScript Authoring Guide 2.0

JavaScript Authoring Guide brought to you by Netscape, up to 2.0!

http://home.netscape.com/eng/mozilla/3.0/handbook/javascript/index.html

JavaScript Authoring Guide 3.0

JavaScript Authoring Guide brought to you by Netscape, including the new 3.0 additions to the langage—the total reference!

http://home.netscape.com/eng/mozilla/3.0/handbook/javascript/index.html

JavaScript Chat Room

A place where JavaScript programmers can come in and talk about JavaScript.

http://www.NETural.com/javascript/chat.html

JavaScript Index

A full site dedicated to JavaScript with lots of resources including newsgroups, JavaScript applets, and documentation links.

http://www.c2.org/~andreww/javascript/

The JavaScript Mailing List Home Page

This is the home page for the JavaScript mailing list, devoted to a discussion of the JavaScript scripting language. It also contains pointers to some JavaScript resources on the Net.

http://www.obscure.org/javascript/

The JavaScript Planet

Full of Javascript examples.

http://www.geocities.com/SiliconValley/7116/

JavaScript Presentation

Provides an overview of JavaScript—historic, extension, and client-side script.

http://www.access.digex.net/~hecker/netscape/majug/ javascript/

The JavaScript Standard Code Group

Allows you to review, design, and submit standard JavaScript code libraries for free use to the Internet community.

http://www.c2.org/~andreww/javascript/jsscg.html

The JavaScript-Sweden Site

This site provides links to many JavaScript tutorials and examples.

http://www.ostrabo.uddevalla.se/dis/javascript/

JavaScript Tip of the Week

This site provides a weekly cool set of JavaScript tips or tricks to help you on your way to JavaScript bliss.

http://www.gis.net/~carter/therest/tip_week.html

Just Changing the Background

Provides a JavaScript function that enables the author to fade a background between 2 given hex colors. Can be "stacked" to fade more than 2 colors.

Similar to the multiple tags that were used for hokey animations under Netscape 1.1 (yes, this is hokey, too).

http://fly.hiwaay.net/~gbaysing/javascript/
background.js.html

Movie Guide to Kalamazoo Theatres

Provides a movie guide to local theatres in the Kalamazoo, Michigan area using frames and JavaScript to update form elements dynamically.

http://www.sapien.net/guide/

Netscape + Sun = JavaScript Press Release

Netscape and Sun Announce Javascript™, the Open, Cross-Platform, Object Scripting Language for Enterprise Networks and the Internet.

http://home.netscape.com/newsref/pr/
newsrelease67.html

Netscape Developers Conference

This site includes information about advanced JavaScript, introduction to JavaScript, JavaScript for database connectivity, and other JavaScript-related topics.

http://home.netscape.com/misc/developer/conference/
proceedings/

News comp.lang.javascript

This newsgroup functions as a resource question and answer forum.

news:comp.lang.javascript

news livesoftware.javascript.developer

This newsgroup functions as a resource question and answer forum.

news://news.livesoftware.com/
livesoftware.javascript.developer

PubNet multiple search

This is a multiple search engine using JavaScript, multiple frames, and Windows TEST 2000 JavaScript & Frame example. This self-grading JavaScript exam provides the student with immediate feedback on test performance. Correct answers and guidance to reference material can be obtained at the end of the test.

http://www.jchelp.com/test2000/test2000.htm

Research Group "Analysis"

Research Group "Analysis" provides lots of undocumented features and good tips for advanced JavaScript programmers.

http://www.mpg-ana.uni-potsdam.de/local/js/

Selector

Other example of graphics selector.

http://www.att.com/homes/cameron/javascript/Selector/

Simple Little Things To Add To Your Pages

This site provides a plug & play JavaScript library.

http://tanega.com/java/java.html

Timothy's JavaScript Examples

This site currently has over two dozen JavaScript examples that have been tested with Netscape 2.0 & 3.04b running on Win 95. Also included are various links to many of the JS resources on the Net.

http://www.essex1.com/people/timothy/js-index.htm

Tom Wittbrodt's Frame Targeting Examples

This site provides examples of how to target frames with JavaScript.

http://members.aol.com/tomwitt/framemkr.htm

The Unofficial JavaScript Resource Center

This page features links, tricks, and advanced stuff.

http://www.ce.net/users/ryan/java/index.html

VRML 2.0, Part I: E. JavaScript Reference

This site describes integrating JavaScript with VRML 2.0. It provides functions called when events come into the script, access to fields within the script, logic to operate on the fields, and the ability to send events out from the script.

http://webspace.sgi.com/moving-worlds/spec/part1/ javascript.html

Web Design Tips and Tricks

This site provides a plug & play JavaScript library and more HTML & JavaScript tricks.

http://www.winmag.com/web/tips/

Yahoo!

Yahoo index of JavaScript.

http://www.yahoo.com/Computers_and_Internet/ Languages/JavaScript/

Games Created with JavaScript

Welcome to MISSED!

This is a JavaScript-based parody of Myst. Extensive use of frames.

http://www.lhouse.com/~jbloomberg/play/play/missed.html

Virtual BlackJack

A virtual blackjack program written in JavaScript. Features session score saving, graphics interface, and more.

http://www.cyberdragon.com/cgi-bin/php.cgi/bj/index.shtml

mastermind

This is a clone of the classic board game Mastermind that is made just to look into the world of JavaScript! The game is self-instructive!

http://www.dreamlink.se/mastermind/

The Amazing JavaScript Maze

The Amazing JavaScript Maze Game. Navigate through a maze to get to the end! Gameboard can be expanded to a variety of game ideas.

http://www.tisny.com/js_maze.html

Bram's JavaScript Life Page

This is a very sophisticated demonstration of what can be done with JavaScript. It requires Navigator 3.0 beta 4. A simulation of the game Life—uses 100% pure, unadulterated JavaScript, with no helper applications, plugins, or Java whatsoever.

http://earthweb.com/~bram/life.html

Cryptarithms, Mathematics, Education, Fun

Cryptarithms are puzzles obtained from arithmetic identities by replacing digits with letters. The goal is to recover the original identity. This JavaScript setup has a stack to remember and, when needed, to retrieve the state of a puzzle making it a much better tool than paper and pencil.

http://mars.superlink.net/abogom/st_crypto.html

Cypherspace

An interactive cryptogram game written in JavaScript. Features include 100 different cryptograms, an automatic hint button, a solving timer, and online help. Using Netscape cookies, the program remembers your best solving time and records the cryptograms you've already solved, and automatically chooses a new one.

http://www.netvoyage.net/~tgrupe/crypto.htm

Index